NUTRITION OF FINCHES
AND OTHER CAGE BIRDS

by

Robert G. Black

ISBN 0-910631-01-8

Printed for the Publisher by
Copple House Printing & Binding
Lakemont, Georgia 30552

DEDICATION

This book is available to the aviculturist today only because thousands of dedicated researchers have gleaned each bit of knowledge contained herein from days, years, and decades of painstaking effort. Every success meant a thousand failures had passed before. Every answer brought only a dozen new questions. But, bit by bit, the pieces of the nutritional puzzle are being pieced together. As you read this volume, remember that every fact in every sentence represents a lifetime of effort and dedication by someone in the past. With my deepest respect and most profound admiration, I dedicate this book in part to those individuals.

The remaining part of this dedication is one of sadness, for behind each new nutritional fact and discovery lie the littered bodies of countless numbers of birds and animals sacrificed so that we might gain this knowledge. The untold suffering endured by these countless millions of living creatures that were the subjects of this nutritional research must give pause to every thinking person. I cannot condemn this use of experimental animals, for I see no other way of gaining the information needed to prevent far greater needless suffering in the future caused by the malnutrition of humans, birds, and animals. Yet, I must ask why the Infinite Wisdom guiding our human evolution gave us no other means of gaining this knowledge. With my sincerest thanks and humble gratitude for the gift of their lives to further our knowledge, I also dedicate this book to those countless birds and animals that died in serving us so well.

CONTENTS

FOREWORD

The study of nutrition is an intimidating pursuit. The more one learns of nutrition, the more complicated and incomprehensible it seems. The complex interactions of all of the necessary nutrients in their cooperation to provide the necessities of life to an organism are completely mystifying. We have no scientifically supported idea yet why most of these chemical compounds act as they do or what governs their actions and use by the body. We can only describe what happens in the body, not what motivates it to happen. Only one religious philosophy has even explained this process to my satisfaction. That is the teaching of the Rosicrucian Fellowship headquartered in Oceanside, California.

The study of nutrition is a very new science. Though the earliest nutritional reference I have encountered dates from around 2700 B.C. from a treatise on herbal medicine during the reign of the legendary Chinese emperor Shennung, it was only in 1931 that vitamin C was definitely isolated and identified. Virtually all detailed knowledge of nutrition and nutritional requirements is a product of the twentieth century. Though such knowledge may have been known to the most advanced of ancient and prehistoric civilizations, as evidenced by their few remaining artifacts, any records of such knowledge have been totally

7

and probably irretrievably lost. Since recent human history indicates that at least fifty years are required for the widespread acceptance of any new discovery, we can be sure that most of the nutritional discoveries of the last few decades will not be totally accepted and utilized for many more years. Nevertheless, all of the information that I could locate is presented in this volume for your information and use.

Our current knowledge of nutrition represents only a very small part of what there is to learn. We have barely touched the surface of potential nutritional knowledge. Much of what is presumed to be true today will undoubtedly be proven false at some time in the future. Yet, slowly but surely, the knowledge of what maintains life is expanded, to the benefit of all who will learn and put that knowledge to use. Regardless of what discoveries should come in the future, the 1930's, a time of economic disaster, will always be looked upon as the golden age of nutritional discovery.

As mountainous and unending as the study of nutrition may be, at some point, a student must fall back, consolidate his knowledge, and begin teaching others something of what he has learned. I have reached that point. Should all writers wait until they felt confident in every aspect of their subject, no writing would ever be done. One person can never know everything about any subject, no matter how specialized. We can, at best, only chip away at our ignorance and try to drag others, kicking and screaming all the way, into our field of knowledge.

Most of the writing thus far on avian nutrition has been so generalized or full of inaccuracies as to be almost useless. What few books have delved deeply into the nutritional requirements of birds have been so extremely technical as to be almost incomprehensible to the average reader. Virtually no research has been done on the specific nutritional requirements of any bird of avicultural interest, though the Department of Avian Sciences of the University of California, Davis, is making a good start. Most of the information offered in this volume for cage birds must be inferred from the study of domestic fowl and laboratory animals. This is regretable, but unavoidable. To make matters worse, even knowledgeable veterinarians and researchers still parrot outdated avicultural literature in attributing a problem as common and disastrous as egg-binding to cold weather or wet nests, when it is totally and completely a symptom of nutritional deficiency.

Very little of the information presented in this volume is the result of my personal research and experimentation. When this is the case, it is clearly stated. Most of the following information comes from the books listed in the bibliography, and I am most deeply indebted to these authors and their publishers for the wealth of nutritional information contained in their works.

It is indeed unfortunate, however, that the most knowledgeable authorities have written no book comparable to this for the use of the average breeder of cage birds. Their writing has been primarily for medical and nutritional journals, and the resulting information definitely has not filtered down to the breeder and amateur aviculturist. Untold millions of birds in captivity have died over the last century solely as a result of this lack of known and available nutritional information.

I must honestly acknowledge that I am certainly not the most qualified to write this book. My gift is in finding, reading, digesting, and presenting the known material in common terms for the average bird fancier. My formal training is in International Affairs and Linguistics. My vocational training has been in management, teaching, horticulture, and aviculture. Nutritional study has always been a very peripheral part of my fields of interest. Nevertheless, the need for this information is so great that I plowed into it full force, and you are reading the result.

To look at this another way, there is no other person with the same background, training, and interests that I possess. These will combine in this book into a unique form that no one else could duplicate. The combination of experience, knowledge, and presentation that is gathered together in these pages, could not be duplicated by anyone else. Perhaps the information presented in this particular form will be able to enlighten most of those who read it. As with most material of this type, this information will be outdated before it is even published.

Many of the nutritional experts looking over this volume will be horrified at several of the book listings by popular authors in the bibliography. These books are directed to the natural food and health food advocate, and have the advantage of explaining in common terms the nutritional concepts that no average reader could possibly understand in the more professional and scholarly presentations. I can only express the greatest of admiration for these authors who have brought nutritional knowledge in understandable form to anyone who chooses to read it. Without the availability of their publications, I would never have started the study of nutrition. Are they unprofessional, disdainful of many nutritional professionals, and even way off base in some of their beliefs and presentations? Certainly! But I have seen the equal of intolerance and foolish statements in the most professional of nutritional textbooks. If such senseless intolerance must result in battle, let he who is free from sin cast the first stone.

In this volume I have decided against including extensive footnotes to credit my sources of information, since I have discovered by experience that this practice detracts greatly from the cohesiveness and clarity of the information presented. Virtually all of the knowledge found in this book is attributable to the volumes listed in the bibliography and can be researched more deeply in them. It has taken me many years to discover and collect these volumes, many of which are now out of print. Collectively, they represent a wealth of nutritional information that is unavailable in most large libraries.

In this volume, I will destroy many cherished beliefs, bury old wives' tales, and also commit my own grievous blunders, for which I will surely be held accountable. Yet I strongly feel that any ray of light that stabs through the dark cloud of nutritional ignorance is of supreme value to every aviculturist. If I am proven wrong and foolish, I will happily correct inaccuracies in the future. For at least I've tried, and in erring brought forth the truth.

PART ONE

NUTRITION BASICS

CHAPTER 1

INTRODUCTION TO NUTRIENTS

Most of our knowledge of the nutrition of birds is the result of studies done in human nutrition or in the nutrition of rats, mice, chickens, and guinea pigs for information leading to further knowledge of human nutrition. The original work that has been done with birds is mostly in reference to the nutrition of chickens and other domestic fowl. As a consequence, though the needs of a bird for any specific nutrient may not be absolutely and finally proven, if humans, rats, and chickens need that nutrient, all logic and experience point to its need by all birds, in addition. Many nutritionists will not accept this concept, but in order to have anything to say on the nutrition of cage birds, I am forced to make this extension of knowledge into unproven areas. Based upon the known unity of all nature with respect to biological functioning, I feel fully justified in doing this.

In discussing the subject of nutrition of cage birds, it is imperative to begin at a basic level. Even so, words unfamiliar to the average reader must be used occasionally and will be explained as completely as possible. This will assure that no one is left behind hopelessly confused in what is admittedly a confusing subject. The glossary defines all terms used in this book relating to nutrition and the other subjects covered in this work that may be unfamiliar.

Everyone is aware that food contains nutrients that are necessary for life and growth. Any statement beyond this will run into ignorance, heated debate, disbelief, and even ridicule. What comes as a particular surprise to many is the fact that the exact same nutrients that are necessary for people are also necessary for birds. Consequently, this volume is directed to the bird breeder's nutrition as much as it is directed to the nutrition of the birds.

The primary task of any aviculturist is to provide food to the birds maintained and to know what constitutes suitable food for the species kept. Without access to the food, the birds certainly cannot eat it and begin the nutritional process. Empty feed dishes and forgotten rations serve no purpose. To the contrary, they assure the eventual death of the birds from starvation. In addition, the food of one species may be a disaster for another species not equipped by nature to digest it.

Yet, the specific nutrients required will be the same for all birds. Some will get these nutrients from seeds, some from insects, some from fruit, and some from flesh and carrion. Yet, the basic nutrients needed and ingested are the same for all avian species. Only the quantities of each nutrient needed at the different stages of life will vary from species to species, as well as among individuals within the same species.

Consumption of the food is the next requirement. As elementary as it may sound in the writing and the reading, food must be eaten to perform the wonders of life and growth. The birds must eat the food you provide, and you must provide foods that will be eaten. A food not consumed is not a food at all, but merely a complex combination of chemical compounds. An offering left untouched by the birds is worse than nothing. It may provide a breeding ground for fungi and bacteria, and it is money totally wasted, since few of the items that we feed our birds are free. Money thrown away cannot go to purchase foods that the birds will eat. Also, food uneaten is time wasted in the purchase, in the preparation, and in the provision.

Contrary to human experience, taste does not seem to play a primary role in the food consumption of birds. The energy level of the diet seems to be of primary importance in determining food intake in most birds. Nevertheless, as anyone who has ever maintained a canary or finch will confirm, birds do have definite likes and dislikes where taste is concerned in their food supply. The breeder must cater to these specific preferences on the part of individual birds and strains of birds.

Birds are much like people in that they will seldom try anything new and unfamiliar. If you want to introduce some birds to a new, highly nutritious food that all of your others are eating and love, here is a simple, safe, and effective method. First, remove all other food from the birds' cage. Place a small amount of the desirable new food in the cage, thus enforcing a fast on the birds. Fasting is a healthful process, enabling the body of the bird to eliminate toxins and wastes. Fasting also is an aid to healing, freeing the body's metabolism from digestion to rebuilding damaged tissues. It should not be confused with starvation. The enforced fast should last a maximum of eight hours for the smallest finches, sixteen hours for a larger bird, such as a cardinal or bullfinch, and may go for several days in large parrots. Longer than these periods of fasting will begin starvation, which is to be avoided under any circumstances.

Usually, the birds will test the newly offered food within a few hours, as they get hungry and find nothing

else to eat. If they have gone the full period mentioned
above without touching the new food, return their normal
diet at least a half hour before nightfall so that they will
not be without food in the crop for the night. The next
morning take away all food again, leaving only the new
offering. In my experience, by the third day they will
be cleaning up a fairly large portion of the new food each
morning. When it is gone, return all normal rations for the
rest of the day, plus a little more of the new food. By the
fifth or sixth day, most birds will be eating the new food
regularly, and you have succeeded. I have found from experience that small finches will be eating a new food in
three hours, Java Rice Birds and budgerigars in 12 hours,
and conures in 48 hours.

During this process, never take away the birds' water,
and be sure to watch them closely for signs of distress.
If a bird still will not eat the new food when anything
else is available, it simply does not consider the new offering palatable and won't eat it voluntarily under any circumstances. It that situation, you are well advised to give
up and feed something else of comparable nutritional
value.

Once a food is eaten, the next necessity is digestion.
This is a complex process of breakdown from whole foods
to basic nutrients. Food passes from the beak into the
esophagus, then into the crop, or diverticulum. The crop
serves as a food storage area, and food moves from there
through the lower esophagus to the proventriculus. This is
the true glandular stomach, also called the forestomach.
Hydrochloric acid and digestive enzymes pour in at the
proventriculus and create a highly acid mixture which
passes into the gizzard.

Before complete digestion can take place, food must
be broken down into the tiniest of particles, literally into
a mush. Humans accomplish this by chewing their food.
Seed eating birds have a gizzard for the same purpose. The

gizzard is a very powerful muscle that grinds seeds against each other, against its horny lining, and against gravel or grit the bird has consumed. As the food is ground into finer particles, the hydrochloric acid and digestive enzymes picked up in the proventriculus further break down the food particles.

Food then moves into the duodenum, the first section of the small intestine, where it is mixed with enzymes from the pancreas which can digest proteins, fats, and carbohydrates. Since the duodenum cannot tolerate this highly acid mixture, and the pancreatic enzymes will not function in an acid environment, the duodenum must release antacids and alkalis into the food mass to neutralize the acidity. Bile is also added from the liver and emulsifies the fats and oils into fine particles. The small intestine then completes the digestive process by breaking down the food particles into their basic, microscopic constituents.

This process of digestion can vary greatly, depending upon the variety of bird and its diet. Should any link in this chain of food breakdown occur, subsequent absorption into the bloodstream will be impossible and the bird will starve to death, regardless of the quantity of food consumed. Many deficiencies and diseases will halt the function of one necessary component of the digestive process, thus rendering the entire system useless.

Absorption is the next necessary step before the avian body can make use of the food consumed. The crucial importance of proper nutrient absorption cannot be overemphasized. Absorption takes place molecule by molecule through the membrane of the intestinal wall, and any substance which interferes with this absorption will prevent the bird from getting the nutritional benefit of the food consumed. Nutrients that cannot be absorbed, regardless of the reason for non-absorption, are simply passed through the rest of the digestive tract and eliminated.

The mechanism by which the intestinal wall rejects or accepts a molecule for absorption is largely unknown. Yet, we do know that this selectivity occurs. Calcium, for example, is usually absorbed, but when calcium is attached to the oxalic acid molecule as found in raw spinach, the resulting molecule is completely unabsorbable. Minerals are absorbed much more readily when they are chelated, meaning attached to an amino acid molecule, or to another compound, such as ascorbic acid. This may be getting a bit ahead of the proper order for explanation, but such examples are necessary to illustrate the complexity of the absorption process.

Occasionally, a substance harmful to the body may be absorbed. These items we call poisons. Lest we consider this overly bizarre, keep in mind that no life form or function is absolutely perfect, or life would last forever. The lungs, for example, will absorb carbon monoxide into the bloodstream many times more rapidly than they will absorb oxygen.

Many things can interfere with proper absorption. Any poison or foreign bacteria which invade the digestive tract and set up a reaction in the form of diarrhea will wash the nutrients through so rapidly that they will not be in contact with the intestinal wall long enough to be absorbed. Also, any substance which coats the lining and plugs up the absorptive surface will prevent absorption.

The smaller molecules, such as those of the simple sugar glucose, are more easily absorbed than the very large, complicated molecule of a substance such as vitamin B-12, or cobalamin. For this reason, an over-abundance of glucose from carbohydrate foods may be undesirable and fattening, while an excess of cobalamin may be desirable to insure the minimum absorption for optimal health. Never forget that eating does not mean absorption. The eating of a food is only the first step in the nutritive process.

Once a nutrient has been absorbed into the bloodstream, it will circulate until it is taken out by a cell through the membrane of the cell for use as a fuel for energy, a building block for cell growth and replacement, or storage for future use. How each cell can identify its various nutritional needs and selectively withdraw them from the bloodstream is a complete mystery.

The physical and chemical processes in which the body uses the nutrients absorbed for growth and energy are called metabolism. Metabolism varies greatly from individual to individual, even within the same species. This will be covered more fully in the discussion of biochemical individuality. We are all familiar with people who are cold even in temperatures of eighty degrees Fahrenheit, and others who frolic in short sleeves at fifty degrees in perfect comfort. These differences are the result of a slower or faster rate of metabolism, in this case the burning of food for heat energy, in particular.

Such differences in metabolism bear little correlation to the amount of food consumed. The successful absorption of the nutrients, by contrast, definitely, strongly affects the rate of use, since nutrients not in the bloodstream certainly cannot be metabolized. Age will usually result in slower metabolism, with any lack of nutrients further harming the body's operation.

There can be no such thing as perfect nutrition at the cell level. Each cell needs a set supply of each individual nutrient, but is totally dependent upon what the blood supply brings it. This, in turn, depends on what has been absorbed, which depends on the efficiency of digestion, which also depends on the nutrients available in the food supply, etc. Consequently, every cell operates continually at what we may call a suboptimal level of nutrition. Sometimes inadequately supplied with a nutrient, at other times oversupplied, it is a wonder at times that any cell continues to function to the use and benefit of the total organism.

All nutrients in the body's metabolism work together to supply the formula for life in each bird and in each of its cells. No nutrient performs its functions alone, but in concert. Since the nutrients occur together in foods, a deficiency of one vitamin, for example, will surely mean that others are also deficient. This interaction of nutrients is one logical argument against the use of single, synthetically produced vitamin supplements. In nature no vitamin occurs alone, but always in association with other vitamins, minerals, and other food factors. They are found together, consumed together, and work together in the body. A single nutrient in supplement form may not work as well in the body because it upsets this natural balance. It does seem that the biological activity of artificial vitamins is less than that of the natural compounds, for reasons that are not yet clear. Nevertheless, chemically, down to the last atom, an artificially made vitamin is identical to its natural counterpart.

Biochemical individuality is a term that seems calculated to frighten away anyone not having a Ph.D. degree. Yet, it simply says in concise form that every individual is different in its body chemistry from every other individual. Everyone easily recognizes that species are different in appearance, and may have different body characteristics and differing needs for nutrients. It is also easy to see that outwardly individuals within a species are different. In birds, colors, personality, size, shape, and behavior readily can be seen to be different in members of the same species. Yet, the greatest differences are not external, but within the body and its biochemistry. Dr. Roger J. Williams has written extensively on this subject, and I highly recommend his published works on the subject of biochemical individuality.

Dr. Williams has shown that within an average population of ten individuals in one species, the normal requirement for nutrients will vary greatly in all of those individuals. The unusual member of the sampling will be one that requires far less of a nutrient than the others for normal, healthy life, and one other that will require far more than the others. On the same nutrient amount, most individuals will be perfectly healthy, but one may suffer and die from a severe deficiency.

This proven concept of biochemical individuality effectively shatters any rationale in the Food and Drug Administration's Recommended Daily Allowances for individuals. Neither human beings nor birds are nearly so uniform as the Government would have us believe. There is simply no such thing as an "average" bird, any more than there is an "average" human being.

This individuality concept must be kept in mind when you observe your birds. Almost everyone has had the experience of owning ten birds of a species and seeing one die for no apparent reason, while all others remain in perfect health, all receiving exactly the same care and diet. The biochemical individuality of the birds is the reason. The one that has died is the individual with a far higher requirement for one vital nutrient, a requirement that your diet could not provide. This high requirement, if not filled, can also make a bird more susceptible to invading disease microorganisms in any case of deficiency.

This whole area of biochemical individuality is without a doubt nature's method for insuring the survival of a species. Though an individual may have an extremely high requirement for one nutrient, it may have a corresponding extremely low requirement for another, or it may synthesize the needed nutrient internally. Therefore, if major disaster should occur in the food supply, with a huge drop in the availability of some nutrients, numerous individuals are sure to survive to perpetuate the species because of their very low body requirement for the nutrients in short supply. True, most individuals in the species may die from malnutrition in such a case, but the few will always survive to replenish the species.

To illustrate this from my own experience, I once purchased a dozen Fischer's Lovebirds in beautiful condition and vibrant health. They were truly the nicest Fischer's I have ever seen. Within a few weeks, trouble began to show up — puffiness, erratic actions, lack of muscle control, and eventual death. These lovebirds were on the same diet as I had always fed lovebirds, finches, doves, and cardinals. All other birds around them were in good health, yet one by one, all but two of the Fischer's died.

The symptoms left no doubt that they were suffering from a severe nutritional deficiency. This strain, all raised by one breeder, obviously had a very high requirement for a particular nutrient that my diet was not supplying in sufficient quantity. I was unable to track down which nutrient they required in such quantity. The remaining two proved to be both hens, apparently without this high nutrient requirement. They proceeded to build a nest and have laid dozens of infertile eggs. Both have remained in perfect health on my standard diet.

A commonly known human example of this phenomenon is evident in the history of sailing ships of the centuries before 1900. At that time, scurvy or acute vitamin C deficiency was the scourge of the seas and the dread of every sailor. The cause and cure were completely unknown and the fear of scurvy rode the waves on every vessel afloat. Sea voyages might last three to six months or more without the ship touching land. After the first few weeks at sea on navy or merchant marine rations, the first men would become ill with scurvy. These were the unusual individuals on the high side of the requirement for vitamin C. At the end of six months, many men would have died, with most of the rest left ill with scurvy. And yet, a few always survived the longest voyage with no touch of scurvy, obviously those individuals with such an extremely low requirement for vitamin C that they could go for months in perfect health with virtually no intake at all. Some writers have suggested that these few could actually synthesize their own vitamin C, and this is certainly a reasonable concept that deserves extensive study. One suspects that the men who became captains of their ships after many sea voyages were among these few, since only they could survive so long under conditions of severe vitamin C deficiency, enabling them to get the needed experience on the sea.

In a chilling and sobering statistic, Irwin Stone in his book *The Healing Factor* recounts the now famous voyage of Ferdinand Magellan in 1519. Magellan set sail with a fleet of five ships on his voyage of circumnavigation of the earth. Three years later, he returned to Spain in triumph, but with only one ship and only 18 members of his original crews. The rest had all been lost, hundreds of men, primarily to scurvy. I highly recommend Stone's book as by far the best I have encountered on the subject of vitamin C.

There are undoubtedly as many different diets for birds as there are aviculturists. The very fact that birds successfully breed on such a wide variety of dietary offerings testifies to the fact that nutrients are widespread and the diets are nutritionally complete for the birds that are breeding successfully. However, many of the minor and major problems in the breeding attempts are the direct result of deficiencies in one or more nutrients. As previously stated and well worth repeating, if there is a deficiency of one nutrient, there must surely be deficiencies of others, also.

I shudder at the frequent recommendations of canary fanciers to withhold egg food, greens, or other special foods during non-breeding periods, when the hen is sitting, or at times when feeding the young. And yet, this practice does recognize the fact that there is a decided difference in nutritional needs from merely maintaining a bird in good health to breeding the same bird. The maintenance diet needs only sufficient protein and other nutrients for repair and replacement of damaged cells and feathers, while the breeding diet requires far more protein and other nutrients for the proper development of the young birds from egg to maturity in a few weeks. Egg laying and molting will increase the protein requirement, though not nearly to such an extent as feeding a nest of young.

The birds instinctively recognize this change in need and always consume far more high protein foods when feeding nestlings. There is no need for the aviculturist to attempt to regulate this intake in any way. A bird on a balanced, nutritious diet will never overeat of any one item at any time. In this respect, the birds exhibit far more good sense than most people do. You can safely feed your birds all they will clean up of any food if they are in good health and breeding.

As an example, there are many references in avicultural writings concerning limiting mealworms in avian diets. In my breeding of birds relishing these, the Brazilian Red-Crested Cardinals, I have fed the birds mealworms free choice at all times. While they are feeding young, never in my memory have I lost a nestling or adult from malnutrition. With the delicate finches, I offered the Lesser Mealworm, Alphitobius diaperinus, free choice. The number they will consume in a day in feeding a growing nest of young is unbelievable, yet I have never noticed the slightest bad effect from this practice. Quite the contrary, the fertility, hatchability, and young fledged in both the Cardinals and finches all represented 100% of the eggs laid. As a result, I tend to look with suspicion upon any recommendation to limit either variety of mealworm. However, there is no doubt that a bird starved for them may overeat to the point of illness.

Any bird starved for a certain nutrient or food item may very well overeat of an item containing the needed nutrients before the craving is satisfied. This is a particular danger with grit and salt, for an excess of either may be fatal. Therefore, extreme care must be taken to give only very small quantities of a new food when a bird is known to be suffering from nutritional deficiencies.

For the record, in order to satisfy those who will at this point be wondering if I really practice what I preach, you are hereby informed that all of my birds, from Gouldian Finches to quail, receive the same diet year-round, breeding or not. They consume far less during non-breeding periods and totally govern their own intake of the various foods I supply. The birds are never forcefully rested, but choose their own rest periods from breeding as they feel the need for it. To reiterate the point, birds are not as foolish as most aviculturists seem to think. Their instincts represent far more knowledgeable guidance than we as aviculturists can provide.

A breeding diet must not only contain a greater percentage of protein, but also increased amounts of the vitamins and especially minerals necessary to support the rapid and sustained growth in the nestlings. The last thing needed is increased carbohydrate intake. Carbohydrates contribute nothing to growth — they are the energy foods. Nestlings do not need much energy, since this is supplied in large part by the parental brooding. For this reason, mixing high carbohydrate foods with high protein items as nestling foods is a very ill-advised practice. Such high carbohydrate items as bread crumbs dilute the protein in a food such as egg. The little protein in bread is incomplete and of no value for growth, so it is utilized for energy. Consequently, the parent birds are forced to eat and feed large quantities of carbohydrates which are at best useless to the nestling, and at worst may supplant the protein beyond the minimum necessary for life and growth, thus causing their death from protein deficiency. You may refer to the chapter on protein for a complete discussion of protein values.

In nature no species exists on a diet of totally dead matter. Even the carrion eaters are consuming vast quantities of living bacteria. Any diet devoid of living material with only cooked or preserved foods will be a diet missing some vital ingredients. Though the prepared commercial mixtures are well balanced generally and a blessing of convenience for the breeder, they are not complete diets. The deficiencies show up in constant feather plucking and cannibalism of birds confined to such diets. Only by eating living tissue can they satisfy the craving for nutrient items as yet unidentified, but missing in the commercial mixtures.

For a number of years, a strong debate has existed among bird breeders as to the necessity for grit in the diet for the various species of birds maintained in captivity. Obviously, the softbills don't need it at all. Any seed eating bird traditionally has been provided with grit. My feeling is that this is a definite necessity for any bird that swallows its seeds whole, without husking them. In other words, all doves, quail, and other gallinaceous birds need a ready supply of grit. However, my own experimentation indicates that this may not be necessary for those birds that husk their seed. This would include all finches and the seed-eating psittacines. I have maintained Society Finches, Zebra Finches, Gouldians, Cordon Bleus, Star Finches, Cutthroat Finches, Green Singing Finches, and Strawberry Finches for periods of six months in perfect health with no grit. This would indicate that at least for these species grit may be dispensable. I cannot at this point make this a flat, all-inclusive statement until the birds can be raised, maintained, and successfully bred for at least a year without the provision of grit.

For Americans used to the English system of measurement in pounds and ounces, the use of weight measurements in nutrition will need a short explanation, since the metric system is still not universally taught in this country. Many of these nutrients are needed only in microscopic quantities, and the metric system is ideally suited for the measurement of these tiny amounts. The metric system provides weight measurement in grams, milligrams, and micrograms which serve the purposes of nutritional writing quite well. One ounce is equal to 28.35 grams. One milligram is one one-thousandth of a gram. One microgram is one one-thousandth of a milligram, an infinitesimal amount. One microgram is the approximate amount of cobalamin, vitamin B-12, contained in one whole chicken egg.

The term "pH," used in several nutrient discussions, is a common measure of acidity and alkalinity. It means "potential Hydrogen." A pH of 7 is a neutral solution. A pH of 4.6 is quite acid, and a pH of 8.2 is very alkaline. The pH of the food residues and the body fluids is a vitally important factor in health.

Finally, in the discussion of specific nutrients in the form of minerals, you will find occasional references to biological transmutation. This is the ability of living organisms to change one basic element into another within the body. A careful consideration of the work of Louis C. Kervran should convince any thinking person that this transmutation of basic elements in not only possible for living organisms, but occurs routinely. How it occurs is still a complete mystery, and no nutritional work has yet taken this phenomenon into extensive consideration. The conventional student of chemistry will dismiss this new science only at his peril. The proof is already in if one will only look at the currently available facts. Even so great a genius as Albert Einstein never discounted such a possibility in science, for his work was solely with inorganic elements and their atomic structure.

These are the basic avian nutritional concepts to keep in mind while reading the more detailed information on each individual nutrient. Once you have thoroughly digested all of the material in this volume, I can highly recommend many of the books in the bibliography for further, more detailed study of the science of nutrition.

CHAPTER 2

WATER

Water is seldom listed among the nutritional requirements of living things, but this substance is the most basic of all needs in nutrition. There are life forms that live without air or oxygen, but none can live without water. Though water is so often taken for granted, it is the most essential nutrient and the first requirement for life. The turnover and exchange of water in the body exceeds that of any other nutrient. A 10% reduction in body content of any other nutrient usually will cause no noticeable effect, but a 10% reduction in water in the form of body fluids will cause symptoms of severe dehydration. A 20% reduction in body fluids is fatal.

Birds and other animals have three primary sources of water. First, the actual drinking of water is the main source. A number of factors may affect this source of water for cage birds. The growth of bacteria may make it unpalatable, and birds frequently will refuse to drink warm water. Cool, clean water is a necessity for avian nutrition. At times, outside water sources for birds, such as a continually dripping faucet, may harbor the growth of algae. These are tiny, green, one-celled plants that are harmless to the birds if eaten and are actually an excellent nutritional addition to the diet. Algae are nothing to be concerned about, since they grow in any natural water source in profusion.

The second water source is the food itself, since food contains a considerable quantity of water. Vegetables, of course, have the highest percentage of water. Tomatoes contain about 94% water, and cucumbers are 96% water. Carrots and onions contain 88%, and bananas and sweet corn are relatively low in water among the fruits and vegetables with a 76% water content. Spinach greens are about 90% water, and kale has a water content of about 87%.

Nuts and grains contain far less water. Cereal grains range from 11% to 13% water, with a water content in millet of about 12%. The oily seeds and nuts contain the least water of any food items, usually a maximum of about 5% in such items as safflower seed, sunflower seed, and almonds. Walnuts, peanuts and pecans contain even less water. If you've ever wondered why nuts make you thirsty, even when they're raw and unsalted, their low water content is the reason. It also follows that nuts are your best nutritional buy, since the water content is so small and the other nutritional contents are so high. As you might suspect, a whole egg, even hard boiled, averages 74% water, though some will test at about 65% water content.

The third source of water for the body is the internal metabolism. As proteins, fats, and carbohydrates are metabolized, water is created as a by-product of this process of energy production. For example, about one pound of water will be formed as one pound of fat is metabolized. Obviously, this is not a large amount in comparison to the body's needs, and this water source is minor in the life of most birds and animals. In some desert creatures, such as kangaroo rats, for example, this can be a very significant part of the body's needs for moisture.

Budgerigars, the common grass parakeets so familiar as pets, can go for an incredible length of time without water. In proven tests, they have lived in perfect health for periods of 120 days — four months — without a drop of water. Their sole water sources were the small content in their feed and the by-products of their heat and energy production. The budgerigar has an extremely well developed internal system for water conservation, perfectly adapted for desert life.

The body content of water may vary considerably at different times even within the same species. Chicks one week old may have a body water content of 85%, but this gradually decreases to 55% at maturity. The percentage of body water is closely related to the fat content of the body. The more fat stored within the body, the less will be the percentage of water content. This is why the normal variation from 50% to 75% water content in the human body can be so large. The average human body water content is 60%.

Two-thirds of the body water is within the cells. The blood is 80% water, but this is less than 8% of the total water content of the body. The kidneys are very efficient in conserving water, and they will resorb enough water routinely to maintain blood volume at a normal level. The water content of the birds' droppings varies a great deal, even within different strains of the same species. From 50% to 70% seems normal for chickens, and a similar amount can be expected in cage birds. Birds with very firm droppings, such as budgerigars, probably have less than 50% water content in their droppings. Under conditions of starvation, a bird can use up almost all of its glycogen or stored carbohydrate reserves, half of its protein and 40% of its total body weight and still live. However, the loss of only 20% of the water content of the body will kill the bird.

A bird will never voluntarily consume an excessive amount of water, since the body's needs are very closely controlled by factors that are not yet completely clear.

The water consumed is absorbed very rapidly, and it is lost through the kidneys and through evaporation in breathing. Water performs a very important function for the body in the regulation of body temperature, since water evaporation removes excess heat. Whenever the body begins to overheat, the bird will begin to pant. This evaporates far more moisture and results in greater cooling. Humans accomplish the same cooling effect through sweating when the body becomes overheated. The evaporation of one quart of sweat will dissipate 580 calories of heat. The panting of birds and the higher water evaporation at higher temperatures greatly increase their need for water. The difference in temperature from 70 degrees to 90 degrees Fahrenheit may increase water consumption by 100%.

Water serves several other functions in the body. In its most important function, it acts as a solvent and carrier for body nutrients, including monosaccharides, amino acids, phospholipids, vitamins, and minerals. These items will be covered in detail in the following sections. Water also carries the hormones and enzymes necessary for the proper functioning of every cell in the body. Water further serves as a lubricant, especially in the joints, and acts as a catalyst for many metabolic reactions.

Water carries a variety of substances in solution that are completely invisible, even under a microscope. These are dissolved minerals and compounds that the water picks up as it flows and exists in liquid form. Rainwater will pick up minerals and oxygen as it falls through the air. Unfortunately, minerals absorbed in this way are often the poisonous pollutants, such as lead, or toxic compounds, such as sulfuric acid. Ground water will absorb minerals wherever it flows, and this content is often a substantial source of minerals in the diet. Two minerals commonly found in water are chlorine from water treatment and inorganic iron from ground deposits. Both of these will destroy vitamin E on contact. Make every effort to exclude them from your birds' water supply. Refer to the section on vitamin E for more information on this vitamin.

Water is also the carrier of the waste products of the cells. These include carbon dioxide, nitrogen compounds from the breakdown of proteins, and other compounds that are poisonous or excess to the body's needs. These waste products are carried to the lungs and kidneys for excretion. Some also go to the liver where they are incorporated into the bile for excretion into the intestinal tract.

The most obvious symptom of a water deficiency in finches and cage birds is squinting. This characteristic seems to be specific for dehydration. The only other time you will notice this is if something is sprayed or placed directly into the bird's eyes. Squinting is a red flag of warning, and I cannot count the number of times birds have warned me of a water problem by this characteristic physical reaction. Normally, a bird without water for 24 hours or less will begin squinting, and this symptom is obvious at a glance from several feet away. More severe dehydration and death are just a step away from the act of squinting.

Only once has squinting failed to develop within 24 hours of water deprivation in my experience. In an act of sheer stupidity, I moved several finches to a new cage with all food items, but neglected to give them any water. It was 48 hours before I discovered this error, yet the birds still were not squinting, and they showed no sign of dehydration. Of course, they were down at the water as soon as it was placed in the cage. They were thirsty, but clearly were not suffering from lack of water. I can only attribute this to the fact that the temperature was cool during this period and stayed at about 55° Fahrenheit (13° C.) This apparently enabled the finches to conserve their water reserves very efficiently. During hot weather, such an extended period without water probably would have resulted in death.

The body contains far more water than any other substance. There is no substitute for water in the body's metabolism, and I cannot overstress the importance of a continuous water supply for the birds. If an emergency should occur that does away with almost all of your time for bird care temporarily, make sure that the birds have water along with some basic food item, such as millet for finches. All else can wait in an emergency. You can check a hundred cages for water and millet in five minutes, and a few days of such limited nutrition will not hurt healthy, adult birds in the least.

CHAPTER 3

PROTEINS

The modern world owes a Dutch chemist from Utrecht by the name of Gerrit Jan Mulder a humble note of thanks. In 1838 after many experiments, he announced his conclusion that all living plants and animals contain a certain substance without which life is impossible. Though Mulder didn't know what was in this substance, he was certain it was vital to life and named it protein, from a Greek word meaning first place. It took another hundred years for the first amino acid constituent of protein to be discovered and named.

Since that time, research has uncovered a great deal of information about proteins, and a summary of the known material will constitute this chapter. Hundreds of different types of protein have been identified and named. As examples, the main protein in corn is zein and the main one is milk is casein. Albumin is a protein in egg white, and hemoglobin is a vital protein component of the blood.

Protein is the raw material used by the body for building tissues. Muscles, toenails, beaks, feathers, and the bird's body organs are composed largely of protein. Protein is the second most plentiful substance in the body; only

water is more abundant. Without protein, there can be no
initial building of body tissue, nor can there be replacement of cells that wear out and die from use, damage, or
disease. Proteins are composed of the most complex
groupings of molecules known to science. Only living cells
can make proteins; they do not casually form from inorganic chemical reactions, such as the sun's energy striking
the earth or through the force of lightning.

The protein metabolism of all species of birds, mammals, and reptiles is very similar. The main differences
are in the nature of the end products of protein metabolism. Nevertheless, as Paul Griminger has stated in Chapter
12 of *Avian Physiology* in reference to birds, "Information on wild species is extremely scanty."

The protein cycle begins with plants. Only plants can
take up the necessary nitrogen and combine it with carbon,
hydrogen, and oxygen to form proteins. Birds and animals,
including insects, eat this plant material, extract the protein from it, and utilize it for their own bodies. This process is extremely complex, and much has yet to be learned
about the make-up and utilization of proteins. When an
organism dies, the proteins in its cells are broken down by
bacterial and chemical action into their component parts,
and the cycle is complete.

Each of these complex proteins is made up of substances called amino acids. Amino acids are the building
blocks of proteins, and each type of protein contains
different amino acids in differing quantities. The hemoglobin molecule, for example, contains 574 amino acids
in the globin portion of the molecule. The nitrogen of the
amino group is unique to protein and constitutes an average of 16% of the amino acid molecules, which are the
building blocks of all proteins. Nitrogen makes up a low
point of 15% of the amino acids in milk, and a high point
of 18% of the amino acids of nuts.

In the process of digestion, the digestive system breaks down the ingested proteins into their component amino acids. These amino acids are then absorbed through the intestinal wall, molecule by molecule. They pass into the bloodstream and are absorbed by each cell, recombined, and used by each cell of the body in the necessary quantities. Once absorbed by the cell, the amino acids are used to build, repair, and replace its parts, or to divide for growth of the tissue.

Amino acids are divided into two major headings: the essential amino acids, and the non-essential amino acids. The term essential when applied to amino acids means that the body cannot make them in sufficient quantity from other materials on hand, and that they must be consumed in the form of food. Non-essential amino acids can be manufactured by the body's organs by breaking down other food components and amino acids, or by combining them in the correct amounts. Keep in mind that all of the amino acids are necessary to the body, but those termed essential cannot be made in sufficient quantity within the body. In other words, it is essential to get them in the food supply. Frequent misunderstanding results from the use of the term "essential" in this sense. Proteins which contain all of the essential amino acids are referred to as complete proteins; those lacking one or more of the essential amino acids in sufficient quantity are referred to as incomplete proteins.

Extensive nutritional research has proven conclusively that all of the essential amino acids must be eaten within a few hours time in order for the body to use them for tissue building. They can be retained chemically unchanged for only a few hours. If the amino acids in the body are not used, either because of incomplete supply or excess supply, they are filtered out of the blood by the liver. The liver strips away the nitrogen, converts it to uric acid, and the body disposes of it through the kidneys. The remaining components of the amino acid are utilized for energy or stored as fat.

Within the plant kingdom, virtually all of the proteins are incomplete or at best unbalanced, partly lacking one or more of the essential amino acids in sufficient quantity. Soybeans and nuts are the most complete protein foods in the plant kingdom. When several different types of plant material are eaten, the protein content of one will complement that of the other. That is, one plant will supply the amino acids that the next one is lacking. Much as North Americans may chuckle over the Mexican diet of tortillas and frijoles, the corn and beans they represent are ideally complementary in their protein content. No one will ever suffer from a protein deficiency from eating an adequate quantity of corn and beans at one meal. Kwashiorkor, an abdominal bloating disease caused partially by lack of complete protein, is not common in Mexico, but endemic in Central Africa, where millet is the staple food with no other vegetative source to complement the incomplete protein in millet. And yet, millet is one of the better sources of complete protein in the plant kingdom. A completely vegetarian diet with no animal-derived food from any source can still supply complete, balanced protein to the body, with a knowledgeable blend of various vegetative sources.

Proteins from any animal source are mostly complete proteins, with gelatin being a notable exception. They contain all of the essential amino acids in adequate quantity for utilization by the body for optimal health. For this reason, the use of animal protein is stressed in many works dealing with nutrition.

While plant sources are normally low in the percentage of protein that they contain, animal sources are usually much higher in that percentage. Most grains, for example,

contain from 11% to 13% protein, most of which is incomplete. Insects, by contrast, are an extremely good
source of complete protein. Grasshoppers are 60% complete
protein. The dry weight of an earthworm is about 72%
pure, complete protein. With this in mind, it is easy to see
why nestling birds thrive and grow so rapidly on a diet of
insects.

Though many of the available writings disagree for
one reason or another, most of the current publications on
the subject of nutrition list ten amino acids that are
termed essential. These essential amino acids cannot be
synthesized by the body at a rate sufficient to meet the
needs for growth and maintenance. Alphabetically, these
are arginine, histidine, isoleucine, leucine, lysine, methionine, phenylalanine, threonine, tryptophan, and valine.
Other works in disagreement will usually list two additional
amino acids, cystine and tyrosine. Histidine and arginine
apparently are not essential to all avian species, nor to
humans at all times. Histidine is essential for human
infants, however. Glycine, usually considered as non-
essential, has been proven essential for chicks. It is probably essential for many avian species. Therefore, it seems
obvious that no hard and fast rule will apply on essentiality
to all species at all times. Most authorities consider the
grouping of ten as the definitive list under most circumstances. These, then, are the amino acids that must be
taken together, in adequate quantity, at the same time, in
order to perform the tasks required by the body.

In any protein complex, the essential amino acid
present in the smallest relative amount is called the limiting amino acid. Methionine is the limiting amino acid in
soybeans. Wheat's limiting amino acid is lysine, and corn
lacks tryptophan in adequate quantities.

Some of the important amino acids so far identified
that are generally agreed to be non-essential are alanine,

aspartic acid, cirrulline, cysteine, cystine, glutamic acid, glycine, hydroxyproline, hydroxyglutamic acid, norleucine, proline, serine, taurine, and tyrosine. Glycine, as one example, is the principal amino acid in sugar cane. Though they are definitely necessary for nutritional purposes, the body can manufacture each of them from one or more other amino acids. Any nutritional supplement specifying these non-essential amino acids in its ingredients is playing upon the nutritional ignorance of the aviculturist.

In reading on the subject of protein, you frequently will see references to the sulfur-containing amino acids. There are three primary sulfur-containing amino acids. They are methionine, cysteine, and cystine. Another one of less importance is taurine. Cystine is a primary protein component of the protein keratin, from which feathers are formed. Fully 20% of the amino acid content of keratin is cystine. These four amino acids all contain sulfur as a mineral component.

Collagen is the vital connective tissue that holds tissues of the body together. With poorly formed collagen, the cells literally come unglued. One-third of collagen is made up of the amino acid glycine. Proline and hydroxyproline make up another one-third of the amino acid content of collagen. This connective tissue can be boiled with water or acid to produce the common food item called gelatin. Lest we call the view of collagen as a glue too simplistic what other glue do we have that will glue water together, as gelatin does?

There is also a great degree of importance attached to both the individual non-essential amino acids and to the individual essential amino acids in the body's metabolism, apart from their use as protein constituents. For example, tyrosine alone is used in the thyroid gland for the production of thyroxine. Also, tyrosine is the foundation for the dark pigment melanin, so common in birds and animals.

The amino acids join together by what are called peptide linkages to form all proteins. Water is necessary for protein breakdown in the digestive tract, and it is a by-product of protein synthesis from the individual amino acids. Glycine is the simplest of these amino acids, and myoglobin, an oxygen-carrying protein within the muscle cells, is considered a simple protein. Yet, myoglobin is so complicated that only in 1961 was the complete composition and structure discovered. Myoglobin contains nineteen different amino acids in varying amounts to form a total of 150 amino acid units. The most complicated proteins can have thousands of amino acid units in their make-up.

Intestinal bacteria can change the amino acid histidine into histamine, a toxic compound. This histamine can be absorbed into the blood, giving characteristic allergy symptoms. Also, breakdown of tissue protein in times of food scarcity forms histamine as a by-product. The liver can destroy histamine in the bloodstream by means of an enzyme called histaminase. Also, vitamins B-6, C, and pantothenic acid all have an antihistamine effect. Histamine is found in many soft tissues and in small amounts does seem to perform a useful function, particularly with respect to the functioning of the brain.

High temperatures used in drying some foods lower the protein value in them, since some of the essential amino acids are destroyed by high heat. For example, 90% of the tryptophan is lost in high heat drying of foods. For this reason, prolonged cooking or baking of foods is unwise either for birds or people, quite apart from the loss of vitamins in such cooking.

The richest sources of protein for finches and other cage birds are, of course, the animal sources. These are naturally the most expensive. No good source of animal protein is cheap, since any member of the animal kingdom must first consume a huge quantity of either plant or other animal material in order to incorporate sufficient protein into its own body. The members of the animal kingdom concentrate the protein from the plant kingdom and thus serve as good sources of complete protein themselves.

Hard boiled eggs are one of the most reasonably priced complete protein foods obtainable for your birds. Eggs average about 13% high quality, complete protein. To prepare them for the most complete consumption, shell the eggs and mash the white and yolk together thoroughly. Since this will result in a fairly damp mixture, prone to spoil rapidly, I recommend the addition of a dry protein supplement to the egg at a ration of about one teaspoon per egg, mixed thoroughly. Soy protein extract is very good, and gelatin can also be used, though it is not a complete protein food, lacking the essential amino acid tryptophan. Either of these dry products will sharply and advantageously increase the protein content of the mixture. You may add one teaspoon of any powdered vitamin-mineral supplement to this mixture to excellent advantage. Theralin and Vionate are two of the better known commercially available vitamin-mineral supplements on the American market. When thoroughly mixed in this manner, with both the powdered protein and vitamin-mineral supplement, the egg will not spoil even under very hot, humid conditions. It will dry out and harden first. This characteristic of this particular egg mixture is invaluable to the aviculturist who must feed his charges only once a day. The addition of any oil, water, or high carbohydrate product will cause rapid and total spoilage of this mixture.

I have formulated a supplement with a high protein base, designed specifically for mixing with Vionate. This supplement also contains additional vitamins A, D, E, and cobalamin, which I felt Vionate to be low in for avian nutrition. Zinc is also added, since Vionate contains none. This commercially made mixture has resulted in exceptional quality in my own birds when mixed in the prescribed manner with hard boiled egg and Vionate. Many aviculturists now use it consistently and have reported excellent results in their breeding.

Mealworms are another ideal protein source from the animal kingdom, though they are far too expensive for continuous feeding to birds as inexpensive as Society or Zebra Finches. It is far more economical to reserve them for use with the rarer finches and softbills. To repeat my disagreement with an established old wives' tale, I firmly feel that it is impossible to overfeed mealworms to a well nourished pair of birds. In raising Brazilian Red-crested Cardinals, I have always offered pairs feeding young ones and on maintenance diets all of the mealworms they want free choice. While I raised these birds, fertility, hatchability, and successful fledging were all 100%.

The dry dog foods are an ideal source of inexpensive, complete protein. Getting most cage birds to try this food after lightly soaking it may be a trick in itself. These birds are very stubborn about trying anything new, particularly when the food is damp. Softbills are usually far better subjects for the feeding of dog foods.

From the plant kingdom, sunflower seeds supply about the highest protein content of any commonly fed plant material in aviculture, averaging about 26%. The sunflower seed protein is more nearly complete than that of most plant material, also. Obviously, finches with their small beaks will not easily shell a sunflower seed, but shelled seed is always available from health food stores and nutritional centers. Be sure to get raw sunflower seed, not the toasted specialty item. Don't let the price scare you away, because pound for pound, sunflower seeds are one of your greatest nutritional values. Though it may take finches some time to get used to sunflower seeds, once accustomed to them, the birds will consume them as readily as millet. Sunflower seed is certainly far more nutritious than any cereal grain. In offering shelled sunflower seed at the wild bird feeder, you will be rewarded by many softbilled birds coming to the feeder. I have watched Red-headed Woodpeckers sitting with newly fledged young ones on the feeder, stuffing them with the shelled sunflower seeds. All birds instinctively recognize these seeds as a nutritional delicacy. The larger doves all consume them greedily, and Green-winged Doves are particularly fond of them.

I have maintained non-breeding Society Finches on a diet of only shelled sunflower seed, white proso millet, and water for many months in perfect condition. This is strictly a maintenance diet for finches, however, as it is very deficient in such nutrients as vitamins A and D and will allow no breeding whatsoever. Any eggs laid will fail to hatch with embryos dying in the shell. If one in a hundred does succeed in hatching out, the protein content of this simple maintenance diet is insufficient for successful rearing to healthy maturity. Restoration of the egg mixture previously described to this diet will result in 100% fertile clutches, hatches, and young fledged within one week. More clearly, hens laying one week after egg supplementation begins will lay fertile, hatchable clutches, and will raise their young to maturity.

Peanuts are rich in protein, with an average value of 25%. If fed to birds, peanuts should always be raw, never roasted, and particularly never roasted in oil and salted. As a protein source for the price, however, peanuts are hard to beat. Most large food stores will carry shelled raw peanuts at a reasonable price.

Any of the nuts are ideal sources of plant protein that is among the most complete of any found in the plant kingdom. The price is high, however, and economics will usually prevent the average fancier from offering them to finches on a regular basis.

The protein surprises of the plant world are pine nuts, also called pignolias, and soybeans. Pine nuts average 33% protein, while soybeans contain more than 35% well balanced protein. The pignolias are a nutritional specialty item, and you can expect to pay a relatively huge price per pound for them.

At times, you may run into the term "crude protein" as a percentage of the nutritional contents of an item. This term includes all parts of the food that can be considered as proteins, with a nitrogen base, regardless of whether they are digestible. In many cases, substantial portions of the listed crude protein content may be indigestible and valueless to avian nutrition. This type of protein would constitute only bulk in the diet, and as far as can be determined, bulk is not required in the nutrition of birds.

Protein deficiency is, unfortunately, the most common problem encountered in the care and handling of cage birds. Feather plucking, loss of weight, egg eating, poor feathering, and loss of young in the nest may all be symptoms of such a deficiency. Without sufficient protein, the replacement of lost tissue is slow and may stop completely. The bird will become listless, lose weight, and eventually will die.

Absorption of amino acids in the intestine of a chick is dependent upon the presence of vitamin B-6, also called pyridoxine. If that vitamin is deficient, the amino acids cannot be absorbed. Consequently, even though the diet may be rich in protein, it is completely unabsorbable, and the chick will die of protein deficiency.

The body of a bird is predominantly protein. From one-fifth to one-quarter of the fat free body of birds is protein. When you consider that much of the remainder is water, all of the minerals, vitamins, and carbohydrates are but a small part of the total. In addition, up to one-third of the total protein of a bird may be in the form of keratin in the feathers. All muscles, organs, hormones, enzymes, and antibodies are formed from protein. The importance of protein in cage bird nutrition cannot be over-emphasized.

Feather plucking is the most obvious warning symptom of protein deficiency. Feathers are almost pure protein, with traces of minerals. In cases of deficiency in the diet, the bird's only other source of protein is from destroying the feathers and body of its neighbors or itself. Feather plucking in finches is usually started by protein deficiency. A diet of the standard finch seed mixes, grit, and minerals in the form of mineral blocks or cuttlebone is deficient in the essential amino acids lysine and tryptophan, not to mention the severe vitamin deficiencies it represents.

Loss of weight is an indication that the protein portions of the body are being used for energy to maintain body heat and energy. Muscle tissue is broken down first, since it is the least necessary for life. This breakdown may stem from several causes, chief among them the inability to digest food and extract the protein and other nutrients from it, possibly as the result of disease microorganisms. A deficiency of protein in the food will cause a gradual loss of weight, as the body robs one of its parts of protein to keep another going.

When protein and its constituent amino acids are broken down for energy by the bird's metabolism, the result is a great deal of excess nitrogen. This must be converted to uric acid for excretion by the kidneys. This necessary function causes a strain on the metabolic system, and can easily lead to excess water consumption and a much higher water content of the droppings. In mild diarrhea of this type, a microorganism may not be directly responsible for the watery droppings.

Birds starved for complete protein can rarely be induced to breed. If they do, this so robs the hen of her meager protein resources that she may instinctively eat her own eggs as a source of replacement protein. Lest this be considered highly unusual, remember that it is one of nature's ways of maintaining population balances among the myriad species of life. If the protein content of the food supply were insufficient for two adult birds in the wild, it could not possibly be available for raising and supporting a nest of young ones. The breeding is thus terminated at an early stage by the female's egg eating. To do otherwise would only put an added burden on the hen when the young would be sure to die of protein deficiency anyway.

Protein requirements vary at different stages in the life of a bird. The requirement for a newly hatched bird for its first week of growth is very high. During the second, third, and fourth weeks, the young make their growth to a nearly full-sized body, mostly feathered, depending upon the species. This three week period is the most critical in terms of protein requirement. If the diet is deficient for more than a couple of days during this period in either the quantity or quality of the protein consumed, the nestlings will be sure to die. You can prevent this only by assuring that the parent birds have available to them all of the high protein food they will consume. When the growing body is increasing in size so rapidly and feathers are forming all over the body at the same time, the need for relatively huge quantities of protein is constant and crucial.

After this period of maximum growth, the protein requirement gradually decreases. This will be noted in the decreasing amount of protein food consumed. Though feathers are still growing and the body structure maturing, the bulk of the growth is completed at the end of the fourth week in most finches and other small birds. In the feather development, amino acids play a part in the color formation as well as the structure of the feathers. To repeat a prior example, melanin, the pigment responsible for dark browns and black, is derived from the amino acid tyrosine.

Once the bird reaches maturity, the protein requirement is much smaller, just enough to replace lost cells in the body and maintain the feather structure. You will note that mature finches not breeding and not in a molt will consume very little high protein food, less than one-quarter teaspoon per day for each finch. By contrast, when feeding a nest of growing youngsters, a pair may clean up as much as three tablespoons of high protein food per day. A molt will again increase the amount of protein consumed, since the body requires larger amounts of protein for the formation of feathers.

When the hen is forming eggs, the protein requirement once again will increase. Eggs in themselves are rich in protein, since they must contain the full complement of protein necessary for the development of the embryo from one cell to a fully functioning baby bird in only about two weeks time.

Though the individual amino acids cannot be retained in the body for long, once they have been incorporated into the body's protein complexes, they act secondarily as a food reserve. The proteins form an emergency reserve food supply that may be called upon from time to time. In cases of simple protein deficiency or disease, as mentioned before, the body can break down the protein components of the muscles to provide repair material for the vital organs or to provide energy when it is necessary to prevent death, as in cases of starvation. Once the emergency has passed, the body will replace the protein and rebuild the depleted muscle tissue.

It seems to be impossible to get an excess of balanced protein in the diet. More protein than the body needs will never cause any problem, provided the vitamins and minerals necessary to break it down and utilize it are available in sufficient supply. Any excess over the need for amino acids is broken down by the liver and used for energy by the body's cells.

Nevertheless, excessive intake of one or more of the essential amino acids in pure form can cause an amino acid imbalance or toxicity. This will result in less food intake and a decrease in growth. This will occur only in controlled nutritional experimentation, not with any natural, protein-rich food. In such nutritional testing, methionine has been shown to be the most toxic of the essential amino acids.

Utilization of the protein consumed may be adversely influenced by a number of factors. Disease has already been mentioned as a factor in the inability of a digestive system to digest the food and absorb the amino acids of digested protein. The intestinal lining can also become coated with some substance that prevents the amino acids from passing through into the bloodstream. A variety of vitamin and mineral deficiencies will have a similar effect.

Any lack of essential vitamins and minerals may prevent the proper absorption and utilization of amino acids once they are made available by the digestive process. The vitamins and minerals are necessary at all levels of digestion, assimilation, and body-building. They make the creation of new tissue possible, while at the same time they may constitute vital and indispensable parts of that tissue. Separate chapters are devoted to thorough discussions of all of the vitamins and minerals, though you can hardly discuss one aspect of nutrition without mentioning others, since all facets of the nutritive process are interrelated.

A finch in a cage is helpless in the face of your lack of knowledge of its protein needs. Protein is vital to its life. There is no substitute for that protein. It must be complete to be properly utilized, and it must be eaten in sufficient quantity. Neither the quantity nor the quality may be compromised without disastrous results. Adequate protein is one of those indispensable keys to keeping and breeding healthful birds. Never forget that protein deficiency is by far the most common deficiency encountered in cage birds.

CHAPTER 4

FATS

This chapter contains many terms that seem calculated to curl the hair of all but Yul Brynner. Yet, the explanations of many authorities are presented here in the most logical and concise forms I could manage. For one who has never yet delved into the subject of fats and their nutritional importance, the first reading will not be totally assimilated. Once the contents of this chapter are thoroughly digested, however, no reference to fats that you encounter in the future will ever again be a mystery. We are indeed fortunate that enough material is available from research over the years to give us a good idea of the functions of fats and their metabolism. Such is certainly not the case with many of the other known nutrients.

Fats in the diet serve three primary purposes. First, they are a source of energy for the body's needs for heat production and muscle action. Secondly, fats serve as carriers for the fat soluble vitamins, essential fatty acids, and minerals. Third, they are the food storage mechanism for the body. In addition, fats remain in the digestive system longer than other food constituents and act to suppress

52

the appetite, since they are digested rather slowly. Researchers have discovered that in maintaining chickens, a small amount of fat added to the diet will increase the efficiency of energy utilization and incorporation into the avian body. This will hold true even when the total energy value of the two diets is the same.

A dietary intake of food over and above the body's requirement for energy, growth, and rebuilding of cells is stored as fat. This stored fat is a reserve source of body heat and energy when the caloric value of the food is insufficient, as it is during a temporary fast. This stored fat also acts as a cushion for the body, particularly for the vital organs. The kidneys are especially well protected by a fat cushion. Fat stored under the skin helps to protect muscles and nerves. It is also important in maintaining the body temperature and insulating the body from environmental changes.

Fats and oils may come from either animal or vegetable sources in the diet. The term fats generally refers to those substances that are solid at room temperature, while oils are liquids at room temperature. One word, lipids, refers to fats and oils together. The term lipids will be used frequently in the continuation of this discussion to refer to the fats and oils as a group.

Animal fats are predominantly solid at room temperature, while sources from cold-blooded creatures and plants are predominantly liquid. Fish, for example, contain mostly oils. Since they are cold-blooded, fats would stiffen their body tissues, and could be deadly. All whole fats and oils have varying combinations of what are called fatty acids, which themselves may be in the form of either oils or fats. For example, more than thirty different fatty acids occur in the butterfat of milk.

A slightly more technical way of presenting this distinction is with the terms saturated and unsaturated when applied to the fatty acids. Note the following drawing of stearic acid, a saturated fatty acid:

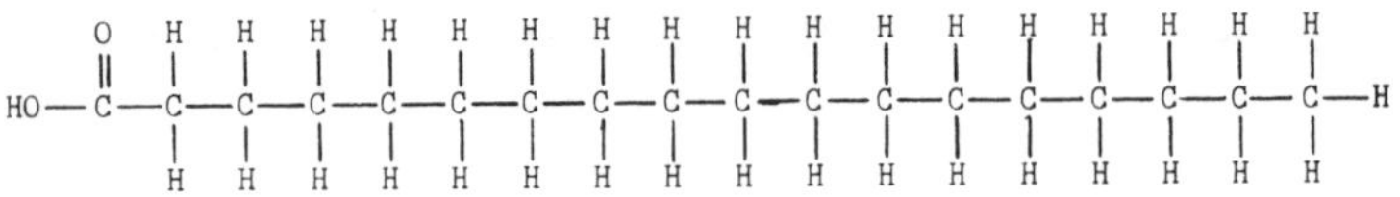

$$
\underset{\text{HO}}{\text{HO}} - \overset{\displaystyle O}{\underset{\displaystyle H}{\overset{\|}{C}}} - \overset{H}{\underset{H}{C}} - \overset{H}{\underset{H}{C}} - \overset{H}{\underset{H}{C}} - \overset{H}{\underset{H}{C}} - \overset{H}{\underset{H}{C}} - \overset{H}{\underset{H}{C}} - \overset{H}{\underset{H}{C}} - \overset{H}{\underset{H}{C}} - \overset{H}{\underset{H}{C}} - \overset{H}{\underset{H}{C}} - \overset{H}{\underset{H}{C}} - \overset{H}{\underset{H}{C}} - \overset{H}{\underset{H}{C}} - \overset{H}{\underset{H}{C}} - \overset{H}{\underset{H}{C}} - \overset{H}{\underset{H}{C}} - \overset{H}{\underset{H}{C}} - H
$$

Stearic Acid

H = Hydrogen
C = Carbon
O = Oxygen

Diagram No. 1

Such a saturated fatty acid contains all of the hydrogen atoms it can carry. Every available bond is solidly filled, so the compound is saturated and a solid fat as a result.

Unsaturated fatty acids may be monounsaturated or polyunsaturated. This means that one or more of the double hydrogen bonds are empty and not attached to a hydrogen atom. This makes the resulting molecule more flexible, and therefore that fatty acid will be a liquid. Each of these double bond linkages will hold two additional atoms, either hydrogen atoms or others.

The term monounsaturated means that one of the possible double bond linkages is empty, leaving room for two additional atoms. The following illustration of oleic acid, a monounsaturated fatty acid, will illustrate this concept:

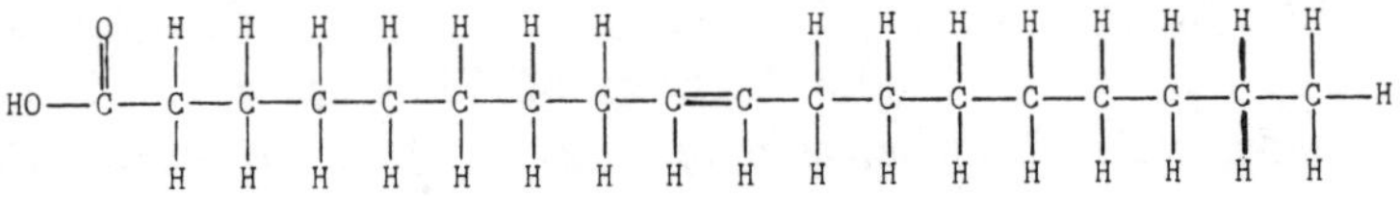

Oleic Acid

Diagram No. 2

Oleic acid constitutes from 70% to 75% of the fatty acids
in olive oil, 50% or more in peanut oil, and 40% of beef,
lamb, and poultry fat. Most of the common monounsaturated fatty acids have the double bond linkage in the
ninth position, between the 9th and 10th carbon atoms
as it is in oleic acid.

The designation polyunsaturated indicates that two or
more of the double bond linkages are empty, leaving room
for four, six, or more additional atoms. The following
drawing of a linoleic acid molecule, a polyunsaturated
fatty acid, will illustrate this explanation.

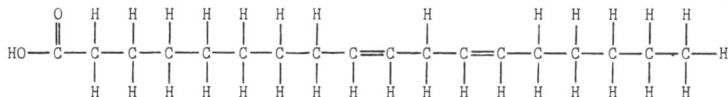

Linoleic Acid

Diagram No. 3

Linoleic acid is chemically described as 9, 12 octadeca-
dienoic, meaning that it has a chain of 18 carbon atoms
with two double bond linkages at the 9th and 12th carbon
atoms.

As shown in the illustrations, the fatty acids are chains
of carbon atoms which may or may not have hydrogen
atoms attached. At one end of the chain, three hydrogen
atoms are attached to the last carbon atom. This is referred
to as a methyl group. The other end of the chain of carbon
atoms is an acid group, also called a carboxyl group. This
structure is characteristic of all fatty acids. This drawing
of the palmitic acid molecule, a saturated fatty acid, points
out these characteristics.

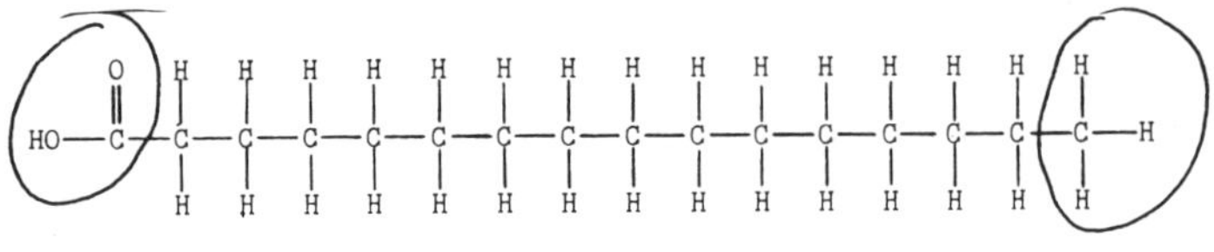

Palmitic Acid

Diagram No. 4

Fatty acids can be short-chain, with less than twelve carbon atoms, long-chain, with twelve to eighteen carbon atoms, or extra long-chain with twenty carbon atoms or more. Short-chain fatty acids occur mostly in milk fat and coconut oil. The shortest chain in the butterfat of milk is butyric acid, with a chain length of only four carbon atoms. Extra long-chains occur mostly in fish oils.

Saturated fatty acids can be any chain length from four to eighteen or more. The most common ones are stearic acid with eighteen carbon atoms in the chain, palmitic acid with sixteen, myristic acid with fourteen, and lauric acid with twelve carbon atoms in the chain.

Three of the fatty acids are essential, all of them polyunsaturated: linoleic, linolenic, and arachidonic. They will be covered in detail separately. The other common fatty acids are palmitoleic, oleic, timnodonic, and clupanodonic.

With the exception of the essential unsaturated fatty acids, birds have no known requirement for dietary fat. Experimental hens were deprived of fat in the diet for 19 months. They showed no long-term difficulties, and at the end of this period, their eggs hatched normally.

When oxygen atoms attach themselves to the open linkages of the unsaturated fatty acid molecule, the fat becomes rancid. This is called oxidative rancidity, and the resulting compound is called a peroxide. All fats have a strong tendency to form peroxides, which are toxic in the body. Peroxides can destroy enzyme systems and break down red blood cells. In nature, natural antioxidants prevent this from happening. The most common and best antioxidant is vitamin E, which occurs naturally with unsaturated fats. This oxygen-caused rancidity results in a large decrease in the energy value of the fats. Do not handle any fats in copper equipment, since copper is a catalyst for oxidative rancidity.

Fats can also turn rancid as a result of the actions of microorganisms. This process is called hydrolytic rancidity. Hydrolytic rancidity does not interfere with the fat's nutritional value.

The process of hydrogenation forces hydrogen through a lipid to fill the open linkages in the unsaturated fatty acids. This alters the oils to a less unsaturated or completely saturated state and prevents oxygen from attaching itself to these linkages. In the case of linoleic acid, a polyunsaturated fatty acid, partial hydrogenation changes it to the monounsaturated oleic acid, which is not a dietary essential. Hydrogenation greatly increases the storage life of a fat product. Nutritionally, hydrogenation is a disaster because of its destruction of linoleic acid.

Whether fat stored in the body is predominantly saturated and solid or predominantly unsaturated and more liquid is dependent upon its source. The body stores both types. Any fat made by the body from excess carbohydrates in the diet through the process called lipogenesis will be solid and predominantly saturated, since the body is unable to form linoleic acid, the primary unsaturated fat in the body's metabolism. Birds are able to form oleic acid for storage. Fats stored from an excess fat intake in the diet will be softer, containing a portion of linoleic acid. Any human or bird deriving all of its excess calories from unsaturated fats will have very soft, flabby fat on the body. Though this may be a social disaster, it is far superior from a nutritional point of view. Fatty acids are not excreted in the urine, so their food value depends on their absorption in the intestine.

The body, whether bird, mammal, or fish, stores fat because it is the most efficient energy storage method in nature. A given weight of fat furnishes 2.25 times as much energy when metabolized as the same weight of either protein or carbohydrate. Fats are the most concentrated dietary source of energy, yielding 9.4 calories per gram, compared with only 4.15 calories per gram for protein and carbohydrate. Consequently, fat storage is 2.25 times more efficient for energy in the body than the other energy sources available. For this reason, when muscle tissue begins to be metabolized in a sick bird, you can be sure that all fat reserves not essential to life have been utilized completely. Only the fats vital to the maintenance of life will remain. In starvation to death, the fat content of the body will not drop significantly below 4% of the total body weight. The adipose tissues contain the stored cellular fat in both birds and people.

In 1814 the French chemist Michel Eugene Chevreul discovered that whole fats are composed of fatty acids and glycerol, also called glycerin. The suffix -ol indicates an alcohol in any chemical name. This noteworthy discovery has been the basis of all subsequent knowledge gained about the structure of fats. One, two, or three fatty acids can attach themselves to the glycerol base. If only one fatty acid is attached, the compound is called a monoglyceride. Two fatty acids attached to the glycerol is a diglyceride. If the maximum of three fatty acids is attached, the resulting fat is a triglyceride. The following drawing will illustrate the structure of a triglyceride:

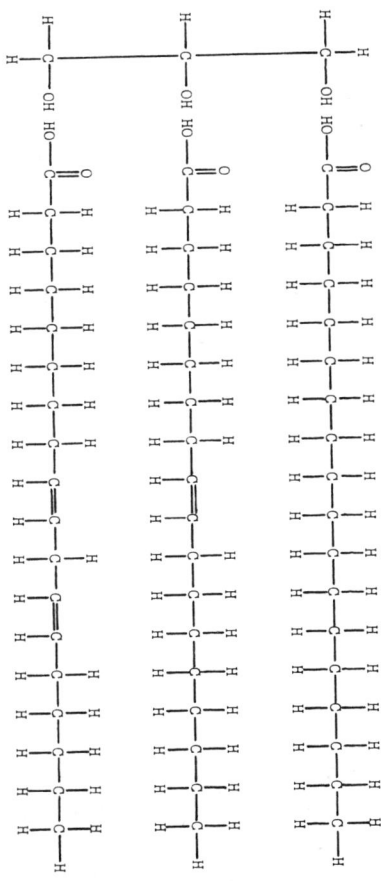

A triglyceride molecule showing three attached fatty acids: Stearic Acid, Oleic Acid, and Linoleic Acid

Diagram No. 5

Either saturated or unsaturated fatty acids can be attached to the glycerol in any combination. This allows thousands of different kinds of fats and oils to be formed. Glycerol is the only part of the triglyceride molecule that can be converted to glucose for the direct energy needs of the cells. The fatty acids, whether saturated or unsaturated, must be radically transformed by the body's metabolic processes first.

In digestion, enzymes split off the fatty acids from the glycerol. The outer positions will be stripped off first. The middle position will be taken away less rapidly and sometimes not at all. In birds, the resulting monoglycerides of the saturated fats are absorbed by the intestines more easily than the free saturated fatty acids.

When glycerol joins with a fatty acid, the resulting compound technically is called an ester. Fats which are simple lipids are esters of glycerol and fatty acids. Any esters formed by the combination of any alcohol other than glycerol and fatty acids are called waxes.

The term compound lipids refers to those fats with a glycerol base, two fatty acids, and the third available position having another chemical group, such as the B vitamin choline, linked with it through phosphoric acid. This combination forms lecithin, one of the most important and well-known compound lipids.

Phospholipids are complex fats linked chemically to phosphorus, and they are found in all plant and animal tissues. They are especially abundant in nervous tissue and may constitute up to 30% of the dry matter of the brain tissue. Triglycerides and phospholipids make up the vast majority of circulating fats in the bloodstream.

Lipids circulating in the blood come from three sources. Intestinal absorption and synthesis, primarily in the liver, are the two primary sources. The third source is from the mobilization of fat deposits when caloric intake is insufficient for body needs. Of the portion absorbed into the bloodstream from the intestine, half of the fatty acids are linked into cholesterol and phospholipids. The rest will remain as glycerides or free fatty acids. Fats also may be attached to amino acids in the blood for easier transport through the bloodstream. These are known as lipoproteins.

The term cholesterol is familiar to everyone thanks to its notoriety in relation to heart and circulatory diseases. No discussion of fats would be complete without mention of it. A thorough, unbiased look at cholesterol indicates that it is definitely not the boogieman the news media would have us believe. Cholesterol is an essential constituent of blood, nerves, the brain, and other parts of the body. The body's own cells, especially in the liver, manufacture cholesterol at the relatively high rate of two to three grams per day. This is more than four times as much as the average diet is likely to contain during the same period. It should be obvious, then, that a low cholesterol diet may be little more than a fool's panacea. A really excessive intake of high cholesterol foods can, of course, increase the blood's cholesterol level, but nothing is going to stop the body's cells from manufacturing it. High dietary intake may suppress normal body synthesis of cholesterol, but a low dietary intake will increase body synthesis.

A diet rich in polyunsaturated fats, particularly linoleic acid, and adequate vitamins and minerals, is unlikely to cause any abnormal buildup of cholesterol deposits. Since all nutrients work together in the nutrition of man or birds, a deficiency of any will cause misappropriation of some others. This is what happens in the dangerous depositing of cholesterol in the circulatory system. It is definitely not normal for cholesterol to form in deposits of this type. Such abnormalities are virtually unknown in

so-called primitive societies where refined food products
are unknown. See the sections on chromium, vanadium
and vitamin E for further information on circulatory and
heart needs in nutrition.

Inadequate fat intake can cause excessive water retention. Deficiencies of the fat soluble vitamins will also be
likely, since the fats are carriers of all of the fat soluble
vitamins. Also, the intestines cannot absorb vitamins A,
D, E, or K without the presence of fat. With this
background in lipids, attention turns next to the essential
fatty acids, which perform the functions of a vitamin and
are referred to frequently as vitamin F.

The Essential Fatty Acids — Vitamin F

There are three of the fatty acids that are termed
essential in the nutrition of birds and people. These are
linoleic acid, linolenic acid, and arachidonic acid. Though all
three are termed essential, linoleic acid is the only one that
seems to be absolutely essential for birds. With an abundance of linoleic acid in the diet, the body can synthesize
arachidonic acid from some of it. If quantities of linoleic
acid are insufficient, this process cannot occur. In the presence of a variety of necessary vitamins and minerals, the
body can also synthesize linolenic acid from an abundant
supply of linoleic. Without linoleic acid, nothing will happen, and death will be the eventual result. Enough linoleic
acid in the diet of chickens negates the need for any of the
others. The essential fatty acids perform the functions of a
vitamin in the body and are referred to in many writings
as vitamin F. Especially in Europe, vitamin F is a common
designation for the essential fatty acids.

As previously discussed, linoleic acid has two double
bond linkages open and available. Linolenic acid has three
available double bond linkages, and arachidonic acid has

four available double bonds. Arachidonic acid forms one percent or less of most animal fats and less than one percent or none in vegetable fats.

Vitamin E is very closely associated with these essentail fatty acids in nature. Natural vegetable oils are rich in vitamin E, which performs as an antioxidant. This action prevents oxygen from forming peroxides and other toxic compounds by its oxidative actions on the fatty acids.

The outstanding function of the essential fatty acids is structural. They are required for the proper formation of the internal structure and cell membranes of every cell. The myelin nerve sheaths and connective tissues in the body also require essential fatty acids for their formation. They are critical for the health of the blood and arteries and vital for healthy nerves. Without the essential fatty acids, there would be no growth.

Linoleic acid, in particular, combines with other substances in the body in order to perform its functions. When combined with phosphorus, linoleic acid has its greatest biological activity. Such a combination occurs in lecithin.

Other dietary factors being equal, an increased dietary intake of linoleic acid will lower blood cholesterol levels. It helps to protect against excessive water loss in an animal and has also been shown to be a protective factor against radiation damage. Linoleic acid is necessary for both growth and reproduction. A deficiency in chickens will produce a striking reduction in the size of eggs laid.

It is significant that linolenic acid will reduce the adhesiveness of the blood platelets. This lessens the danger of a clot. Linoleic acid alone will not perform this function. This is obviously one of the reasons for the continued classification of linolenic acid as essential.

For cage birds, the commonly fed oily seeds are excellent sources of the essential fatty acids, particularly of

linoleic acid. Safflower is by far the best, since safflower
oil ranges from 70% to 75% linoleic acid. Sunflower seeds
are also an exceptionally good source, as are all walnuts.
Flax is probably the best source of linolenic acid.

In feeding canaries a variety of seeds free choice in
equal amounts, the seeds I have offered are white proso
millet, canary, rape, flax, and shelled sunflower. The flax
seed dish is invariably the first emptied, with the sunflower a close second. Last emptied are the dishes of
canary, millet, and rape, in that order. Given a choice, the
canaries will eat very little rape, preferring to get the oils
in their diet from flax and sunflower. Obviously, this
gives canaries a very high calorie diet which demands
adequate exercise to forestall serious obesity. Yet, the
birds always can be trusted to choose a diet nutritionally
balanced from a wide variety of offerings.

Human needs for linoleic acid are larger than for most
animals, as evidenced by the content of milk. Human milk
will contain two to four times as much linoleic acid as does
the butterfat content of a cow's milk.

In experiments with rats, diets lacking in the essential
fatty acids will cause numerous symptoms of deficiency.
The rats show retarded growth, a higher metabolic rate,
and changes in their skin and fur. Dryness and scurfiness
in the skin and fur would be called dandruff in humans.
Kidney disorders and kidney stones were common. With
respect to reproduction, the problems were severe. Males
were frequently sterile. In females the litters were resorbed,
labor was prolonged with hemorrhaging, and litters were
underweight and sickly. Experiments with chickens have
shown much the same symptoms and results.

A deficiency of the essential fatty acids together
with the fat soluble vitamins, in particular vitamins A and
D, is the cause of the common problem in cage birds
known as eggbinding. In this condition, the tissues of the

oviduct are neither elastic nor sufficiently lubricated to permit the passage of an egg. The unfortunate result is an egg stuck in the oviduct. If not forcefully removed, this immobile egg will inevitably cause the death of the bird. One case of eggbinding indicates a bird that probably is not eating all of the dietary offerings. Several cases indicate a major deficiency in these fat soluble factors, and the diet must be supplemented immediately to prevent any further recurrence of eggbinding.

It is vital to the lives of cage birds that their diets contain sufficient amounts of the essential fatty acids. Though cereal grains have a good quantity in the germ of the seed, this represents only a tiny oil content for seeds of this type. No whole cereal grain is an adequate source of the unsaturated fatty acids. As was proven by the experiments discussed on rats, breeding is impossible without a sufficient quantity of the essential fatty acids in the diet.

CHAPTER 5

CARBOHYDRATES

Carbohydrates are a third primary source of energy for birds, animals, and humans. In quantity consumed and energy value extracted, the carbohydrates usually rank first in the diets of most species of birds commonly maintained in aviculture. The carbohydrates function primarily as a source of energy in the avian body for heat and muscle work, but can also be stored to a certain extent.

Most carbohydrates are plant products formed by photosynthesis, using sunlight in the presence of chlorophyll. Technically, the plants turn light energy into chemical energy by combining carbon, hydrogen, and oxygen in a complex series of reactions. When metabolized, they yield carbon dioxide and water in the body as by-products. Molecular energy is the subsequent conversion of that chemical energy stored in the molecules of food into kinetic energy for muscle action. The dry matter of most plants ranges from 60% to 90% carbohydrates.

As surprising as it may seem, there is no definite, known, nutritional requirement for carbohydrates in the diet. Fats or proteins can substitute, if perhaps less efficiently, for the known functions of carbohydrates in metabolism. Nevertheless, it is fortunate that most species can digest and utilize carbohydrates easily, or the available food supply would be drastically reduced.

Carbohydrates are classed under several headings, depending upon their chemical structure. They range from very simple in their structure to incredibly complex. This structure determines whether the carbohydrate is digestible, absorbable, and capable of being utilized by the body. The properties of these carbohydrates depend totally upon their molecular structure.

The food carbohydrates are classified as sugars and starches. The sugars are subdivided into several categories, depending upon their structure. The simplest of these sugars are called monosaccharides. These are the simplest carbohydrates. By far the most important in nutrition is glucose, which will be covered in more detail later. It is found in pure form in honey. Another important one is fructose, also called fruit sugar. As the name implies, this sugar is found primarily in fruits. Three other monosaccharides are mannose, galactose, and ribose. Ribose is a constituent of the vitamin riboflavin and of the nucleic acids.

Glucose, fructose, and galactose are the major forms of carbohydrate circulating in the bloodstreams of avian species. In experimental chicken diets, over 10% of galactose content in the diet will produce toxicity in the form of a central nervous system disorder characterized by convulsions. Over 50% of the diet as galactose causes severe kidney damage, convulsive seizures, and death. These ill effects occur only in nutritional testing, however, certainly not on any normal diet.

The term disaccharide means two monosaccharides linked together to form a more complex sugar. The disaccharides are the simplest of the multiple sugars. Three of these are important in nutrition, but cannot be absorbed from the digestive tract until broken down into their constituent monosaccharides.

Sucrose is the most important of these disaccharides and is formed by the combination of one glucose molecule and one fructose molecule. Sucrose is our common white sugar extracted from sugar cane or sugar beets. In the process of digestion, an enzyme called sucrase or invertase splits these two joined molecules and releases the free monosaccharides glucose and fructose.

Maltose is the second important disaccharide. It is composed of two glucose molecules linked together. The enzyme maltase breaks these apart in the small intestine and releases two molecules of glucose for each molecule of maltose.

Lactose is of great importance in human nutrition, since it is milk sugar. For birds, however, lactose has a very low energy value because they lack a sufficient quantity of the enzyme lactase to break it down or hydrolize it. Lactose is composed of one glucose molecule and one galactose molecule joined together. Lactose is the only carbohydrate of animal origin that is significant in the nutrition of humans. It is much less soluble than other sugars and is therefore digested much more slowly.

The oligosaccharides are technically those multiple sugars that contain from three to six molecules of simple sugar. Most writings will omit this term and use the word polysaccharide to mean any complex sugar with three or more monosaccharide units.

The polysaccharides are those carbohydrates with over six monosaccharide molecules joined together. Starch is the only polysaccharide that can be used efficiently in metabolism where birds are concerned. Nutritionally, it is the most important carbohydrate. There can be more than a thousand simple monosaccharides, such as glucose, in a polysaccharide carbohydrate chain. The resulting carbon chain formation can be straight or branched. Rice, wheat, corn, and millet contain about 70% starch. Even as much as 40% of beans and other seeds is starch. Cereal grains are the most important source of starch, but tubers, such as potatoes, are also important sources.

In the digestive process, the complex carbohydrates are split into monosaccharides through the action of the specific enzymes needed for each type of simple sugar in the carbohydrate chain. This splitting process is called hydrolysis. Hydrolysis occurs quite rapidly under the influence of enzymes. The enzymes act as catalysts only. They speed up the reaction, but are not altered in structure by so doing. The digestive tract can absorb only the resulting monosaccharides.

One of the organic acids formed during carbohydrate oxidation is required for complete oxidation of fats. Therefore, a fat cannot be completely metabolized without some carbohydrate in the diet. The products of incomplete fat oxidation are short-chain acids called ketones. An accumulation of ketones can cause the blood and urine to become acidic. Ketones are excreted as salts, so excretion may lead to severe sodium losses. This will reduce the blood's ability to carry carbon dioxide and can result in coma in severe cases. This usually occurs in humans during starvation or severe fast when the body is metabolizing stored fat, or possibly in a very high-fat diet.

Glucose is the most common monosaccharide, and it is by far the most important in the nutrition of birds and animals. Glucose is the blood sugar for all animals and is controlled in this function by the body within very narrow limits. It is the basic source of energy in all animals. Glucose occurs in two structural forms, called the open-chain form and the ring form. Both are equal in all respects nutritionally and metabolically. Glucose is highly soluble, neither acid nor alkaline, and the tissues utilize it directly. It can be converted to other monosaccharides as necessary in a reversible process.

Hydrolysis, the splitting of starch and complex sugars into monosaccharides in the digestive system, results in the addition of water as they are broken down. Thus, one gram of starch after hydrolysis will yield more than one gram of absorbable monosaccharides. The liver can synthesize glucose from short-chain organic acids that form during the oxidation of carbohyrdates and amino acids. Also, the liver can convert other carbohydrates into glucose. Pure glucose metabolism will yield less energy than will starch metabolism, because of the addition of water in the digestion hydrolysis. The average energy content of both pure glucose and starch together is usually considered to be four calories per gram.

At the cell level, energy becomes available when glucose is broken down in the tissues. This occurs in a series of steps, with many intermediate reactions. The process is similar to a reversal of photosynthesis. All of these biochemical changes involve many enzymes and co-enzymes. Incomplete breakdown of glucose in the cells forms organic acids. Complete oxidation, by contrast, yields only carbon dioxide and water.

The energy released at each step in the breakdown of glucose forms high energy phosphates. Adenosine triphosphate is particularly important in this process. It serves to soak up excess heat energy from glucose and fat breakdown. It might be called a storage tank for energy within the body.

The body can store carbohydrates in the body in the form of glycogen. It is a polysaccharide, similar to starch. For this reason, glycogen is sometimes called "animal starch." Glycogen is stored in the liver and muscles. During muscular exercise, lactic acid is formed from carbohydrate breakdown. It enters the blood and is carried to the liver, which can convert it back to glycogen.

The skeletal and smooth muscles use their glycogen reserves for energy on a continuous basis, but cardiac muscle does not. The heart muscle preserves its glycogen reserves and uses blood glucose primarily for the energy requirements of its work and maintenance. Surprisingly, in response to a 48 to 72 hour fast, avian heart muscle glycogen levels will double or even triple.

In times of fear or anger, the adrenal glands will release adrenalin, also called epinephrine. This hormone stimulates the rapid breakdown of glycogen in the liver. The consequent release of glucose raises the blood sugar level, allowing an almost immediate surge of extra energy for coping with the emergency triggering the emotion.

Insulin is a hormone produced by the pancreas which facilitates the entry of glucose into tissue cells. A lack of insulin causes a rise in the amount of glucose in the blood. Insulin also stimulates the formation of glycogen through direct absorption of the glucose by the cells, and also by stimulating certain enzymes, thus removing excess glucose from the blood.

Several noted authorities have stated that excess metabolizable energy, once absorbed, cannot be excreted by the animal body, but must be stored as fat. Another authority has called this into question by affirming that a large amount of galactose, one of the monosaccharides, will be absorbed rapidly, accumulate in the blood and tissues, and result in much of the galactose being excreted in the urine. I suspend judgment here; you may feel free to consult your family biochemist to resolve the contradiction.

The gross energy of a food is all the energy value that can be measured, including that which is indigestible to the birds. For example, cellulose, though an energy source, furnishes only bulk in the avian diet, since birds do not possess the enzyme cellulase in the digestive tract for breaking it down. Cellulose is completely unabsorbable. Authorities seem to agree that bulk is not a requirement in the avian diet, at least not in the diet of chickens. The insect skeletal material called chitin is also completely indigestible by chickens. Digestible energy is that value that can be broken down by digestion and absorbed. The term metabolizable energy refers to digestible energy corrected for losses such as in the excretion of nitrogen wastes. These two energy references are the most important where avian nutrition is concerned.

The best sources of carbohydrate content in the diet of seed-eating birds will be the cereal grains: wheat, millet, oats, canary, etc. For softbills, lories, and similar feeders, fruit will be the best source. In preparing mixed foods from which birds cannot separate protein from carbohydrate, it is unwise in the extreme to dilute a high protein food with additional carbohydrate. Leave carbohydrates in their natural form or feed them separately. I strongly advise against mixing bread crumbs with hard boiled egg, for example, as a nestling food. Such a practice forces the birds to consume excess carbohydrate in order to get the protein content they crave, particularly while feeding young ones. As previously mentioned, no bird will ever suffer from a carbohydrate deficiency. Carbohydrates in any form are simply not necessary in the nutrition of birds, though you can hardly keep from feeding some carbohydrate foods. Overloading cage birds with high carbohydrate foods is a sure road to illness and death.

As a final note, a Rhode Island Red chicken requires energy in the amount of about 360 calories per day with its high rate of metabolism. Small birds, such as finches, consume a vastly greater proportion of calories with relation to their body weight. In translating this consumption to the calorie intake of a human adult, it is rather evident that the statement, "He eats like a bird," is hardly a compliment. Rather, it is in reality the grossest of gluttonous insults.

PART TWO

THE VITAMINS

CHAPTER 6

INTRODUCTION TO VITAMINS

Casimir Funk coined the term "vitamine" in 1912 to name those elusive substances containing nitrogen (amines) that were necessary for life (vita). He was a Polish biologist working at the Lister Institute in London at the time. Later, when researchers discovered more specific vitamins and found most to contain no nitrogen, the final "e" was dropped from the word. The familiar spelling that we now use was the result.

Vitamins are defined as relatively complex organic substances essential in small amounts for the control of metabolic processes. In order to be classified as vitamins, they must be dietary essentials rather than products of synthesis within the body. They function as intact, free chemical compounds or as coenzymes in metabolic reactions in a variety of ways. The vitamins serve primarily as catalysts without which another chemical process in the body cannot occur. This is undoubtedly the most important function of most of the vitamins.

Vitamin C is one of the most versatile of the vitamins in its proven functions, but it is technically not a vitamin for birds, since they synthesize internally all that they require with a few exceptions noted in the section on this vitamin. As examples, vitamin C is vital to the formation of collagen, the material that holds individual cells and tissues together as functioning units. It also serves as a chelator that attaches itself to a mineral and transports it for use by the cells of the body. Vitamin C can also attach itself to poisons and carry them out of the body, including such toxic metals as cadmium. Since this compound is not a vitamin for most avian species, it will be referred to by its chemical name, ascorbic acid, in most further references.

Vitamins are classified into two groups. The first group consists of the fat soluble vitamins. These are found in fatty compounds and are carried by fats. They are not soluble in water and are usually found dissolved in fats. Vitamins A, D. E. and K are all in the fat soluble group. The essential fatty acids also fall within the fat soluble vitamin group. These have been referred to as vitamin F in some writings in the United States, and they are known by this designation in Europe. I have included these essential fatty acids in the chapter on fats, but this is not meant to lessen their importance as a true member of the fat soluble vitamin group.

The second group of vitamins is the water soluble vitamins. This includes ascorbic acid and all of the B complex. As the name implies, these vitamins are soluble in water and can be washed away easily with water. Cooking them in water dissolves them out of the food. The only thing the B-complex vitamins have in common is that they are all water soluble. Because of this, the "B" designations are gradually being dropped in favor of the chemical names of the individual vitamins. I have followed this modern practice in covering the individual vitamins in this volume. Though the formal names may cause a little short term confusion, over the many years of the future the new method of naming will be far more advantageous.

One may also note three other letter designations for vitamins or compounds that have been used rather frequently. Vitamin P is usually known as the bioflavonoids and is found in close contact with ascorbic acid. Vitamin G is an old, but formerly common name for one of the members of the B complex, now known as riboflavin. Similarly, vitamin H is another name for biotin, also a B complex vitamin. A complete chart of all known historical vitamin designations is included in *Nutrition of the Chicken*, one of the volumes listed in the bibliography.

There are three other newer vitamin designations that the reader may encounter in further reading on the subject of nutrition. The compound referred to as vitamin M is apparently a part of the folacin group. Vitamin L-1 is a factor derived from liver and believed to be essential for lactation. It may be related to anthranilic acid, as reported in *Nutrition of the Chicken*. Vitamin L-2 is a factor derived from yeast which is necessary for lactation in mammals. It is probably a compound called adenosine, again as reported in *Nutrition of the Chicken*. I do not recommend the use of these terms until research has proven the true chemical structure and biological need for these compounds.

The destruction of vitamins and other nutrients is a serious problem in food processing and cooking. Any amount of processing destroys vitamins, removes minerals, and alters the chemical structure of fats and proteins. High heat accounts for most of this damage. These accumulated alterations of foods have resulted in widespread nutritional problems. This section will discuss a few of the specific effects of cooking and processing, and the sections on each vitamin will cover the available information on that particular nutrient.

The tryptophan-niacin relationship is an example of
the far-reaching effects of any food processing. Though
most protein components are stable in heat, one of the
essential amino acids is not. This is tryptophan, and it will
be destroyed by heat. A longer period of exposure to heat
and higher heat accelerate this destruction, which renders
all of the protein in the cooked food incomplete. Since
incomplete protein can only serve as an energy source in
the process of metabolism, the required body growth and
repair will not occur until sufficient tryptophan appears in
the diet to complement the remaining essential amino
acids. Individual amino acids, of course, have some specific
functions in the body apart from their combined role in
tissue formation. Since the body can synthesize niacin
from an adequate supply of tryptophan, a niacin deficient
diet that also lacks tryptophan is an invitation to severe
niacin deficiency symptoms. This is only one of the
complex interrelationships found in the study of the individual nutrients.

In addition to this problem with niacin, four other
vitamins in the B complex are destroyed or badly depleted
by cooking. Thiamin is the most easily destroyed by the
heat of cooking. Folacin is from 50% to 90% destroyed in
cooking, and high heat will destroy it completely. Pyridoxine is also partly destroyed by cooking and completely
destroyed by very high heat. Dry heat, such as that used in
baking, will completely destroy pantothenic acid. All
enzymes are destroyed in heat also, though the results of
this are still unknown.

Cooking any food in water dissolves some of the water
soluble vitamins into that water. At least twelve vitamins
are affected in this way. If the cooking water is then incorporated into other foods, the vitamins are salvaged.
Since most cooking water is discarded, the loss of vitamins
in this manner is considerable.

Most items that are cooked are first cut up or peeled in some manner. This opens the food to another vitamin destructive process in the form of oxidation. Vitamin C is especially susceptible to this oxidative destruction, though this vitamin is inconsequential in the nutrition of most cage birds. Oxidation will render biotin inactive, and thiamin is also very susceptible to oxidation damage. Vitamin A will be destroyed by oxidation, in addition. Much of this destruction occurs on contact with oxygen in the air. The longer vitamin compounds are exposed to the air, the greater will be the destruction.

Light, acids, and alkalis are three other destructive influences on some of the vitamins. Riboflavin, for example, is particularly susceptible to destruction caused by exposure to light. Other vitamins are destroyed by exposure to either acid or alkaline solutions. The chart on the next page lists the destructive factors with a partial list of those vitamins affected by each destructive factor. It should be obvious from this that most vitamins are rather unstable compounds and great care must be taken to preserve them in the foods offered to your birds.

Many of the commercially available vitamin-mineral preparations for birds are prepared for mixing with the seed or drinking water. I cannot support either method of supplementation. Supplements in the drinking water are at least 75% wasted in splashing, bathing, and discarding when fouled by the birds. Powdered supplements mixed in the seed are probably at least 90% wasted in birds that shell their seed. Only by mixing a supplement completely with a soft food acceptable to the birds can you be assured that the birds will get the benefit of the supplementation. This is the method of supplementation that I use for my own birds, and I have found it very effective with a minimum of waste. I estimate my supplement waste at about ten percent; this translates to a 90% rate of consumption by the birds.

PARTIAL OR TOTAL LOSS OF VITAMINS

DESTRUCTIVE FACTOR	WATER SOLUBLE VITAMIN LOSS	FAT SOLUBLE VITAMIN LOSS
Wet Heat	Ascorbic acid, folacin, pyridoxine, thiamin	— —
Dry Heat	Ascorbic acid, folacin, pantothenic acid, thiamin	E
Oxidation	Ascorbic acid, biotin, folacin, pantothenic acid, thiamin	A, D, E, K, F
Acids	Pantothenic acid	K
Alkalis	Biotin, cobalamin, pantothenic acid, pyridoxine, riboflavin, thiamin	E, K
Visible Light	Folacin, riboflavin	K
Ultraviolet Light	Pyridoxine, riboflavin	A, E
Storage	Ascorbic acid	— —
Freezing	Pyridoxine	— —
Trace Mineral Exposure	Ascorbic acid	A
Rancid Fats	— —	D, E, K

As important as the vitamins are in nutrition, most act simply as catalysts for the completion of a biological reaction. Only a few are actually incorporated into the structure of the body, primarily the essential fatty acids and choline. Without the minerals, the vitamins are mostly useless. Nevertheless, they are vital to life and to the health of birds maintained in captivity. The specific functions of each vitamin are covered in the sections on each particular vitamin. My only regret is that so little information on birds is available to pass along to you.

The suspicion that vitamins may perform more esoteric functions than the strictly physical job of a catalyst is strengthened in viewing special photographs of the structure of vitamin crystals. Photographing them with magnification under polarized light reveals an unknown world. These micro-photographs reveal a pattern of structure and color that surpasses the appearance of any abstract art in beauty and design. The incredible, breathtaking beauty of the photograph of pantothenic acid, in particular, is proof of the unseen worlds that exist around us in the most delicate and perfect of structure. A number of photographs of the vitamin crystals were published in GEO magazine, Volume 2, the July, 1980, issue.

CHAPTER 7

THE FAT SOLUBLE VITAMINS

VITAMIN A

Back in the year 1912, researchers concluded that a fat soluble substance was necessary for growth. It was named vitamin A. In 1919, the yellow pigments in vegetables were discovered to have the same effects, and by 1928 carotene was identified as a strong precursor of vitamin A. By 1930, the chemical structure of vitamin A had been identified, and the pure vitamin was almost colorless. This vitamin is measured in International Units or United States Pharmacopoeia Units at present. These two measurements are equal in potency. They represent the amount of vitamin A or its precursor that will cause a specific growth response in rats with depleted vitamin A reserves. The recent adoption of a new, different system to measure vitamin A potency is discussed later in this section.

Compounds with vitamin A activity come in several different forms. Vitamin A alcohol is called retinol, while vitamin A aldehyde bears the name retinal. Vitamin A acid is known as retinoic acid. Retinol can be oxidized to retinal in a reversible reaction. Retinoic acid is formed from retinal, and it cannot be converted back to that form of vitamin A. With regard to vitamin A activity, retinal has 90% of the potency of retinol, and retinoic acid has about 60% of the potency of retinol. Retinol is stored in the liver combined with a lipoprotein, but the body cannot store retinoic acid. Preformed vitamin A in these three forms is found only in animal products.

Fortunately, vitamin A is stable under normal storage and food preparation. Heat, light, acid, and alkali will not break down the structure of vitamin A. However, it is unstable to oxidation, especially under hot, humid conditions, and it will oxidize in the presence of rancid fat. Also, exposure to ultraviolet light will destroy vitamin A, as will contact with trace minerals.

Research has identified ten vitamin A precursors or provitamins which are called carotenoids in plant material. Carotenes are a part of the larger class of carotenoids, and for the sake of convenience, the term carotene is usually used to mean the vitamin A precursors or provitamins. Animals which consume these compounds form vitamin A from them. The presence of the provitamins in fruits and vegetables and their potential vitamin A value is directly proportional to the depth of color of the green and yellow pigments in them. Many of the yellow and orange pigments are the provitamins. Green pigment is not a precursor of vitamin A. The green chlorophyll occurs everywhere with these yellow pigments and masks their yellow color. This accounts for the fact that so many tree leaves turn yellow or orange in the fall, after the chlorophyll has broken down. The carotenoids in their natural form participate in lipochrome production, which gives many of the colors to avian feathers. Any deficiency in carotenoids will lead to inadequate pigmentation or to color changes in developing feathers. I need to stress at this point that not all yellow pigments are vitamin A precursors. In animal products such as butter and eggs, the depth of color is never an indication of vitamin A content in any way.

The vitamin A precursors, collectively referred to as carotene, are absorbed through the intestinal wall after digestion frees them from the plant cells. They are converted to one of the vitamin A compounds in the intestinal wall. This conversion is far from complete, however, since only about one-third of the absorbed carotene is converted to vitamin A. Some carotene enters the blood without conversion and is stored in the fat as carotene. Some conversion of carotene to vitamin A also takes place in the liver and lungs. Carotene is subject to destruction in the presence of unsaturated fatty acids, but antioxidants, such as vitamin E, will protect the carotene from this form of destruction. Carotene is also destroyed by high heat, such as that used in frying.

Preformed vitamin A is found only in animal products after the animal has consumed carotene and converted it to vitamin A, or consumed it in other animal sources, such as insects. Most of the preformed vitamin A in the food supply is combined with palmitic acid, one of the fatty acids, as vitamin A palmitate. The palmitate is split by enzymes to form free retinol for intestinal absorption. Any of the many factors which promote fat absorption also promote the absorption of vitamin A. Unfortunately, mineral oil in the digestive tract will absorb both vitamin A and carotene and carry them out of the body. Vitamin A undergoes many changes in form from the point of absorption until it is finally utilized in the cell.

In research with chicks, investigators have noticed a variety of factors that will affect their requirement for vitamin A. Variations in the amount of vitamin A deposited within the egg will affect the later requirement of the hatched chick. Disease, stress, and genetic differences can all increase the requirement for this vitamin. Inadequate protein intake, variations in the potency of any supplement, and destruction in the feed through processing and oxidation will all affect the requirement for vitamin A. Problems at the absorption level caused by destruction of vitamin A from disease or other factors, lack of bile salts for absorption, low absorption due to low fat levels in the diet, or damage to the intestinal wall will all affect the vitamin A requirement.

Vitamin A serves a wide variety of functions in the cells of the body, serving numerous metabolic roles. All outer skin cells and mucous membranes depend upon it for their integrity. The eyes will not function without a constant, adequate supply of vitamin A. Reproduction depends on sufficient vitamin A, in addition to its use in the mucous membranes of the reproductive organs. This vitamin is necessary for the stability of cell membranes. Vitamin A also seems to be necessary for the release of some enzymes, including one without which the body is unable to synthesize glycogen, the storage form of carbohydrate in the body.

The health and proper functioning of the mucous membranes in birds, animals, and humans cannot be maintained without vitamin A. The epithelial, or surface, cells must have a sufficient supply of vitamin A or they will degenerate. This includes all mucous-secreting cells. The degeneration of these cells in a deficiency of vitamin A occurs with a dry layer of hard keratin forming. With this dry degeneration, the ability of the cell to secrete mucus is lost, and the hairlike cilia on the cell surface are also lost. Vitamin A is believed to be necessary for the formation of a carbohydrate found in the mucus. Once the cell ducts are clogged up by keratin, the outer layers of cells pile up, leaving a layer of hard, horny, keratinized cells in place of the normal, round, moist, ciliated, mucous cells. This degeneration leaves the cells open to serious bacterial and viral infections that are usually the cause of eventual death in a severe vitamin A deficiency.

Normal growth depends upon a sufficient supply of vitamin A. Any bird or animal deprived of vitamin A will cease to grow when its stored vitamin A reserves are exhausted. This growth failure will appear before any other symptom of deficiency. Bones will fail to grow, while nerve tissue, which does not require vitamin A for growth, continues to grow and expand. This will cause pressure on the nerves where they are protected by bones, with severe pain as an obvious result. When vitamin A is restored to the diet, the bone growth is stimulated. In addition, for reasons that are not yet clear, a deficiency of this vitamin may cause defective formation of nervous tissue.

The several forms of vitamin A within the body are in some uses specific for a specific function or reaction in the body. Retinoic acid, for example, will carry out all of the functions of vitamin A except for vision and reproduction. This vitamin A acid cannot prevent night blindness, eventual complete blindness, nor reproductive failure. Retinal is the form required for use in the eye. Such specific requirements have at the same time facilitated and made more difficult the unraveling of the mysteries of vitamin A functioning in the body.

The best understood function of vitamin A, in the form of retinal, is in the ability of the eye to adapt to darkness. In the retina of the eye, retinal combines with the protein opsin to form the compound called visual purple, or rhodopsin. This visual purple is the photoreceptor pigment in the rod cells of the retina. When light strikes the retina, it bleaches the visual purple to visual yellow, in the process separating the retinal from the opsin. This stimulates the optic nerve. During this process, some of the retinal is changed to retinol, which is reconverted to retinal. A small amount of retinal is lost in these chemical changes and is replaced from the blood. The vitamin A content of the blood determines the speed of regeneration of the visual purple. This rhodopsin, allowing vision in dim light, regenerates in darkness. Vision in dim light is not possible until this cycle is complete. The speed of this adaptation in sight is directly related to the amount of vitamin A available. Vitamin A is also present in the cones of the retina, but they are not so sensitive to the amount of available vitamin A.

This vitamin plays a vital role in reproduction, also. Either the vitamin A alcohol, retinol, or the aldehyde form, retinal, must be present for normal reproduction. In female mammals, a deficiency will cause the resorption of the fetus. The keratinization of the mucous cells of the reproductive tract is a common result of vitamin A deficiency.

When hens that are fed only retinoic acid begin laying, the rate of egg production, egg size, and all other factors are normal, but the eggs contain no vitamin A. Retinoic acid is not deposited in the egg by the hen's reproductive system. The eggs will be fertile, but after two or three days of incubation, the embryos will always die at the same stage of development. If the hen's diet is restored by a retinol supplement, hatchability is also restored immediately. Eggs can even be injected with retinol before incubation begins, and they will hatch normally.

If retinoic acid alone is fed to growing chicks, growth will be normal, but the chicks gradually will become blind. This condition is not permanent, however, Supplementation with retinol restores sight within two days, even after months of blindness.

Research has shown that the vitamin A intake of humans is below recommended levels more than is true for any other nutrient. A deficiency will show up only after the liver's reserves of vitamin A have been completely depleted. In such a deficiency the skin will become dry and rough, especially on the shoulders, with an accompanying loss of appetite. Night blindness will appear, there will be hardening and opacity of the cornea of the eye, and the tear glands will stop secreting their fluid. Because of damage to the mucous membranes, a deficiency will make the body highly susceptible to respiratory infections, and there will be adverse changes in both the reproductive tract and the gastrointestinal tract caused by cell keratinization. In juveniles, growth will cease, and the tooth enamel layer on new teeth will not form. Hard work in hot weather will always raise the body's requirement for vitamin A. Also, in any protein deficiency, utilization of vitamin A will be depressed, since many proteins are involved in the body's utilization of this vitamin. A large number of enzymes that are also proteins are needed at many stages of vitamin A metabolism.

A number of deficiency symptoms appear in young chicks and will probably be very similar in all avian species. If the laying hen has been well supplied with vitamin A, a considerable amount is carried through her egg to the embryo, and the newly hatched chick can grow and develop normally for several weeks on this stored supply. Once any stored reserve is exhausted, growth will cease, and the chicks will appear drowsy, weak, uncoordinated, and emaciated. Ruffled feathers and anorexia or loss of appetite will also be evident. If the deficiency is severe, there will be severe ataxia, or loss of muscular coordination, such as occurs in severe vitamin E deficiency. The beaks, shanks, combs, and wattles will also be very pale in color.

Adult chickens will exhibit much the same symptoms from vitamin A deficiency with a decrease in egg production, longer length of time between clutches, and reduced hatchability. They will also have a watery discharge from the eyes and nostrils, and the eyelids will stick together. The eyes fill with a white material and a severe deficiency eventually will destroy the eye. Vitamin A deficiency is also the major nutritional factor causing blood spots in eggs.

Time and again, you will read and hear of the dangers of an excessive intake of vitamin A. As far as I am concerned, this is a paranoia of fools. Though an excess intake of vitamin A to the point of toxicity is possible, it is rare in the extreme. It is impossible to get an excess of vitamin A on any normal, natural diet. Only in the naturally occurring vitamin A content of salt water fish liver and sea mammal liver is the vitamin A content sufficient to cause toxicity symptoms. Beef liver is a very rich source of this vitamin and it will contain about 45,000 International Units in 100 grams, a small, average serving of just under four ounces. Polar bear liver, by contrast, is a notoriously rich source of vitamin A. An average serving of 100 grams contains 2,000,000 International Units of vitamin A, enough to cause serious toxicity symptoms. Nevertheless, in any excess intake of vitamin A, recovery from all symptoms is rapid and complete as soon as the excess intake is stopped. You may feel certain that for every one person getting an excess of vitamin A in the world today, there are at least 10 million with a serious deficiency.

The commonest form of hypervitaminosis A, as a toxic excess of vitamin A is called, is in infants. Well-meaning mothers have been known to give their children a teaspoon of concentrated, synthetic vitamin A daily, when only one drop is recommended. The effect is cumulative, and over a period of months this will cause a variety of toxicity symptoms. Even so, it takes from six to fifteen months for such an excess to manifest itself as toxicity symptoms. Such symptoms may include nausea, diarrhea, scaly skin, weight loss, and skeletal pain. Toxic reactions can only be caused by the preformed vitamin, not by the precursors.

An excess of vitamin A can be excreted both through the kidneys and the intestinal tract. When consumption is above the body's ability to excrete the excess, toxicity symptoms will appear. In chicks this will take the form of weight loss, decreased food consumption, and sores around the mouth, nearby skin, and feet. Bone strength will be greatly decreased with bone abnormalities. The eyelids will be swollen and crusted to the point of being sealed. Death will result if the excess continues. Such ill effects will occur only under conditions of deliberate overdose under experimental conditions, certainly not on any normal diet.

The richest sources of preformed vitamin A are liver, the fish liver oils, and to a much lesser extent egg yolks. Eggs are the only animal source of vitamin A likely to be in the cage bird diet of the average aviculturist. Cod liver oil is an excellent source, but because of its tendency to become rancid, I do not recommend its use unless immediate consumption can be assured. Cod liver oil contains about 4,000 International Units of vitamin A per gram, but is a relatively poor source when compared with other processed fish and mammal liver oils. Tuna liver oil contains about 150,000 International Units per gram, while whale liver oil has an astonishing 400,000 International Units per gram.

Fruits and vegetables will contain no preformed vitamin A, only the precursors as the yellow and orange pigments, collectively termed carotene. Carrots and dark green vegetables are good sources. Spinach is an especially good source of carotene, as is kale to a lesser extent. Some fruits will increase their carotene content with storage, and mangoes are a notable example of this.

Within the last few years, a new system of measuring

vitamin A potency has been adopted and will gradually replace the old designations of vitamin A in International Units. Now retinol equivalents, expressed in micrograms, are used to measure vitamin A activity. Dietary retinol is considered to be 100% utilized. Beta-carotene, the most active of the carotenoid precursors of vitamin A, yields about one-sixth the utilizable vitamin A activity of retinol. Therefore, one microgram of beta-carotene is equivalent to 0.167 micrograms of retinol. The other provitamins are considered to yield only one-twelfth the activity per unit that retinol yields. When the provitamins are the sources of vitamin A, the retinol equivalents may contain a sizable error factor. You may expect to see this new system of vitamin A measurement in use much more widely in future years, and it eventually will completely replace the old International Unit measurement system.

In conclusion, adequate vitamin A should be on the mind of the bird breeder constantly. Fruits, vegetables, and greens are appreciable sources of the provitamins for avian nutrition, but egg yolks will be the best for the pre-formed vitamin. Yellow corn fed raw, another good source of provitamin A, is relished by many birds, but white corn has virtually no provitamin A. Even the best all-vegetarian cage bird diet could benefit from vitamin A supplementation. As previously stated, a deficiency of vitamin A is considerably more likely than an excess. An excess in normal cage bird feeding is a virtual impossibility, while a deficiency is a probablility. Unless you habitually feed your birds polar bear liver or whale liver oil, you can completely discount the possibility of vitamin A toxicity from any natural food. Use synthetic vitamin A with caution, of course, since most recorded cases of vitamin A toxicity were caused by overdose with the synthetic compound. Vitamin A is one of the most likely deficiencies to occur in birds maintained in captivity.

VITAMIN D

It is fortunate for all of the birds and animals maintained in captivity that our knowledge of vitamin D in
nutrition has progressed so far since its initial presumed
existence in 1918. In that year, a British nutritionist by
the name of Mellanby presented the first evidence for a
fat soluble factor that would prevent and cure rickets. The
relationship between sunshine and what we now call the
sunshine vitamin was not established until the late 1920's,
and vitamin D was not isolated in crystalline form until
1930. Other names given to this vitamin in the past have
been the antirachitic factor and the rickets preventative.

There are several chemically distinct forms of vitamin
D. The two primary forms are known in common terms
as vitamin D-2 and vitamin D-3. From vegetable sources
comes the compound known as ergocalciferol or vitamin
D-2. Ergocalciferol is also known by the name viosterol in
some writings. Cholecalciferol is designated vitamin D-3,
and it comes only from animal sources. Vitamin D is a
necessary nutrient for all creatures with a bony skeleton.
This nutrient traditionally has been measured in terms of
International Units, and one milligram contains 40,000
International Units. The designation of potency in vitamin
D has changed recently. Future nutritional sources will
list the intake of vitamin D as micrograms of cholecalciferol rather than as International Units.

I will stress several times in the subsequent discussion
that only vitamin D-3 is biologically active in birds. Vitamin D-2 is effective for most mammals, but is not a useful
nutrient for birds.

The deficiency disease caused by severe vitamin D
deficiency in humans is known as rickets. Similar symptoms
occur in animals and birds and will be covered in detail
later. Until the 1920's rickets was an epidemic disease in

England, particularly in the crowded industrial areas. In some areas as many as 80% of the children were suffering from rickets. This is a disease in which the bones are defectively formed due to inadequate deposits of calcium and phosphorus in the bones. Bones in infants consequently remain soft and pliable and fail to harden normally. When weight is placed on these bones, as when a child begins crawling and walking, the bones bend under the weight they are not structurally able to handle. When walking begins before the bones harden, bowed legs are the result. Also, the ends of the bones become enlarged as they flatten with the weight put on the poorly calcified ends. This causes such deformities as knock-knees. Rib deformity and beading can also result in a concave chest, which causes severe crowding of the chest cavity and its organs. There is rapid enlargement of the head as the fontanels or soft spots fail to close. Growth is retarded, and teeth erupt late which are poorly formed and decay easily. The symptoms of rickets are slowly reversible on a diet with adequate vitamin D intake.

Vitamin D is a fat soluble substance in the diet. If fat absorption is poor, the amount of vitamin D absorbed will also be poor. This vitamin is absorbed only in the presence of bile, and absorption seems to be complete for both types of vitamin D in the human body. As vitamin D in the diet increases, magnesium absorption will also increase. Absorption in birds takes place primarily in the duodenum, the first section of the small intestine, and is facilitated by the presence of fat and bile salts.

Vitamin D can be formed by irradiation of precursors, or provitamins, with short wave ultraviolet light. The ultraviolet light changes the molecular structure enough to form active vitamin D. This is possible either in natural sunlight or under artificial ultraviolet light. Ergocalciferol, the plant form of vitamin D, is formed by irradiation of the provitamin ergosterol. The irradiation of 7-dehydro-cholesterol, found only in animal tissues, forms chole-calciferol or vitamin D-3, the only form of the vitamin of value for the nutrition of birds. The discovery that such ultraviolet irradiation of either chicks or their diet will prevent and cure rickets dates back to 1923.

The formation of vitamin D in the form of cholecalci-ferol on the skin is the same in birds, animals, and humans. The precursor, or provitamin, 7-dehydrocholesterol, is synthesized within the body and travels to the skin surface via the hair or feather follicles or via the roots of the scales. When exposed to the short wave ultraviolet rays of the sun, this compound is converted into cholecalciferol, vitamin D-3, on the outer layers of the skin. The skin then resorbs the modified compound into the circulatory sys-tem for use within the body. This resorption takes some time, and a shower or bath immediately after a sun bath will wash away most of the newly formed vitamin D before it can be absorbed.

This sunlight-formed vitamin is of vital importance to birds and animals in captivity, since vitamin D occurs so irregularly in their diets. The skin of the legs and feet of a chicken will contain about eight times as much provita-min D as does the body skin, to assure the maximum possible skin synthesis of vitamin D-3. Contrary to older beliefs, the preen gland does not contain any appreciable amount of provitamin D that will be deposited on the feathers. From eleven to 45 minutes in the sun for a chick is sufficient to prevent rickets, and no further supplemen-tation will aid growth. This irradiated 7-dehydrocholesterol has been shown to be twice as active metabolically as the mixed vitamin D in cod liver oil.

All authorities state that excess irradiation will form compounds that are toxic or antagonistic to vitamin D-3. I am unable to discover exactly what constitutes "over-irradiation," but presumably this is not a problem related to natural irradiation from sunlight.

This skin synthesis of vitamin D-3 is subject to many problems, primarily concerning the ability of ultraviolet light to reach the skin. The British problem with rickets, also common in the United States and other countries in the temperate zones, resulted from the lack of winter sunlight in the higher latitudes and more severe weather conditions throughout the year. Ultraviolet rays cannot penetrate fog, clouds, smog, smoke, window glass, window screening, clothing, or skin pigment. The presence of any of these factors reduces or eliminates completely the vitamin D available through irradiation. Children living in the deep mountain valleys of Switzerland in the Swiss Alps frequently showed symptoms of rickets, while children in the higher elevations that received sunlight were immune.

Nature created darkly pigmented skin for human beings native to the tropics to cut down on the ultraviolet reaching the skin. When this dark skin is moved to a northern temperate climate zone, the possibility of skin formation of vitamin D by irradiation is drastically reduced. Black people are consequently more likely to suffer from a vitamin D deficiency than are white people.

The intestinal absorption rate of calcium is greatly increased by adequate vitamin D in the dietary intake. Vitamin D is carried in the body attached to a blood protein. In some way it seems to cause an elevation in the calcium and phosphorus levels of the blood to a supersaturated point at which calcification will occur. The blood carries vitamin D to the liver, where it is converted into an active metabolic form. This must occur before it can induce the synthesis of the calcium-binding protein which is necessary for intestinal absorption of calcium. Though both forms of vitamin D will perform this func-

tion in mammals, in birds only vitamin D-3 will act as the
precursor of this essential hormone which promotes
calcium absorption, bone formation, and eggshell formation
in chickens and other birds. The fact that injected calcium
was built into the bone tissue even in severe vitamin D
deficiency proved conclusively that the usage of vitamin D
in the body took place at a different location. This was
proven later to be in the absorptive process, and vitamin D
is not involved in the actual transport of calcium.

Calcium uptake in the cells causes an increase in an
enzyme that leads to release of phosphate into the blood
at the same time. Both calcium and phosphorus are then
available simultaneously for bone and eggshell formation.
The failure of bone calcification is more often caused by a
lack of phosphate than of calcium. Vitamin D increases
the rate of phosphate absorption and stimulates its resorption from the kidneys. If this did not occur, all phosphorus
would be lost in the urine.

The vitamin D requirement in birds depends on the
sources of phosphorus in the diet, amounts of calcium in
the diet, the ratio of calcium to phosphorus, and the
extent of exposure to direct sunlight. The optimal dietary
ratio is two parts of calcium to one part of phosphorus.
If these limits are any broader or narrower, the vitamin D
requirement will increase. Vitamin D-3 is needed for
normal egg production, calcification of the eggshells, and
hatchability. In my own nutritional experimentation, a
supplement of powdered vitamin A and D, with all other
conditions remaining the same, resulted in a substantial
increase in the size of the clutch of eggs in Society Finches.
Whereas the average clutch had been four to five eggs,
within a few days, the newly laid clutches began to average
from six to seven eggs. I suspect that the vitamin D was the
primary reason for this increase.

Any deficiency of vitamin D-3 in growing chicks will

produce the symptoms of rickets. Growth will be retarded with severe weakness in the legs. The beaks and claws will become soft and pliable. The chicks will take a few unsteady steps and squat to rest, swaying slightly as if they lacked complete equilibrium and sense of balance. Feathering will also be poor, and there will be abnormal blackening of the feathers in the colored breeds of chickens. In any continuous, chronic deficiency, there will be a variety of skeletal disorders, including a downward curving spine and beading of the ribs.

Symptoms of vitamin D-3 deficiency will begin to appear from one to two months after the beginning of a deficient diet. First, there will be an increase in the number of thin shelled and soft-shelled eggs. Soon after that symptom, egg production will decrease and there will be a very noticeable reduction in hatchability. Hens may experience the loss of the use of their legs until an egg is laid, which will usually be soft-shelled. Then, leg use will return to normal. Hens will sit in a characteristic squat, resembling the posture of a penguin, and their beaks, claws, and bones will become soft and pliable.

Vitamin D is stored only in limited amounts, primarily in the liver. Though aquatic species store sizable amounts of vitamin D in the liver, birds and other land animals do not. Though all liver is a good source of vitamin D, the liver of sea fish abounds in this vitamin. The richness of cod liver oil is well known, as it has about 10,000 International Units of vitamin D per 100 grams of cod liver oil. Comparatively, however, this is a relatively poor source, since swordfish liver oil may have one million International Units of cholecalciferol per 100 grams, and bluefin tuna liver oil can have as much as four million International Units of vitamin D-3 per 100 grams.

Fortunately, vitamin D is very stable to most nutritionally destructive forces. It is not destroyed by oxidation

as vitamin A is, though it will be destroyed by the formation of peroxides in the presence of rancidifying fats.
Vitamin E, acting as a natural antioxidant, will prevent the
destruction of cholecalciferol from oxidative reactions. In
the body's metabolism, there is a definite antagonistic relationship between vitamin D and hydrocortisone, a hormone secreted by the adrenal glands.

A dietary intake of about 400 International Units per
day is presumed to be an adequate intake for humans, subject to the calcium and phosphorus relationship to the requirement already mentioned. Five times this amount is
enough to cause retarded growth. At this rate of 2000
International Units per day, other toxicity symptoms may
appear. Vitamin A will protect against any symptoms of
toxicity even with this high intake. An excess of vitamin D
is technically called hypervitaminosis D. This condition
will cause the resorption of calcium and other salts from
the bones and abnormal deposits of calcium in the soft
tissues of the body. Very high levels of intake in chicks
will cause kidney damage due to the calcification of the
kidney tubules. The symptoms of a gross intake of vitamin
D with resulting vitamin D poisoning are nausea, loss of
appetite, vomiting, cramps, diarrhea, and tingling in the
fingers and toes.

Vitamin D intake in cage bird nutrition must be in the
constant attention of the aviculturist. Since birds cannot
utilize ergocalciferol from plant sources, only the cholecalciferol, vitamin D-3, synthesized on the skin or obtained
from animal foods in the diet, will supply the need for this
vitamin. If birds are maintained indoors exclusively, the
first source of cholecalciferol is lost completely. The
needed, ultraviolet light will not be present in normal incandescent or fluorescent bulbs, nor will it pass through
window glass or screens, In this case, all vitamin D-3 must
come from dietary sources.

Of the animal derived dietary sources, only eggs are commonly fed to cage birds. Presumably, insects would be a good source of vitamin D-3, but I can find no written confirmation of this as yet. Dairy products will contain vitamin D, but this is predominantly as ergocalciferol and of little value to the birds. Liver is always a good source, but is certainly not a common item in cage bird nutrition.

Cod liver oil mixed in the diet is favored by some, but it will turn rancid so rapidly with exposure to air that I do not recommend its use in avian feeding. Nevertheless, if this oil can be provided in a readily consumed form, it is probably the best source of vitamin D-3 in an easily available form. If no alternative is available, I would recommend mixing cod liver oil in an item that will be consumed within fifteen minutes. Because of the danger of rancidity, I would not trust cod liver oil over a much longer period.

The only logical solution to the problem of vitamin D-3 deficiency is dietary supplementation with this vitamin, preferably as a dry, powdered addition to an already accepted soft food. Supplementation in this manner assures that the vitamin will be consumed and that waste will be held to a minimum. It also assures that no deficiency will develop and that rancidity or spoilage will not create a problem. Judging by my nutritional study and knowledge of cage birds and their feeding. I suspect that the deficiency of vitamin D-3 is the second most common deficiency that will be encountered in the maintenance of cage birds. Only protein deficiency is more likely to occur.

VITAMIN E

Vitamin E was discovered as a fat soluble factor necessary for health by Evans and Bishop in 1922. It was not isolated and identified until 1936 as a result of research by Evans, Emerson, and Emerson. The technical name for vitamin E and its close chemical relatives is tocopherols. There are seven natural tocopherols which occur together, named after the first seven letters of the Greek alphabet: alpha, beta, gamma, delta, epsilon, zeta, and eta. The one which is by far the most biologically active is the alpha-tocopherol, and it alone receives the common designation vitamin E.

There is still wide disagreement over the activity of the other six related tocopherols, but all researchers agree that if they have any biological activity at all, it is minor in comparison to d-alpha-tocopherol, the nutritional necessity that we call vitamin E. Some researchers claim no biological activity at all for the remaining six tocopherols. Though these other tocopherols occurring in nature have no officially recognized equivalency to d-alpha-tochopherol, research has indicated that the relative potencies seem to be about 40% of alpha-tocopherol, for beta-tocopherol, 10% for gamma-tocopherol and 1% for delta-tocopherol. The usage of the mixed tocopherols in early vitamin E testing would account for the early research failures in vitamin E supplementation.

Vitamin E has been synthesized since the late 1930's, but again there is wide disagreement as to the efficacy of the artificially produced vitamin. All researchers agree that the biological activity of the synthetic form is less, but how much less is in heated argument. Some authorities claim that the synthetic vitamin, called dl-alpha-tocopherol, has only one-fifth of the biological activity of the natural form. The "l" after the "d" must be used to signify the synthetic form, and any vitamin E preparation will clearly state this difference, if you can understand the label.

Since vitamin E is a very unstable compound, it is customarily put into acetate form to improve its stability for storage and use. Fortunately, vitamin E is stable to acids and to heat, so cooking losses are minimal. Nevertheless, it is destroyed on exposure to oxygen, ultraviolet light, alkalis, iron salts, and lead salts.

The measurement of the natural and synthetic forms of vitamin E is different. The natural form has been measured in International Units, while the synthetic form was measured in milligrams. One International Unit equals one milligram of dl-alpha-tocopherol activity.

The future designations of measurement for d-alpha-tocopherol are still in doubt. Any designation of vitamin E activity in the near future will be stated in milligrams relative to the natural d-alpha-tocopherol. Farther in the future, you may see the biochemical designation RRR-alpha-tocopherol replace the term d-alpha-tocopherol for the natural vitamin, and the term all-rac-alpha-tocopherol replace the dl-alpha-tocopherol designation for the synthetic vitamin. These are new terms adopted in biochemistry to more closely describe these substances.

Though vitamin E is found in small quantities in a wide variety of foods, any processing destroys part of it. As much as 86% of the vitamin E in whole wheat is removed in refining it to white flour. There are no truly rich natural sources of this nutrient. The most reliable sources are whole cereal grains, eggs, seeds, nuts, and deep green leafy vegetables. For herbivores, alfalfa is the most reliable source. Most of the vitamin E available for human or animal diet supplementation is distilled from oils that are to be used in the manufacture of paints. One ton of vegetable oil must be refined to produce only one cup of vitamin E. Because of the large amount of processing

necessary, vitamin E is usually the most expensive of the
vitamin supplements available. Since this is a fat soluble
vitamin, it is stored in the body for use in times of scarcity
in the diet.

Vegetable oils have a respectable quantity of vitamin
E, with the cold pressed oils considered richer than the oils
extracted under heat. Normal wet cooking, such as boiling, will not destroy the vitamin E content in foods, but
dry heat is a vitamin E disaster. Though any exposure to
air slowly destroys vitamin E, baking will destroy as much
as 47% of the food content of this nutrient.

The needs of various species for vitamin E vary a great
deal, as might be expected. Human needs are considerably
larger than those of the mammals, as evidenced by the content of human milk. Human milk has over twice the vitamin
E content of cow's milk. Significantly, in both cows and
humans, the colostrum, milk produced by the mammary
glands for the first few days after birth of the young, is
ten times richer in vitamin E than is the milk produced
later. Surprisingly, no one has ever succeeded in producing
a dietary deficiency of vitamin E in goats. Apparently the
goat's body is able to synthesize all that is needed by the
animal.

Digestion can be a major block to the body's utilization of vitamin E. It is not well absorbed in the best of
conditions. Best estimates indicate that less than half of
ingested d-alpha-tocopherol is absorbed. In the digestive
tract it protects vitamins A and C from oxidation. In any
problem with fat digestion, vitamin E and all of the other
fat soluble vitamins are not freed for absorption. As a
result, they are excreted along with the undigested fats.

A number of critical functions have been discovered
for vitamin E over the years since its discovery. The acceptance of these functions by all authorities has been a long,
slow process and is still not complete. It was only in 1959

that the Food and Drug Administration even admitted and stated that vitamin E is a necessary, vital nutrient. As stated in the foreword, about fifty years are required for any new nutritional discovery to become finally accepted. Though this is a tragedy of unimaginable proportions, it is simply human nature at its very worst.

It is most unfortunate that the first discovery of vitamin E function was in relation to sex and reproduction. This immediately got it labeled as a quack panacea in the eyes of numerous people who equate sex with sin. I can have only the greatest of pity for such puritanical morons. As this is written, thorough research and sane examination have finally succeeded in overcoming this ingrained prejudice and in getting across the true value of this nutrient to most reasonable people.

The primary function of vitamin E is as an antioxidant and an oxygen conservator. The tocopherols are the main antioxidants present in all natural fats. In this function, they prevent rancidity. Vitamin E, in particular, of all the tocopherols, unites with oxygen to prevent rancidity in fats. Through this function, it is able to improve the cell's functioning and prolong its life. Lest this be lost in passing, prolonging the life of the cells also means prolonging the life of the total organism. Vitamin E maintains the normal permeability of the cell membranes. Too little permeability causes interference with the cell's ability to feed itself. Too much permeability causes the cell to literally ooze its contents.

The oxygen conserving function of vitamin E has vast ramifications throughout the body, since oxygen is used by every cell in its metabolism. Muscle health is an especially important effect of vitamin E action. Since it conserves oxygen, this nutrient lowers the body's total need for oxygen. The result is a vast increase in muscular stamina and endurance. Rats in experimentation can swim twice

as long before exhaustion under vitamin E supplementation, and their tolerance for high altitude oxygen deficiencies leaves them healthy and active when control speci-
mens with no supplementation have died of oxygen deficiency. This information is obviously of greatest importance
to athletes in the human realm.

Apparently this oxygen conserving function and prevention of destruction of fats by rancidity are the basis
for vitamin E's action in healing. All wounds heal better
and faster with ingested vitamin E and its direct application to injured areas. It has proven itself a miraculous healing agent in the case of severe burns and scarring, but only
if adequate nutrition has also supplied the remaining necessary nutrients for rebuilding damaged tissues. A liberal
application of vitamin E to an injured area twice a day
with additional internal supplementation has on numerous
reported occasions prevented the formation of scars even
in the most severe burns and lacerations. Even in black
people, who have a tendency to form massive keloids,
or scar tissue, vitamin E will completely prevent the formation of scar tissue in cases of severe burns or other injury.
It seems quite likely that the members of our black population have a higher vitamin E requirement than the whites
or orientals.

Interior body scar tissue can be more disastrous than
the cosmetic exterior scars. Research has proven that even
in cirrhosis of the liver, massive internal scar tissue can be
replaced with normal liver tissue with adequate nutrition
and a high vitamin E intake. Even a goiter will not heal
after iodine supplementation without adequate vitamin E
to reduce and eliminate the goitrous internal scar tissue.
Even long standing scars can be dissolved away and replaced
by normal tissue with vitamin E application.

In my personal experience, I can give adequate nutrition and heavy vitamin E supplementation (1000 Inter-

national Units daily) much of the credit for the healing of
my left eye and the prevention of any serious scar tissue.
In a serious carpentry accident in 1978, I had a 16-penny
nail hit directly in the center of my left eye with devas-
tating force. The cornea was lacerated completely across,
the iris injured to the point that it will no longer contract,
and the lens destroyed by the formation of an immediate
trauma-caused cataract. An operation within six hours of
the accident corrected all of the physical damage that it
was possible to correct, including removal of the cataract.
A long period of healing was required, obviously. My ophthalmologist, Dr. Joseph C. Yarbrough, Jr. of Anderson,
South Carolina, remarked to me after the healing was
substantially complete, "When you first came into my
office, I wouldn't have given you a nickel's chance of ever
again having any usable sight in that eye."

The final result? The cornea healed with no obvious
scar. With a tinted contact lens to compensate for the loss
of iris function and lens focus, the eye tests at 20/20 vision.
Though a slight scar on the cornea is visible under magnification, it is not visible nor distorting in my field of vision
in any way. Certainly, I owe a great deal to a very highly
competent ophthalmologist, Dr. Joseph C. Yarbrough, Jr.
Secondly, I owe a great debt of thanks to the Almighty
Creative Forces that we call God and for the many prayers
that aided my healing. But last, I owe this physical healing
and once again perfect vision to superior nutrition and in
particular to heavy vitamin E supplementation during the
healing process.

Another major function of vitamin E is as an anti-
coagulant which prevents untimely clotting of the blood.
This is accomplished without danger of hemorrhaging.
Also, vitamin E seems to have some tendency to dissolve
existing clots. Any deficiency of vitamin E will make the
red blood cells abnormally susceptible to oxidation damage.

Without a doubt, vitamin E has achieved its greatest reputation in the treatment of circulatory diseases. All types of circulatory problems from atherosclerosis to phlebitis, varicose veins, and angina pectoris are aided immeasurably by Vitamin E supplementation in adequate amounts. Vitamin E supplementation in adequate amounts will completely cure angina pectoris.

Much of the older research on vitamin E was done with lack of knowledge concerning the characteristics of vitamin E, and as a result, no value and no health improvements were shown. Current research has indicated that the body has a physiological "dam" that keeps lower amounts of vitamin E confined or inactive. A higher amount is necessary to break down or spill over this physiological dam and perform the resulting physical health improvements. Whereas 400 International Units of vitamin E supplementation may be virtually ineffective, 2400 units can give the greatest of benefits in the body. Since no toxicity has ever been observed for vitamin E, even with supplementation of 3000 International Units daily over periods of years, no one need fear any excess over the body's true needs.

There is one major caution to observe, however. Supplementation for any individual with high blood pressure should begin at low levels under a doctor's guidance. The amount can be increased each week slowly, up to the optimal amount. An immediate, heavy, supplementary intake of vitamin E can further elevate blood pressure enough to cause a heart attack.

There are several other functions of vitamin E in the body that have been identified and proven. Several of the amino acids cannot be utilized without the presence of vitamin E. Also, vitamin E has been proven to prevent radiation damage to vitamin A and the fatty acids. Researchers also feel that vitamin E works closely with the vitamins of the B complex. Phospholipids seem to have a special affinity for vitamin E, and it prevents the formation of free radicals in the lipid cell membranes. In birds it is possible that vitamin E is involved in ascorbic acid synthesis, though this is not yet proven.

Vitamin E is essential to the production of the pituitary, adrenal, and sex hormones. In addition, it prevents these hormones from being destroyed by oxidation as they circulate in the bloodstream. Vitamin E is more concentrated in the pituitary gland than in any other portion of the body.

Vitamin E is destroyed or rendered ineffective by a variety of common antagonists. Inorganic iron of the type in iron rich water will destroy it, and inorganic chlorine, such as that used in water purification, will also destroy vitamin E on contact. Estrogen, the female hormone, will also destroy vitamin E, so those women taking "The Pill" should exercise care that the two substances are not consumed together. Rancid fats in the diet will inactivate vitamin E. And finally, mineral oil dissolves this vitamin and does not readily release it.

Deficiencies of vitamin E cause a variety of problems in birds and animals. Several named diseases in a variety of animals are the direct result of vitamin E deficiency. Mink will die of "yellow fat disease." Lambs will succumb shortly after birth to "stiff lamb disease."

Several different diseases in chickens have been thoroughly studied as symptoms of vitamin E deficiency. Before such diseases fully develop, hens' eggs will exhibit low hatchability, with embryos dying in the shell from the fourth day of incubation on. Egg production will not be affected. There will be a high mortality rate in any chicks that do hatch. Growing chicks will show a severe myopathy, or muscular disease, especially of the breast muscle at about four weeks of age, if the sulfur-containing amino acids are deficient along with vitamin E. In poults there will be injuries in the muscular walls of the gizzard. In all species, vitamin E deficiency results in lipid degeneration.

Nutritional muscular dystrophy is one specific disease caused by severe vitamin E deficiency. This involves degeneration of the skeletal muscles in chickens and other animals. Both selenium and vitamin E are intimately involved with the metabolism of the amino acid cysteine in the prevention of nutritional muscular dystrophy. In tests with guinea pigs, the damage to muscles from muscular dystrophy is far greater when their diets are also lacking vitamin C. Guinea pigs are a true blessing to humanity, for they are the only mammal other than monkeys and one species of fruit-eating bat yet discovered that is incapable of synthesizing its own vitamin C. Consequently, it is forced to get this nutrient in its diet and serves as an excellent subject for the nutritional testing of Vitamin C.

Nutritional encephalomalacia is a second named disease caused by vitamin E deficiency in chickens. In this disease an affected chick is characterized by sudden prostration with legs outstretched, spastic actions, and flexed toes. The head is retracted and often twisted sideways. Another name for this malady is "crazy chick disease." Encephalomalacia is a loss of muscular coordination resulting from hemorrhages and fluid accumulation within the cerebellum of the brain. The head may also curl under the breast. An autopsy will show lesions or injuries in the cerebellum and sometimes in the cerebrum of the brain. This deficiency disease can also be characterized by fluid accumulation under the skin and in the heart and pericardium, the membrane enclosing the heart.

Exudative diathesis is a third vitamin E deficiency disease in chickens. It is an accumulation of fluid in all tissues caused by an abnormal increase in the permeability of the blood capillaries. Selenium, as well as vitamin E, is effective in treating this disease. Oral administration of 300 International Units of vitamin E per chick causes the total remission of exudative diathesis and maintains them for about one week in normal condition.

In rats, vitamin E deficiency interferes with placenta function and causes the death and dissolution of the fetuses. A deficiency in growing rats causes slackened growth with weight stabilizing or declining. Paralysis with dragging of the hindquarters is a symptom of severe deficiency in rats and other mammals.

Vitamin E deficiency in males can be more serious than in females. After 75 to 100 days of deficiency, male rats will become sterile, and this damage is permanent. Testicle degeneration will occur in all male animals as a result of severe vitamin E deficiency, with the same permanent damage to fertility. This could very well be a cause for the frequent reports of infertile pairs of birds in aviculture. Vitamin E deficiency damage resulting in degeneration of the male sex glands is permanent and irreversible where fertility is concerned.

Vitamin E and selenium seem to be interdependent in all of their body functions. Vitamin E will reduce the selenium needs and requirements in at least two known ways. First, it maintains body selenium in an active form and prevents its loss from the body. Vitamin E also prevents the destruction of lipids within the cell membrane. This reduces the amount of glutathione peroxidase, a selenium-containing enzyme, that is needed to destroy the peroxides formed in the cell. See the section on selenium for more detailed information concerning this nutrient interrelationship.

From the above discussion, representing only a limited summary of the information available on vitamin E, the importance of this tocopherol to the nutrition of birds is patently obvious. Vitamin E is one of the first nutrients that aviculturists should consider for diet supplementation in their birds. It is one of the most likely vitamins to be deficient, if human and animal experience are any indication. Unlike the characteristics of most other deficiencies, a severe vitamin E deficiency in males will not be reversible by the restoration of adequate vitamin E in the diet. Never forget this fact, for it means that males will remain permanently sterile.

VITAMIN K

If you have been under the assumption that vitamin K is only one vitamin, you are in for a big surprise. Actually, there are a considerable number of chemical compounds that perform the functions of vitamin K in the body. Researchers use the term vitamin K activity to describe the functions of these compounds. Vitamin K was discovered in Denmark in 1934 by Carl Peter Henrick Dam in his studies of blood coagulation. He named the compound vitamin K after the Danish spelling of "Koagulation."

All compounds with vitamin K activity belong to a chemical group called quinones. This vitamin occurs in three distinct groups called K-1, K-2, and K-3. Any compound in the K-1 group is called a phylloquinone or phytoquinone. These occur naturally in oily seeds and in green leafy plants. They were first isolated from alfalfa meal. The compounds with vitamin K activity in the K-2 group are called the prenylmenaquinones. This group is found in animal tissues and is produced by bacterial synthesis in the digestive tract. A compound in the K-3 group is called a menadione or menaquinone. All of the quinones in this group are synthetically produced. Menaquinone is the simplest compound with vitamin K activity and is a yellow, crystalline powder.

Many of the synthetic forms of vitamin K are water soluble, while the naturally occurring forms are all fat soluble. All vitamin K compounds require the presence of some dietary fat for best absorption. Any deficiency is usually caused by a failure to absorb the available vitamin in the digestive tract. Any lack of bile acids will prevent the breakdown of fat in the digestive system and its subsequent absorption, along with the absorption of vitamin K.

Synthesis of vitamin K by intestinal bacteria occurs in both birds and mammals. However, since most vitamin K absorption occurs in the upper intestinal tract and synthesis is in the lower tract, little of the vitamin available from this source will be absorbed. This leads to coprophagy, since the droppings are rich in vitamin K, as well as several of the B vitamins. In testing done with rats, these animals obtain sufficient vitamin K from coprophagy to prevent any deficiency symptoms. However, if coprophagy is prevented, deficiency symptoms will appear very shortly.

Vitamin K is essential to proper liver function, and the liver is the site of its metabolic activity. The natural, fat soluble forms of vitamin K are stored in the liver, primarily. In the liver, vitamin K is necessary for the formation of four blood proteins which are involved in blood clotting. Any deficiency will prevent the formation of these proteins and make the body susceptible to serious bleeding and greatly prolonged clotting time. After two to three weeks on a deficient diet, the blood of chicks will cease to clot properly. Bleeding and hemorrhages will be visible on the breast, legs, and wings, as well as internally. An affected bird can easily bleed to death from a bruise or small cut. Vitamin K is also involved in the addition of phosphate to glucose to facilitate its conversion into glycogen and its passage through the cell membranes.

Though the natural forms of vitamin K are non-toxic at very high dosage levels, the synthetic menadione can cause the development of toxicity symptoms. Twelve milligrams daily is considered the safe upper limit of intake for human beings, but 10 milligrams at one time will be toxic to newborn babies. In addition, a high vitamin K intake in the diet of hens has been proven to increase blood spotting in their eggs.

The highest natural sources of vitamin K are the dark green, leafy vegetables. Alfalfa is especially rich in this vitamin. Fruits and seeds for avian consumption, particularly the oily seeds, contain some vitamin K as well. Humans apparently have a lower requirement for vitamin K than the animals, since human milk contains only one-quarter the amount of vitamin K activity contained in cow's milk.

Vitamin K is stable in heat, but a variety of influences are capable of destroying it. Mineral oil will absorb it and cause its excretion. Light, acids, alkalis, and oxidizing agents will all destroy vitamin K. Radiation and x-rays are very destructive of vitamin K, and it is also destroyed in the presence of rancid fats.

The small amounts needed in the body of a bird should be supplied in adequate quantity in any dark greens and oily seeds in the diet. Birds maintained on a diet of raw, unprocessed foods should need no supplementation with vitamin K.

CHAPTER 8

THE WATER SOLUBLE VITAMINS

ASCORBIC ACID

The terms ascorbic acid and vitamin C are generally interchangeable in any discussion of nutrition. Ascorbic acid is the scientific term for this nutrient, while vitamin C is the name applied by most writers for the general public. Also, for most birds, it cannot be classified as a vitamin, since a vitamin by definition is an essential chemical nutrient extracted from the diet. For almost all birds commonly maintained in aviculture, ascorbic acid is not a vitamin, since the birds manufacture their own supply in either the liver or the kidneys, depending upon the species. Only man, the primates, guinea pigs, one species of fruit-eating bat, and the birds mentioned in the subsequent discussion are unable to synthesize their own ascorbic acid.

Nevertheless, ascorbic acid fulfills the same functions in the avian body as it does in the human body. It is vital to life. It is a potent killer of viruses and acts as a detoxifier in the blood. It seems to react with any foreign substance in the blood. Ascorbic acid is vital to the formation of the collagen which holds the cells together. Any weakness in this collagen will result in cell separation and escape of the fluids.

In the less advanced species of birds, such as the pigeons, gallinaceous birds, and even the psittacines, the kidneys are the source of ascorbic acid production. In the more advanced species of birds, most of the passerine birds in particular, the source of ascorbic acid is the liver. Most species have not yet been tested specifically to see which organ is the seat of ascorbic acid synthesis. Research by two Indian scientists, C. Ray Chaudhuri and I.B. Chatterjee, indicates sixteen species that are unable to manufacture their own vitamin C and must obtain it from their diet, based upon studies of their enzyme metabolism. If this initial research proves valid in years to come, ascorbic acid will be proven to be a true vitamin for these species. The most well known of these 16 avian species in aviculture is the red-vented bulbul, which was the only known subject of an actual feeding trial on birds with relation to vitamin C. The bulbuls did develop the symptoms of scurvy on a deficient diet. The symptoms were cured by vitamin C supplementation.

In periods of stress, the need for ascorbic acid skyrockets, probably beyond the avian body's ability to synthesize it. In humans, under severe stress, the limited vitamin C storage in the adrenal glands is depleted in a matter of seconds. At times of severe stress, therefore, an addition of ascorbic acid to the avian diet could be of value. In normal maintenace and breeding of avicultural species, however, supplementation with vitamin C is a useless waste. Chicken eggs contain no vitamin C until their incubation begins. As soon as the embryo begins developing, ascorbic acid is detectable in the egg, synthesized by the embryo. The inclusion of vitamin C in many supplements for avian consumption is a condescension to the nutritional ignorance of the aviculturist, not a necessity for the birds.

Vitamin C is the most easily destroyed of all the vitamins. The greatest destruction occurs as a result of exposure to oxygen with the resulting oxidation of the vitamin C. Storage and exposure to trace minerals are very destructive of vitamin C. Cooking destroys much of the vitamin C in foods, also, since it is unstable in heat. Fortunately, freezing does not damage the vitamin C content of foods.

While your birds are safe from scurvy, or acute vitamin C deficiency, you are not. Human beings cannot synthesize their own ascorbic acid. A study by the United States Department of Agriculture indicated that half of the students in the United States were not getting even the daily amount of vitamin C recommended by the U.S. Food and Drug Administration. Many researchers feel that even these recommended amounts are far too low for optimal health.

Bruises are a symptom of vitamin C deficiency in humans. Vitamin C is a vital ingredient in the formation of collagen, a component of all cell walls and connective tissue. With insufficient vitamin C, collagen is poorly formed and separates with the slightest pressure. This separation permits blood to escape into the tissues, thus causing a bruise. If you bruise easily, you have a severe vitamin C deficiency, technically called sub-clinical scurvy.

The human race suffers from what Irwin Stone has named hypoascorbemia, the genetic inability to synthesize ascorbic acid. A vital enzyme link in the transformation of glucose into ascorbic acid is missing in humans and the other species previously mentioned. A staggering amount of needless suffering occurs each day in the human sphere simply because of lack of knowledge on the subject of vitamin C and other facets of nutrition. Nevertheless, anyone who expects immediate results with increased vitamin C intake or supplementation is doomed to failure and disappointment. The rebuilding of the body's cells takes time. It will not occur in a few days or months.

Years are required to correct the damage of past years of
inadequate nutrition.. With a sensible diet and a minimum
of refined food products, the human body will rebuild its
deficient tissues over a period of years. Researchers estimate
that the human body replaces every cell over a period of
seven years. Impatience over the long term has been the
fatal flaw in most research to date on the usefulness of
vitamin C supplementation in the diet. For your reading
and information, I highly recommend the book by Irwin
Stone, *The Healing Factor*.

BIOTIN

Biotin was recognized as a dietary essential first in
1924, but its structure was not understood fully until
much later, and it was not synthesized until 1943. This is
one of the sulfur-containing vitamins. There are at least
five known forms of biotin, and it occurs naturally in both
free and bound forms. The biotin found in animal sources
is bound to a protein and is fat soluble. The biotin occurring in plant sources is free biotin and is water soluble. It
is classified as a water soluble vitamin.

Biotin participates in many biological reactions. The
requirement is extremely small, measured in micrograms,
but for its necessary functions, it is vital. Biotin within the
cells occurs bound to a protein, where it functions as an
enzyme. It is involved in both the synthesis and oxidation
of fatty acids and in the oxidation of carbohydrate. Biotin
is necessary for the removal of the amino groups from
several amino acids before they can be broken down for
energy. It is also necessary in the synthesis of nicotinic
acid and for the synthesis of at least one of the digestive
enzymes. The best established role of biotin in nutrition

is in the addition or removal of carbon dioxide in various metabolic reactions.

Though much remains to be learned about this vitamin, it does not appear that humans need a dietary source, and deficiency is unlikely to occur in humans. Human milk has only one-tenth the biotin found in cow's milk. Intestinal microbial synthesis provides a large quantity of biotin for both humans and mammals. Because of this, it is difficult even to induce a deficiency state in mammals. Coprophagy can be a sizable source of biotin in some mammals, again as a by-product of the microbial action. Any possible deficiency in humans would be signaled by changes in the skin with scaliness and hardening in the region of the eye. Loss of hair and muscular atrophy will follow the skin manifestations. Nausea, loss of appetite, and muscle pains are also symptoms of biotin deficiency. These human symptoms are very similar to those of thiamin deficiency. Excess biotin is excreted in the urine. At times, urinary excretion in humans can be greater than dietary intake. This again indicates a sizable biotin source from intestinal microbial synthesis.

Chickens, by contrast, do not seem to have the advantage of microbial synthesis as a source of biotin, and a diet low in biotin will produce definite symptoms of deficiency. In chicks, skin inflammation is a symptom, and the bottoms of the feet become rough and calloused with deep fissures which may bleed. The toes can die completely and slough off. The tops of the feet and legs show only dry scaliness. Also, sores appear in the corner of the mouth and spread to the whole area around the beak. Eventually, the eyelids become swollen and stick together. In breeding hens, deficiency will cause a reduction in hatchability of the eggs, but no decrease in egg production. These deficiency symptoms in chickens are very similar to those of pantothenic acid deficiency.

Dietary sources of biotin are found in both plant and animal products. Liver, kidney, milk, egg yolk, and yeast are the richest animal sources, with cauliflower, green leafy plants, peanuts, legumes, and nuts the richest plant sources. Grains, meat, and fish are poor sources of biotin in the diet and should not be relied upon for the dietary content. Research has determined that much of the biotin in natural food sources is biologically unavailable. Biotin is stable in ordinary conditions, but some will be lost in cooking, since it is water soluble. Though biotin is stable to heat, alkalis and oxidation will render it inactive. Oxidative rancidity is especially destructive to biotin, though the presence of vitamin E at the same time will prevent most of this destruction.

Symptoms of biotin deficiency can occur either in diets low in biotin or in diets high in raw egg white. Raw egg whites contain a protein called avidin, which binds biotin and makes it nutritionally unavailable. For this reason, raw egg whites are used frequently to induce a biotin deficiency for experimental purposes. Avidin will bind biotin into a protein too large for absorption, and the body is unable to break up this protein. Since it only takes 27 raw egg whites daily to cause a deficiency of biotin in humans, there seems little likelihood of a deficiency developing from this cause in any normal and rational diet. Also, moist heat denatures the avidin, changing it into a form that can no longer bind biotin. Thus, any amount of cooking renders the avidin harmless for human or avian nutrition.

For nutritional purposes in cage bird maintenance, biotin deserves a little closer attention. Without the microbial synthesis, birds are much more likely than animals to develop a biotin deficiency. Particularly for seed-eating birds, grains are a poor source of biotin. The diet must include eggs, greens, peanuts, nuts, sunflower seeds, or another high quality biotin source in order to provide biotin in sufficient quantities. Since so little is needed, there is little likelihood of a deficiency developing in finches or other cage birds on a varied diet.

CHOLINE

Choline is a vitally important compound in the body's functioning and metabolism. Under most conditions, it appears to be synthesized in adequate quantities in humans and animals. Rats, for example, synthesize their own supply of choline in the liver. For this reason, it is technically not a vitamin for many species, including humans. However, in guinea pigs, young chickens, and turkeys, choline is not synthesized in adequate quantity in the body, and it is definitely a vitamin for these species, especially while growing. It seems probable that this will be true for all birds, but only further extensive research can reveal the actual dietary requirement for choline in cage birds. This section is written on the assumption that choline will be proven as essential to other birds as it is to chickens and turkeys.

Pure choline is a strongly alkaline liquid, first isolated by Strecker in 1862. It was shown to be the active ingredient in lecithin in 1932. Though choline is present in relatively large amounts in all foods that contain fat, it is water soluble and is generally classified as part of the B complex of water soluble vitamins. Fruits and vegetables contain virtually no choline, with the exception of legumes. such as beans and peas. Liver, meats, and nuts are good sources, and there is some choline in the cereal grains. Eggs contain a large amount of choline, and the yolk, in particular, is an excellent food source of this vitamin. One large egg will contain about 170 milligrams of choline. For cage bird nutrition, the fatty seeds, eggs, and nuts are probably the best sources.

Choline functions in the body in three primary areas. First, it forms a compound that is necessary for transmitting nerve impulses from one nerve ending to the next. The second primary function is structural in nature. Choline forms an actual part of fat and nerve tissue, and it is an essential part of the fatty compound called lecithin. Unlike other vitamins, so far as is known, choline does not catalyze any reactions or act as a part of any coenzyme in the body.

The third function of choline is in relation to the methyl groups that are a part of the choline molecule. These are loosely bound units consisting of one carbon atom and three hydrogen atoms. The effectiveness of choline is due to the three available methyl groups in each molecule of this vitamin which are detached for a wide range of uses in the body. In order to act as a methyl donor, choline must first be oxidized in the body into a compound called betaine. In this manner, choline plays a vital role in the formation of phospholipids. These methyl groups are necessary to mobilize fat from the liver to be transported in the bloodstream to each of the body cells. In this way, choline prevents the accumulation of fat in the liver. An addition of choline to the diet will prevent the development of a fatty liver. Choline also exerts a protective action in cirrhosis of the liver in alcoholics. A folacin deficiency will exaggerate a choline deficiency, because methyl transfer is affected.

These important methyl groups can also come from other sources, such as the amino acid methionine, or they can be synthesized in the body in the presence of adequate folacin or cobalamin. For this reason, the choline requirement depends largely upon the amount of folacin and cobalamin in the diet. Because of this methyl donor function, the level of methionine in the diet is important in relation to the need for choline, and vice versa. However, in chicks methionine cannot serve this function, and this is probably also true in other avian species.

As previously mentioned, choline is a dietary requirement for growth in chickens and turkeys. A deficiency of this vitamin will result in perosis in chicks. This disease shows its first symptoms as pinpoint hemorrhages and slight puffiness around the hock joint. The leg bones then twist out of alignment, and the leg is unable to support the weight of the bird. The amount of choline necessary to prevent perosis is greater than that required for normal growth. Also, any folacin or cobalamin deficiency will cause a large increase in the choline requirement. In chickens, the perosis caused by deficiency can be cured by folacin, manganese, or choline. A deficiency in chicks is probably caused by inability to synthesize choline in adequate quantity.

The chick's ability to synthesize choline increases with age. Choline supplementation in the diet during this growth period will require supplementation in the diet at maturity for maximum egg production and for keeping liver fat at a low level. Even with lower egg production, however, the choline content of the eggs is not affected. Laying hens can synthesize sizable amounts of choline, so the choline content of the eggs produced will not be reduced, even in a deficient diet.

A number of other facts about choline may be of interest. First, a deficiency in animals will show up first as spots of hemorrhage in the kidneys. Hormones in the body have an effect on the choline requirements. One hormone seems to spare the choline requirement in the body. Because of the presence of female hormones, female rats are much less susceptible to an induced choline deficiency than are male rats.

Choline supplementation in the average cage bird diet should not be necessary. Three items commonly offered to cage birds are hard-boiled eggs, peanuts, and sunflower seeds. All of these are rich in choline. Any fatty item offered in the diet should have enough choline content to prevent any possible deficiency in birds in captivity. This is not a nutrient about which the breeder needs to be overly concerned.

COBALAMIN

The year 1926 marked a major advance in nutritional knowledge with the discovery that large amounts of raw liver would completely cure an invariably fatal disease, pernicious anemia. Three-quarters of a pound of raw liver each day was required to effect this cure. Fortunately, in 1948 vitamin B-12 was isolated from liver as small, red crystals which proved to be the curative factor. Since these crystals contained four percent cobalt, the compound was given the name cobalamin. Several similar chemical compounds exhibit vitamin B-12 activity with cyanocobalamin the most active. This form has a cyanide group attached to the basic cobalamin structure. The cyanide group was used in the original isolation of this vitamin, and it does not occur in the vitamin as it exists naturally in food items. There is no apparent nutritional difference, according to some reports, between the biological activity of cobalamin and cyanocobalamin. Cobalamin is water soluble, and the cobalamin crystals will absorb water vapor on exposure to air.

The best source of cobalamin is liver, which contains about one part per million of this vitamin. Oysters are a good source, and it is also found in kidney, meat, eggs, and milk. Only those and other animal foods are dependable sources of cobalamin. One ton of liver must be processed to get only 20 milligrams of cobalamin. So little cobalamin is needed for human health that intake is virtually always adequate in anyone who is not a strict vegetarian.

Plant material is virtually devoid of cobalamin. The tiny amounts found in some plants, such as comfrey and alfalfa, have been absorbed from the soil after bacteria have synthesized and excreted the cobalamin in that soil. The respectable amounts of this vitamin found in some varieties of seaweed also seem to be concentrated there after synthesis by bacteria associating with the seaweed.

This vitamin is now freely available commercially as a by-product of the antibiotic-producing streptomyces bacteria. Synthesis in the digestive tract by bacterial action is possible if sufficient cobalt is available in the diet. Microorganisms in the human digestive tract can synthesize cobalamin, but the site of this synthesis is too far down in the colon to permit absorption. Many varieties of bacteria and actinomycetes have the ability to synthesize cobalamin.

Any deficiency of cobalamin is usually an absorption problem rather than a dietary deficiency. The cobalamin molecule is complicated and cannot be absorbed without the presence of an intrinsic factor. This factor is a secretion of the cells in the stomach wall and is found in normal gastric juice. It is apparently different in every species. As this factor mixes with food, it releases cobalamin from the protein complexes in which it occurs. Without the presence of this factor, cobalamin will not be absorbed. The only exception to this is in the administration of massive doses, 1000 times the normal amount given. Some of this will pass through the intestinal wall by diffusion. Injection is the best method for immediate supplementation of cobalamin, since this form of administration bypasses the need for the intrinsic factor.

Absorption and subsequent utilization are also affected by other factors. A pyridoxine deficiency will lower the absorption efficiency of cobalamin, and any lack of iron will do the same. Also, in hypothyroidism, low thyroid gland activity, absorption efficiency will be lowered. Once absorbed, cobalamin is bound to a protein in the bloodstream and circulates to the tissues in this form. If absorption is in excess of the blood's capacity to bind it, cobalamin is excreted in the urine. Any limitation of this binding capacity in the bloodstream can also cause a deficiency as the body cells are deprived of the vitamin's usefulness.

Cobalamin is necessary for normal growth, the maintenance of healthy nervous tissue, and for normal red blood cell formation. It is necessary for normal carbohydrate metabolism and also appears to function in both fat and protein metabolism. Cobalamin is essential to the formation of the single carbon units called methyl groups which are incorporated into many of the compounds used by and made a part of the body. Cobalamin has the ability to promote nitrogen retention in the body and thus raises the biological value of protein in the food. Cobalamin has also been effective in the treatment of hepatitis. A complex interrelationship exists between cobalamin and folacin, and also between cobalamin and many other nutrients.

Fortunately, cobalamin is stored to a considerable degree in the liver in an enzyme form. Liver uptake is facilitated by the presence of ascorbic acid, and it is stored at the rate of one to two micrograms per gram of liver tissue. The average storage in humans is around 2,000 micrograms, or two milligrams, which amounts to about a six year supply. Body stores may be as high as 11,000 micrograms, which is 11 milligrams.

A number of other interesting facts are now available

regarding cobalamin. This vitamin is more stable than many other vitamin compounds, but it is destroyed by alkalis. Acids and oxidation have little effect on it. About 70% of the cobalamin in foods will be retained in cooking, and it seems to be completely non-toxic. Injected doses as high as 1600 milligrams per kilogram of body weight have proven completely harmless. The use of the antibiotics Aureomycin and penicillin have stimulated the growth of animals, apparently because they inhibit the growth of organisms that destroy cobalamin.

With particular reference to cage birds, any deficiency of cobalamin will reduce the rate of growth and also decrease hatchability of the eggs, based upon research with chickens. A severe deficiency will result in death. Aviculturists need to pay particular attention to the supply of this vitamin in the avian diets, since cobalamin occurs in no plant sources regularly and in sufficient quantity. A source of animal food such as egg or insects must be provided to fulfill the cobalamin requirement. Alternately, a cobalamin supplement must be mixed with another commonly fed item to insure against deficiency. Most commercial supplements have cobalamin added, since its necessity in nutrition is now universally recognized. Considering the few micrograms required even for a large number of finches, no aviculturist can afford to chance a cobalamin deficiency. Since five micrograms is presumed to be a very adequate daily supply for human beings, one microgram should be sufficient to prevent any deficiency symptom in a large number of finches, when fed on a daily basis.

FOLACIN

The vitamin that we now call folacin has gone through many temporary names and name changes in the past. The most well known of these is folic acid, and this term is still widely used to identify this vitamin. Other common names given to this compound, before exact identification was made, are vitamin M, Factor U, and Factor R. Folacin was discovered during the search for the antipernicious anemia factor in liver. This vitamin exists in nature in both free and bound forms. It is a proven dietary essential for chickens, monkeys, humans, and guinea pigs. Rats do not appear to need this vitamin, apparently producing their own supply through intestinal microbial synthesis. Neither is it a dietary essential for dogs and rabbits. Folacin was isolated and synthesized in 1945.

Folacin is absorbed primarily in the upper part of the small intestine by both active transport and diffusion. Absorption is assisted by the presence of ascorbic acid. A high percentage of the folacin in liver, yeast, and eggs is absorbed, but as little as 10% of the folacin in other foods may be available. The liver is able to store reserves of folacin that are adequate for four or five months.

Substances with folic acid activity, called folates, are synthesized by plants, in animal tissues, and by intestinal microorganisms. The term folate refers to all substances that give rise to folacin in the body. The term folacin is now used to describe only the form from which the active coenzymes are directly derived. Folates occur in foods as a combination of pterin and para-aminobenzoic acid, commonly called PABA. For some time, researchers felt that PABA was a vitamin in its own right, but further research revealed it to be a part of the folate molecule. Folate must go through several changes in the presence of various enzymes and coenzymes to form the citrovorum factor, also called folinic acid. This is considered the biologically active form of this vitamin, and it is in this form that the liver stores folacin.

Para-aminobenzoic acid alone has been found to be an ideal dressing for burns and sunburns, rivaling vitamin E in its positive effects. Arsenic and sulfa compounds will destroy PABA and it has been a prescription item because of its antagonism to sulfa compounds. Another effective use for PABA is in treatment of the condition called vitiligo, characterized by spots of white appearing on the skin, totally lacking in pigment. A high intake of PABA over a period seems to be effective in restoring normal pigmentation to affected areas of skin.

Animals appear to differ greatly in their requirements for folacin. This seems to be primarily due to the animal's ability to utilize intestinal microbial synthesis as a source of folacin. The requirement is small, and humans require less than one milligram per day. Yet, one authority has stated that further research may reveal that folacin deficiency is the most common vitamin deficiency in the United States. In one test, 20% of pregnant women were shown to be deficient in folacin to the point of symptoms of blood poisoning. The need for folacin always increases in pregnancy and in any iron deficiency.

Folacin acts as an intermediary in a variety of biological functions. It aids in the transfer of single carbon units, such as methyl groups, from one substance to another. Folacin is active in the synthesis of parts of the nucleic acid molecules DNA and RNA. Because of this important function, folacin is very important in rapid cell division and growth. It is also involved in normal blood formation and is used in the synthesis of choline, another of the B complex vitamins. One unfortunate action of folacin is to mask the symptoms of pernicious anemia, caused by a cobalamin deficiency, until irreparable damage has been done in the body.

The dietary sources of folacin and the destructive influences on it must both be considered when trying to
assure an adequate dietary intake for cage birds. Of the
items commonly offered to cage birds, only peanuts, walnuts, and wheat are excellent sources. Liver, brewer's
yeast, mushrooms, asparagus, broccoli, lemons, and bananas
are very good sources. A varied diet of whole foods should
contain a sufficient supply to prevent any deficiency.
Processing and cooking losses are disastrous where folacin
is concerned, and the losses will range from 50% to 90%
of the folacin content of foods. Exposure to light will destroy folacin, and high heat also will destroy it.

As previously mentioned, folacin deficiency may be
more widespread than is generally realized. A folacin deficiency may result from inadequate intake, poor absorption of the vitamin, excessive demands, or possibly from
metabolic derangements. Alcohol is a particularly destructive influence on the human body's folacin supply. Studies
have shown that 90% of alcoholics suffer from a folacin
deficiency. A dietary deficiency of folacin will cause the
formation of abnormally large red blood cells and reduced
production of white blood cells. Two named forms of
anemia caused by such blood abnormalities resulting from
folacin deficiency are macrocytic anemia and megaloblastic anemia. Rheumatoid arthritis may be in large part
a human symptom of folacin deficiency, and lack of this
vitamin is suspected of causing such birth defects as harelip
and cleft palate. Almost all of the deficiency symptoms
can be attributed to a failure to metabolize single-carbon
units.

Symptoms of a deficiency in chicks include macrocytic
anemia, poor growth, very poor feathering, anemic appearance, and perosis. Folacin is required for the production of
feather pigmentation in several of the dark colored chicken
breeds. A deficiency in the breeding diet will cause a large

increase in embryonic mortality. Embryos will die within the shell soon after pipping the air cell. Presumably the same symptoms will occur in any cage bird, though research is not yet available regarding specific symptoms of folacin deficiency in cage birds.

GLUCOSE TOLERANCE FACTOR

The Glucose Tolerance Factor is one of the newest discoveries in the field of nutrition. Though it is classfied as an essential trace mineral at present, in all probability it will be reclassified as a vitamin with further research. The trace mineral that is the basis of the GTF molecule is chromium.

This discovery of Trivalent Chromium, also known as CrIII or Cr+++, by Schwarz and Mertz was accidental, as are most major discoveries. The experimentation on laboratory animals suddenly began producing completely unexpected results. Deficiency symptoms disappeared virtually overnight for no apparent reason. Careful investigation revealed that a new laboratory assistant, more experienced than the former, was disinfecting all washed glassware with chromic acid. Even subsequent thorough rinsing left enough residue on the glassware to supply the laboratory rats with the trace amounts of chromium necessary for Glucose Tolerance Factor synthesis.

The GTF molecule consists of chromium bound in an organic form. Trivalent chromium is the center of the GTF molecule. The molecule also contains two niacin molecules and three amino acids — glutamic acid, glycine, and cysteine. In structure, it resembles a hormone. Researchers have not yet determined the exact arrangement of these constituents.

The Glucose Tolerance Factor has been crystallized from brewer's yeast. Unlike cobalamin, GTF is well absorbed in the digestive tract. The body cannot easily synthesize it, but intestinal bacteria may be able to do so with an abundance of chromium in the diet. This factor is apparently completely non-toxic, either by mouth or intravenously.

GTF is released into the blood in response to insulin. The blood carries it to the tissues where insulin is working, and it becomes involved in sugar utilization at that point. GTF works closely with insulin to maintain the delicate balance between hypoglycemia (low blood sugar) and hyperglycemia (high blood sugar).

There is no reason to believe that the functions of GTF in the avian body differ significantly from the functions in rats and humans. A diet with sufficient chromium content should insure that no deficiency occurs in cage birds. Refer to the section on chromium for further information in this regard.

INOSITOL

The study of this vitamin presents an unusual grouping of facts, plus many uncertainties. Though it is classified as a B complex vitamin and was discovered in 1928, very little information exists about inositol. It is one of nine compounds with six carbon atoms closely related to glucose chemically. Of these nine, only nyoinositol is biologically active, and the name is shortened in most reports to inositol.

Most surveys of the known material on inositol will state that the biological significance of this vitamin in human nutrition is unknown. Yet, research has proven that human cells fail to grow without inositol. It is essential

for the growth of liver and bone marrow cells. A number
of other roles have been suggested for inositol, but are not
yet clearly proven. Perhaps the contradiction becomes
more understandable when we discover that the body
seems to be able to synthesize inositol from glucose. That
synthesis occurs within the individual cells, not through
the action of intestinal bacteria. Together with choline,
inositol has the function of preventing the accumulation of
excess fat in the livers of experimental animals. Inositol
seems to work in the body very closely with folacin, pantothenic acid, pyridoxine, and choline. It also seems to
stimulate the synthesis of biotin in the intestine.

Birds and animals have been proven to have a more
positive need for inositol. It is definitely a vitamin for
mice, and severe deficiency symptoms appear when it is
removed from their diet. In an inositol deficiency, mice
will develop an abnormality called spectacled eye, and loss
of fur, failure of lactation, and growth failure will also
appear. Inositol promotes the growth of yeast, and chickens
also seem to require inositol for normal health and development. Deficiency symptoms reported in chicks are
similar to the encephalomalacia and exudative diathesis
of vitamin E deficiency.

Inositol is present in nearly all plant and animal tissues
in fairly high concentrations, certainly higher than those in
which vitamins normally occur. It actually appears to be a
structural component of cells and seems to participate in
one step of the formation of nucleic acids, which are in
turn used to synthesize RNA. Inositol has the added effect
of mobilizing fat from the liver, even when the diet
contains a good supply of choline and other methyl
donors. See the section on choline for a more complete
explanation of methyl donors.

Inositol occurs mainly as a phospholipid in animal cells
in a form sometimes called lipositol. Some fish and sharks

may store carbohydrate as inositol rather than as glycogen in the manner of all birds and land animals. There are large amounts of inositol in the brain, the spinal cord nerves, and in their fluids.

The wide occurrence of inositol in natural foods would make a deficiency very unlikely. Fruits, meat, nuts, vegetables, grains, and yeast are all good food sources of inositol. In the grains, inositol is present in the form of a compound called phytic acid. In this form it occurs as a complex water soluble compound which will bind calcium, iron, and zinc in an insoluble complex, unavailable for use in the body. Sprouted seed may be a better source of inositol than whole grain seeds, since inositol seems to be freed from the phytic acid complex in the germination process. The aviculturist need have no concern about a deficiency of inositol in any normal avian diet.

LIPOIC ACID

Lipoic acid is one of the newest discoveries in the field of nutrition, and it is recognized by most modern sources as a vitamin. Lipoic acid is a sulfur-containing fatty acid which also goes by the name of thioctic acid. It is classified as a water soluble vitamin. Lipoic acid has been identified in five distinct forms. Three of these forms are fat soluble, but all three can be reversibly oxidized to the water soluble beta-lipoic acid.

Researchers have found lipoic acid to be an essential nutrient for several microorganisms. Any possible requirement for birds or higher animals is not yet known. Where investigated, lipoic acid is an essential component of the chemistry of metabolism in very small amounts. No deficiency has yet been induced in experimental animals and any required amount is now assumed to be provided by synthesis within the body.

Lipoic acid occurs in a wide variety of natural foods, and it has been isolated from liver and yeast. In its active form, lipoic acid is bound to a protein. Any requirement for lipoic acid in the nutrition of finches and other cage birds is unknown at this time.

NIACIN

This vitamin occurs in two primary forms in foods. Nicotinic acid is the form of niacin present in plants, and nicotinamide is the metabolic form of niacin occurring in animals. Either of these compounds performs the functions of niacin in the body, but nicotinic acid is apparently not converted to nicotinamide in the body. Niacin is soluble in water. Nicotinic acid was prepared as far back as 1867 in Germany, and it was easily available in this form long before its importance in nutrition was recognized. The term niacin is now used in all nutritional works in preference to the old designation of vitamin B-3.

The white crystalline substance of nicotinic acid was first isolated from yeast and rice bran in 1912, but again, its nutritional importance was not discovered at this time. In 1936, nicotinamide was isolated and the nutritional importance of niacin was fully recognized. The name niacinamide replaces the name nicotinamide many times, but both names refer to the same substance.

The disease which resulted in the push to find and identify niacin is called by its Italian name, pellagra, in English-speaking countries. In Spain it is known as mal de la rosa. It is called black tongue disease when it strikes dogs. The symptoms in order of their occurrence are called the four "D's": dermatitis, diarrhea, depression or dementia, and death. Though pellagra was first described in the 18th century, only in 1917 did Goldberger associate it with the absence of a dietary factor. He was able to cause pellagra by diet restriction. The disease first causes a characteristic skin inflammation, which occurs almost totally on areas exposed to sunlight in a very symmetrical pattern on both sides of the body. There will also be inflammation and redness of the tongue and lips with cracks at the corners of the mouth and inflammation of the mucous membranes, including the mucous linings of the gastrointestinal tract. This gastrointestinal disturbance is the cause of the diarrhea.

Next, the symptoms of mental depression will be evident, including unreasoning paranoia. The severest mental symptoms directly precede death from niacin deficiency. Dr. R. Glen Green of Canada has noted peculiar visual effects in persons suffering from niacin deficiency. Printed words seem to wiggle around, faces change in size, everything looks foggy, the world seems unstable and moving, and buildings seem to be falling on you. These are apparently the first noticeable symptoms in humans of a niacin deficiency.

Niacin is required by all cells in the body. It is readily absorbed in the digestive tract and can be stored in the body to a limited extent. Niacin in the form of nicotinic acid is frequently bound in an unabsorbable form. This lack of availability greatly affects the dietary requirement for this vitamin. Only treatment with an alkaline solution will release this bound niacin for absorption. Diets rich in corn are frequently pellagra-producing diets, since the nicotinic acid found in corn is not absorbable. Nevertheless, in Central America, where corn may constitute 80% of the diet, no niacin deficiency is known. This is because of the alkali treatment used in the preparation of tortillas and other corn products in that area.

Another strong factor affecting the body's requirement for niacin is the ability of the cells to synthesize
niacin from the amino acid tryptophan. This means that
the body's niacin requirement is partly dependent upon
the amount of tryptophan in the diet. Pyridoxine, thiamin, riboflavin, and possibly biotin must be present for
this synthesis to take place, and there are wide differences
in the ability of various animals to effect this synthesis.
Cats, for example, are unable to do it at all. The body cells
can convert sixty milligrams of tryptophan to one milligram of niacin.

Niacin is also a part of two important enzymes in the
body that play a vital role in the release of energy from
proteins, fats, and carbohydrates. Without these two enzymes, the metabolism of carbohydrates, fats, and proteins
is not possible. These enzymes catalyze the oxidation of
glucose, glycerol synthesis and breakdown, the degrada-
tion and synthesis of amino acids, and fatty acid oxidation
and synthesis within the body, among other functions.

A number of additional facts are known with respect
to niacin. An excess intake of pure nicotinic acid in
humans will cause severe flushing, itching, sweating,
nausea, and abdominal cramps. Nicotinamide will not
cause the flushing, but will cause all of the other symptoms. There are several known anti-nicotinic acid compounds that will destroy the effectiveness of this vitamin
in the body. Also, niacin has been proven to be a part of
the molecule of the Glucose Tolerance Factor, a recently
discovered vitamin that contains chromium as its basis.
Finally, niacin can be synthesized by intestinal bacteria
within the digestive tract.

Niacin deficiency symptoms are well documented in
chickens, and similar symptoms in any cage bird will be a
definite indication of possible niacin deficiency. The
primary symptoms in chickens are enlargement of the

hock joint, bowing of the legs, poor feathering, and dermatitis or skin inflammation. There also may be inflammation
of the mouth and diarrhea. In young chicks, all of these
symptoms will heal and become normal with additional
dietary niacin, including the bowed legs. Symptoms for
ducks and turkeys are the same, but far more severe.
Ducks have a niacin requirement about twice as high as
chickens and in a severe niacin deficiency they will become
so bowlegged and weak that they cannot walk.

As with most of the B complex vitamins, liver is an
excellent source for niacin. Beans, peas, and peanut butter
are also good sources for human nutrition. For cage bird
diets, grains, peanuts, and sesame seeds are all good sources.
Any refining will lower the niacin values of food, and
white flour has only 19% of the niacin found in whole
wheat. Since this vitamin is water soluble, any wet cooking
will dissolve it from the food. Fortunately, this is about
the only loss of niacin that occurs. It is probably the most
stable of the vitamin compounds, and it is not destroyed
by acid, alkali, heat, light, or oxidation.

Any appearance of the previously mentioned symptoms
will signal that the avicultural diet is lacking in niacin.
Either a radical change of diet or supplementation with a
balanced B complex supplement then will be required.
A deficiency of one vitamin in the B complex surely signals
the deficiency of others also, since all occur in similar food
sources.

PANTOTHENIC ACID

Though pantothenic acid was isolated in 1938, the
compound was known to exist as a vitamin before that
year. This vitamin is a water soluble part of the B complex,

and in its pure form is a sticky yellow oil. Very rarely, but occasionally, you will see it referred to as vitamin B-5. Pantothenic acid is usually seen outside of its natural state as calcium pantothenate, the calcium salt form of this vitamin. The pantothenic acid molecule is a combination of the amino acid alanine and pantoic acid. There is no scarcity of pantothenic acid in nature, and the name itself means an acid found everywhere.

The characteristics of pantothenic acid make the occurrence of any deficiency problem highly unlikely. It is stable in moist heat in neutral solutions, though it is unstable in acids or alkalis. Little is lost in normal cooking, but dry heat will destroy pantothenic acid completely. Refining removes much of the pantothenic acid content of foods, and half of this vitamin is lost in refining whole wheat into white flour. Though all plant and animal cells seem to contain some pantothenic acid, the richest known source of this vitamin is the royal jelly of honey bees. Other rich sources are liver, yeast, egg yolk, and green leafy plants.

Pantothenic acid is vital to all energy-requiring processes within the body as a result of its central role in the utilization of carbohydrate, fat, and protein. It participates in the release of energy from all three of these energy-yielding nutrient groups. Because of this, low intakes of pantothenic acid will slow down metabolic processes with general harm to the health of the cells. The highest concentrations are found in the most metabolically active body organs — the liver, adrenal glands, kidneys, brain, and heart. This vitamin is also required for the synthesis of fat, and it is important for coping with stress, which increases the requirement for this vitamin. In addition, pantothenic acid seems to stimulate the spontaneous movement of the gastrointestinal tract. Chickens and other birds require pantothenic acid for normal egg production and hatchability.

Pantothenic acid combines with several other substances in the body to form a compound called coenzyme A. This is the form in which pantothenic acid occurs in microorganisms and animal tissues, and it is the form which the body cells use in most biological reactions. Coenzyme A apparently is synthesized within the cells, since it is found only in the cells and not in the blood. Pantothenic acid in this form is necessary for hemoglobin synthesis, and a deficiency of it slows down the synthesis of insulin in the body. Coenzyme A is also required for the breakdown of the fatty acids within the body.

Researchers have examined the effects of pantothenic acid deficiency in experimental animals, and the results in chickens can safely be applied to all avian species kept in captivity. Any deficiency in the hen's diet will result in a shortage of pantothenic acid in the egg and will cause the death of the chick shortly after hatching. Chicks on a deficient diet will exhibit a severe skin inflammation, poor growth, broken feathers, and eventual death. Internal symptoms include spinal cord degeneration and fatty degeneration of the liver. Chicks will appear emaciated and crusty, scab-like sores appear in the corners of the mouth. The margins of the eyelids will be granular and small scabs will develop on them. The eyelids may be stuck together by a sticky exudate. On the feet, the outer layers of skin between the toes and the bottoms of the feet peel off and small cracks appear in the skin. At times, the skin of the feet thickens and becomes horny with wart-like growths developing on the balls of the feet. These symptoms in chicks are very similar to those of a biotin deficiency, and only a close examination of the diet can reveal which of the two vitamins is in such severe deficiency. Ducks will develop anemia as a result of pantothenic acid deficiency, and in humans a feeling of burning in the feet is a symptom of a deficiency of this vitamin.

Such severe deficiency symptoms as those described for chickens will never occur on any natural, varied avian diet. Only purified diets in laboratory experimentation will produce such severe effects. In addition, if the degenerative changes described have not progressed too far, the symptoms seem to be completely reversible. Since pantothenic acid occurs so widely in the food supply and the requirement is so small, the development of any deficiency in cage bird feeding is extremely unlikely.

PYRIDOXINE

This vitamin has been known as vitamin B-6 for a long period of time, but the chemical name of the compound, which is pyridoxine, is gradually replacing the old B-6 designation. The first identification of this vitamin occurred in 1934, and the compound was isolated in 1938. The term pyridoxine is used to designate three separate substances, all of which are biologically active as vitamin B-6. These are pyridoxol, pyridoxal, and pyridoxamine. You may occasionally see the term pyridoxine used synonymously with pyridoxol to refer to the primary form of vitamin B-6. This vitamin occurs as pyridoxol in plant material as an alcohol bound to a protein. It is the primary form of pyridoxine, but unfortunately, it is not readily absorbable. Strict vegetarians who consume no animal material must be extremely careful to avoid a deficiency of pyridoxine caused by poor absorption. Pyridoxal and pyridoxamine, by contrast, are most prevalent in animal tissue and are easily absorbed in the digestive tract.

Vegetable pyridoxol is more resistant to losses from storage and processing than are the pyridoxine compounds from animal sources. Though pyridoxine is somewhat stable to heat, it is partly destroyed by cooking. Very high heat in food preparation will destroy pyridoxine. Both irradiation and pasteurization deplete the pyridoxine content of milk, and freezing will cause a 25% loss of the pyridoxine value. The milling of cereal grains causes losses of as much as 80% to 90% of the pyridoxine value in them. White flour contains about 29% of the pyridoxine value of that in whole wheat. This vitamin is also rendered inactive by oxidation and ultraviolet light. It is unstable to alkalis, but all three forms are stable to acid exposure.

Though the National Research Council recommends two milligrams of pyridoxine per day for an average human adult, the requirement for pyridoxine can vary widely, depending on a variety of factors, including biochemical individuality. Body size will alter the requirement, since a 250 pound male will obviously require a greater amount than will a 120 pound male.

The protein content of the diet is a primary determining factor in the amount of pyridoxine required, since there is a direct interrelationship between pyridoxine and all aspects of protein metabolism. Periods of rapid muscle growth will also increase the pyridoxine requirement. A diet high in the amino acid tryptophan will increase the need for pyridoxine, as will an abundance of the amino acid methionine in the diet. A high content of the compound sugar called sucrose in the diet will also increase the pyridoxine requirement for its metabolism. Finally, increased pyridoxine intake is needed during pregnancy and lactation, or from any exposure to radiation. Conversely, a high dietary intake of choline, the essential fatty acids, biotin, and pantothenic acid will reduce the requirement for pyridoxine.

Pyridoxine is essential in the body in a number of ways. It is vital to the proper functioning of the nervous system. Pyridoxine is vital to protein metabolism, but seems to play no direct role in the production of energy.

In its protein-related functions, it is necessary for the synthesis and breakdown of all amino acids. Pyridoxine is vital to the maintenance of the smooth integrity of the arterial walls and it is essential for the production of many enzymes. It also controls one of the intermediate steps in the body's production of niacin from the amino acid tryptophan.

It is interesting to note that normal dream recall in humans depends to a large extent upon the presence of adequate pyridoxine in the brain. With too little pyridoxine, there will be no dream recall. An excess of this vitamin will cause awakening after every dream with vivid recall of the dream sequence.

Pyridoxine is required for the proper absorption of cobalamin, and in its protein-related functions, it is necessary for the synthesis and proper functioning of both DNA and RNA. Finally, with magnesium, pyridoxine is essential for the synthesis of lecithin, and it has been proven to be effective in the reduction of tooth decay.

In the form of pyridoxal phosphate this vitamin functions as a coenzyme for many biological reactions. Either zinc or magnesium can catalyze the formation of this coenzyme, which is especially important to protein and amino acid transformations. The body can form this compound from any of the three forms of pyridoxine. Pyridoxal phosphate catalyzes three main types of amino acid reactions, one of which is the removal of sulfur from the sulfur-containing amino acids. All amino acid transport systems seem to require this coenzyme. Pyridoxal phosphate also plays a vital role in the synthesis of the blood protein hemoglobin.

Pyridoxine is found in a wide variety of sources in both free and organically bound forms. These foods include muscle meats, liver, vegetables, egg yolks, whole grains, and nuts. Bananas and pecans are respectable sources, and pyridoxine is synthesized in the lower digestive tract by microorganisms existing there. This intestinal microbial synthesis is an important source of pyridoxine for most species. Since pyridoxine is water soluble, virtually no storage of the pure vitamin occurs in the body. However, the body can store some compounds containing pyridoxine. Fully one-half of the amount that the body can store is in the form of glycogen phosphorylase, an enzyme stored in the muscles, which facilitates the release of glycogen from the muscle tissues. Any excess over body needs is oxidized to pyridoxic acid, which is excreted in the urine. This acid will disappear from the urine entirely in cases of severe deficiency.

A variety of deficiency symptoms have been noted in animals suffering from a lack of vitamin B-6. Circulatory and nervous problems form a large group of these noted symptoms. Lesions in the artery walls are common; they fill up with fat and create all the symptoms of arteriosclerosis. Also, a form of anemia occurs because of pyridoxine's role in hemoglobin synthesis. Nerve functioning is severely disrupted, to the point of death in severe deficiencies. Muscular twitchings, irritability, and convulsive seizures are characteristic deficiency symptoms. Weight gains will cease in human infants, and anemia will develop. the severe convulsive seizures caused by pyridoxine deficiency will end in death.

Several other effects of pyridoxine deficiency have been documented. Animals suffering from deficiency will have four times as much dental decay as animals supplied with adequate pyridoxine. Utilization of the iron absorbed seems to be greatly decreased, and abnormal amounts of iron are stored in the body in cases of pyridoxine deficiency. The iron content of the blood will rise and the copper content will decrease in a deficiency situation. Needs for the essential fatty acids increase with any pyridoxine deficiency, and a skin eruption will occur in the area surrounding the nose in humans. Whereas young animals will suffer from convulsions from a pyridoxine deficiency, older animals will exhibit anemia.

A great deal of research on chickens and pyridoxine deficiency has taken place in the years since 1934. The resulting knowledge should be applicable to all cage birds, though direct research on any wild species seems to be nonexistent. A deficiency in chickens causes jerky, nervous leg movements, depressed appetite, and poor growth in growing chicks. Adult chickens will have reduced egg production, reduced hatchability, decreased feed consumption, loss of weight, shrinkage of sexual organs, and involution of the wattles and comb. Death is the final deficiency symptom in chickens. Chicks will be seized by extreme convulsions characterized by great activity with flapping of wings, running around, falling, and rolling around. These severe convulsions will end in death. Though anemia will occur in deficient ducks, this is not a strong symptom of deficiency in chickens or turkeys. A chronic borderline deficiency may cause one severely crippled leg with one or both middle toes bent inward at the first joint.

The first symptoms of deficiency in humans are varied and not all will occur in any one individual. Anyone suffering from at least two of these symptoms as outlined by John H. Ellis, M.D., should begin taking a balanced B vitamin supplement immediately which contains 50 milligrams of pyridoxine. Bursitis and pain in the shoulder joints is a strong symptom, frequently accompanied by cramps in the legs or "charlie horses," particularly while lying on the bed at night. Awakening with a "dead" arm with no feeling and dizzyheadedness at any time are two other symptoms. Swelling of the feet, hands, arms, or any other part of the body is a serious symptom of pyridoxine deficiency, particularly during pregnancy.

As important as these symptoms may be, the hands are the primary focus of symptoms of a deficiency of this vitamin. Swelling that masks the veins and tendons may be accompanied by tingling, numbness, prickling, and extreme sensitivity. Hands and fingers may be so painful and sensitive that a handshake is agony, with the joints particularly affected. The hand may go to sleep when writing and fingers will lose control and drop items held in the hand in a momentary, transitory paralysis. Frequently, the deficiency results in inability to make a fist with the fingers touching the palm of the hand. All of these symptoms are the result of the important role pyridoxine plays in the integrity of the nerves and circulatory system. These symptoms also correspond to the noted minor symptoms in chickens, particularly with reference to crippling of their feet.

Pyridoxine deficiency is a distinct possibility in cage birds. Their high protein requirements for maintenance and breeding will demand a correspondingly higher amount of pyridoxine than is present in cereal grains, for example. Though whole foods are expected to contain any nutrients necessary for their proper absorption and utilization, any cooking or processing will alter this balance. No bird in the wild ever cooks or processes its food in any way, and as a result, wild birds will not exhibit any deficiency of any vital nutrient. Cage birds can and will show deficiency symptoms if the diet we provide them is high in cooked or refined food products. This is particularly true where pyridoxine is concerned.

RIBOFLAVIN

In 1917 researchers realized that the substance they had designated as vitamin B was in part unaffected after heat had destroyed the anti-beriberi properities of the compound. For this reason, they listed the vitamin destroyed by heat as vitamin B-1, and the one stable to heat as vitamin B-2. Though B-2 eventually turned out to be six different vitamins, the designation B-2 remained with riboflavin. Today, the terms riboflavin and vitamin B-2 refer to the same substance, a slightly water soluble orange-yellow fluorescent pigment. Initially, this vitamin also carried the name Vitamin G. It has in the past also carried the names ovoflavin, uroflavin, lactoflavin, verdoflavin, and heptoflavin, depending upon the item from which it was extracted. This vitamin exists in two chemical forms in its biological functions.

Riboflavin is a relatively stable vitamin, quite resistant to acid, heat, or oxidation. However, it can be very unstable to both visible and ultraviolet light and to alkaline substances. Heat in any acid solution will not destroy it, but any alkali will. Thus, baking soda used in cooking will destroy the riboflavin content of the food. Riboflavin was isolated in pure form in 1932, and research then indicated that it was a combination of a protein and a pigment called flavin. Flavin compounds are substances that produce an intense yellow-green fluorescence in water. Riboflavin also contains a simple sugar called ribose, and this accounts for the first half of the name of this vitamin. Riboflavin was synthesized in 1935. This vitamin is not affected by light when it is dry, but light quickly destroys it when in solution. Riboflavin is insoluble in fats and fat solvents, and it produces a strong, green, fluorescence if irradiated with blue or ultraviolet light. The official British spelling of this vitamin differs from the American in adding a final "e" to form "riboflavine."

Riboflavin is not abundant in the diet, and surveys have revealed substantial deficiencies in the American population. Part of this is due to the removal of riboflavin in the refining process, as 80% is removed in refining wheat to white flour. The body is unable to store riboflavin in any quantity, though the liver and kidneys do contain higher concentrations than the other tissues. Yeast is the best source, and milk, liver, eggs, heart, kidney, cheese, green leafy vegetables, nuts, and grains also contain some amounts of riboflavin. Though riboflavin is widely distributed in both animal and vegetable sources, the quantities present are small. Any diet with an appreciable amount of refined foods is likely to be deficient in riboflavin. Cereal grains are much richer sources of riboflavin after sprouting.

No animal has the ability to synthesize riboflavin, but all green plants, yeast, fungi, and some bacteria synthesize it. Some intestinal bacteria can synthesize riboflavin, but this is not an abundant source of this vitamin. A diet high in starch stimulates this microbial synthesis, but diets high in fat or protein inhibit the existence of the producing microorganisms. In the ruminants, however, the entire riboflavin requirement is supplied by the microorganisms existing in the rumen, or first section of the stomach.

The absorption and excretion of excess riboflavin are controlled within narrow limits by the body's nutritional mechanisms. The body absorbs riboflavin through the intestinal wall, and it is attached there to a phosphate molecule. From this point, the blood carries the riboflavin compound to the tissues where it may be attached to a protein molecule. The compound formed in this way is called a flavoprotein. Most excretion of excess riboflavin occurs through the kidneys, and there is no evidence of human or animal toxicity, even at very high levels of dosage. Riboflavin is excreted when protein is broken down and retained when protein is being accumulated.

Riboflavin performs a wide variety of important functions within the body. It is essential to normal tissue growth and maintenance, and it also assists in the metabolism of amino acids, fatty acids, and carbohydrates. Riboflavin must be present in order for the amino acid tryptophan to be converted into niacin. The flavoproteins are important in the utilization of oxygen by the cells, and also work closely with enzymes which contain niacin.

Riboflavin combines with a protein to form over a dozen known important enzymes in the body's metabolism. Before it can function as a part of these enzymes, riboflavin must have a phosphate group attached to it, which is usually added in the intestinal cells during absorption. Riboflavin's enzyme and coenzyme reactions are essential for the release of energy from glucose and the fatty acids. Riboflavin is also a part of enzymes involved in the transfer of hydrogen atoms in the metabolism of protein. As a part of several of these enzymes and coenzymes, riboflavin contributes to their ability to accept and transfer these hydrogen atoms. There are a number of known antagonists that will replace riboflavin in its functions and thus prevent it from functioning usefully in the body. Also, research has indicated that riboflavin is probably required for the formation of melanin in the feathers of birds.

Deficiency of riboflavin has been termed by some experts as the most common vitamin deficiency in America, though this is certainly debatable. Riboflavin deficiency goes by the formal name of ariboflavinosis. In humans the intake must be low for several months for the commonest symptoms of mouth abnormality to appear. The tongue becomes smooth and sore with a characteristic purplish-red color. The lips may become noticeably red also, with cracks appearing in the corners of the mouth. A deficiency in animals will cause a reduction in reproductive capacity.

Pregnant animals will give birth to young showing abnormalities or will abort the embryos. Alopecia, or loss
of hair, may also occur in animals. Such congenital malformations as harelip and cataracts, clearly demonstrated
in animal experiments, will occur if deficiency happens
at a crucial embryonic stage of pregnancy. Growth of the
young will also be retarded.

Problems with the eyes and skin also can be symptoms
of riboflavin deficiency in humans. Eye fatigue, over-
sensitivity to light, blurred vision, and bloodshot eyes are
all symptoms of riboflavin deficiency. A deficiency also
causes a gritty feeling on the inside of the eyelids, burning
eyes, and pupil dilation. Though the skin may become dry
and scaly, a greasy skin inflammation on the face and ears,
or particularly on the scrotum in males, is more likely.
Animals will also experience abnormal growth of the blood
vessels of the eye into the cornea, and the eye may eventually form a cataract.

Symptoms of deficiency in chickens are well known
and should appear similar in all species of birds kept in
captivity. In adult hens, egg production will not be affected
in a riboflavin deficiency. Hatchability becomes poor
within two weeks after hens are fed a deficient diet, and
eggs from severely riboflavin deficient hens will not hatch.
Hatchability will return to normal in about seven days
with adequate supplementation in the hen's diet.

Chicks suffering from a deficiency will have a good
appetite, but very slow growth. Gradually, they become
weak and emaciated. The leg muscles are atrophied and
flabby, and the skin is very dry and rough. Between the
first and second weeks of deficiency, the chicks will have
diarrhea. They don't move around unless forced to move,
and then may walk on their hocks with the help of their
wings. Malfunction of the sciatic nerve causes the toes to
curl inward in paralysis, both when resting on the hocks

and when walking. In an advanced stage of deficiency, the chicks lie with their legs extended. In a marginal deficiency, spontaneous recovery will occur, indicating a reduced requirement for riboflavin with age. If the deficiency is severe enough that the curled toes symptom remains over a long term, the damage to the sciatic nerve is irreparable, and the deformity will be permanent.

On several occasions I noted this curled toe syndrome on fledgling Society Finches in my collection. At the time, as most breeders would, I attributed this to a genetic defect in the two pairs of my Society Finches that occasionally produced such offspring. The benefit of additional knowledge and experience has convinced me that this was definitely a riboflavin deficiency. Since less than one percent of the offspring of my strain of Societies showed this defect, there is little doubt that this reflected an unusually high riboflavin requirement in these few birds, governed by their biochemical individuality.

The information presented earlier in this section and my own experience indicate that a riboflavin deficiency is a strong possibility in any birds maintained in captivity. The only food commonly offered to cage birds that contains a reasonably good amount of riboflavin is hard boiled eggs, particularly the yolk. Yet, this source in abundance together with millet and sunflower seed, both excellent nutritional items, failed to supply enough riboflavin to prevent a severe deficiency symptom from appearing in my finches. The only suggestion I can offer to the breeder is to mix a high potency, balanced B vitamin supplement with some soft food that the birds will eat if you should notice any of the riboflavin deficiency symptoms noted in this section.

THIAMIN

Thiamin was the first of the B complex vitamins to be chemically identified. It was crystallized in pure form in 1926, and its structure was established and synthesized in 1936. Thiamin also carries the name vitamin B-1, and it was called aneurin in years past. Thiamin is a water soluble, white, crystalline substance in its pure form. It is insoluble in fats and fat solvents. Thiamin hydrochloride and thiamin mononitrate are two more stable forms of this vitamin. Several thiamin derivatives have been synthesized, and they are absorbed in the body at a faster rate than natural thiamin. The name thiamin frequently is spelled with a final "e," as "thiamine."

When food refining for increased storage life became common in the middle of the 19th century, thiamin deficiency in the form of beriberi became a major health problem. Until the 1940's, beriberi was the main health problem in Java, Malaysia, Japan, and the Philippines. As late as 1947 thiamin deficiency was one of the two major causes of death in the Philippine Islands. Over 20% of the Japanese Naval personnel suffered from beriberi until 1882 when Tataki changed the diet of the Navy to include more protein, and at the same time inadvertently added additional thiamin to the diet. Beriberi was first recognized as a dietary deficiency disease in Java.

Thiamin is readily available in the food supply and is well absorbed in the body and easily transported. Brewer's yeast, pork, and liver are the three best sources of thiamin. Since these foods are something less than common in the average cage bird diet, whole grains, sunflower seeds, wheat germ, pecans, and other nuts are the best sources for avian nutrition. Most of the thiamin is in the outer coverings of the hulled grain, and the removal of this layer, particularly in rice, has caused an untold amount of suffering in the world. Even in wheat, as much as 77% of the thiamin content is removed when it is refined into white flour. Intestinal synthesis of thiamin does occur as a result of microbial action, but this is not an important source in humans, and occurs too far down in the digestive tract to be absorbed and of value in avian nutrition. Absorption takes place in the first part of the small intestine, and this absorption requires an input of energy. A deficiency of folacin, another of the B complex vitamins, will hinder absorption of thiamin. Also, human milk normally contains less than half the thiamin content of cow's milk, and breast-fed babies can get beriberi if the mother's milk is deficient in thiamin.

The body does not store thiamin in any quantity, but levels of this vitamin in the tissues will increase with supplementation. Any amount present over and above the body's needs will be excreted in the urine. A high fat and protein content in the diet reduces the amount of thiamin required, while an increased carbohydrate intake increases the need for thiamin. Consumption of alcohol and sugar and also smoking greatly increase the thiamin requirement. Alcoholics are particularly susceptible to severe thiamin deficiency. There is no indication of any toxicity from an excess intake of thiamin, even at very high levels.

The first symptom of a thiamin deficiency in humans is loss of appetite, technically called anorexia, and other symptoms appear rapidly. A deficiency of this vitamin has a more profound effect on the appetite than that of any other nutrient, as all interest in food is lost. Nausea, vomiting, constipation, and decreased muscle tone are also early symptoms of deficiency. In babies, deficiency symptoms develop very rapidly and can cause death within hours. Excessive carbon dioxide in the blood causes a bluish color in the skin. Babies suffering from the onset of this severe deficiency have a very fast heartbeat and a very characteristic, loud, piercing cry. The administration of thiamin will relieve all of these symptoms within hours.

Adults will develop the disease symptoms called beriberi, which can come in two forms. In dry beriberi, the patient becomes thin and emaciated. This is also called wasting beriberi. In wet beriberi, also known as edematous beriberi, there is a great swelling and accumulation of fluid beginning at the feet. The accumulation of fluid in the heart muscle leads to heart failure and death. In the wet form of beriberi, tissue wasting still occurs, but it is masked by the accumulation of fluids. Both forms share the symptoms of irritability, vague uneasiness, and disorderly thinking. The most acute symptom is mental confusion which leads to coma.

These symptoms of deficiency result from the functions and utilization of thiamin within the body. These functions are particularly concerned with the metabolism of carbohydrates, but thiamin is involved to a lesser extent in the metabolism of fats and amino acids. There is some evidence also that the presence of thiamin is necessary for the synthesis of the amino acid glycine in the body. For its utilization in the metabolism, thiamin forms a coenzyme that is vital to the metabolism of carbohydrates and fatty acids. Thiamin also activates an enzyme necessary to oxidize glucose before it can be used to produce ribose, a simple sugar component of RNA, and an enzyme necessary for the synthesis of the fatty acids. Thiamin also has a strong effect on the nervous system, in addition to its coenzyme functions.

Symptoms of deficiency in chickens appear about three weeks after the beginning of a deficient diet. The onset of these symptoms in adult chickens is gradual. As in humans, loss of appetite is the first symptom, followed by loss of weight, ruffled feathers, leg weakness, and unsteady gait. Adult chickens may also show a blue comb and polyneuritis, the inflammation of many nerves. Once the loss of neuromuscular coordination occurs, the chickens will die shortly.

Deficiency symptoms in young chicks may appear before two weeks of age, and the onset of such symptoms is sudden. The loss of appetite mentioned earlier is permanent, and the chicks will not resume eating until their thiamin requirement is restored. This thiamin must be either force-fed or injected in order to induce the chickens to resume eating. In a continuous deficiency, muscle paralysis occurs beginning in the toes and working upward. The result is contraction of nerves and muscles which causes a star-gazing position in the chicks. This position is more pronounced than in the manganese deficiency symptom discussed later, with twisting of the neck. After this stage, the chicken loses the ability to stand, body temperature lowers, and breathing slows.

Several factors are important as destructive influences on thiamin. First, thiamin is the most vulnerable of all the B vitamins to destruction from heat. Oxidation, especially in the presence of alkalis, is also quite destructive of thiamin. In Japan the danger of deficiency in the past was great from the consumption of raw fish, as well as the consumption of large quantities of polished rice. Some raw fish contains an enzyme called thiaminase, which splits and thus destroys the thiamin molecule. Fortunately, thiaminase is inactivated by the heat used in cooking.

For the nutritional needs of finches and other cage birds, millet and sunflower seeds are both good sources of thiamin. Contents may vary widely, depending upon the particular species of producing plants. Any whole grain should supply an adequate amount of thiamin for seed eating birds. Since thiamin and the other B vitamins, excepting cobalamin and folacin, are not stored to any great extent in the body, a continuous supply of thiamin must

be present in the diet. Greens will supply some of the
dietary requirement, and pecans and other nuts are also
reasonable sources. Fruits as a rule are poor sources of this
vitamin.

CHAPTER 9

OTHER NON-MINERAL NUTRITIONAL FACTORS

AMYGDALIN

The controversy which surrounds this substance rivals that which erupts upon the mention of nuclear power. This is most unfortunate, since the controversy has virtually ended the possibility of serious research on this substance. Amygdalin has not been proven to be a vitamin as yet, though it is frequently referred to as vitamin B-17. The more well-known name for this compound in therapeutic doses is Laetrile. Need I say more about the controversial nature of Laetrile?

Amygdalin has not been exposed to any extensive research, so its true nutritional value is largely unknown. The raging controversy over its use as a cancer treatment has served to thoroughly squelch any serious research into its true nutritional effectiveness. We will be lucky to hear anything but wild emotion concerning this compound for the next fifty years. Whether amygdalin will be classified eventually as a vitamin is open to question at this time. Too little is known about it to hazard even a guess.

The cyanide in amygdalin's chemistry is said to attack cancer cells selectively. Its cyanide content is broken down through action of the enzyme rhodanese and excreted in normal cells. However, cancer cells do not possess this necessary enzyme, but are surrounded by another enzyme that releases the cyanide from amygdalin, thus destroying the cancerous cell through cyanide poisoning. This presumed train of events is the basis for all of the current controversy over the effectiveness of Laetrile.

Apricot pits are known as the best source of this substance, but most whole seeds of fruits, together with many grains and vegetables also contain amygdalin. For cage birds, millet, buckwheat, and flaxseed are good sources, as are raspberries, cranberries, blackberries, and blueberries.

BIOFLAVONOIDS

The bioflavonoids are a group of water soluble substances that were referred to as vitamin P until 1950. Some writings still refer to them with this designation. They were first suggested as dietary factors in 1936, and hesperidin is probably the most active of these substances. Rutin is also a well known bioflavonoid. These are brightly colored substances found in the peelings and juice of citrus fruits, and in buckwheat, grapes, cherries, apricots, blackberries, and to a lesser extent in other fruits and vegetables. Buckwheat is a particularly good source of rutin. The bioflavonoids appear to be completely non-toxic.

Researchers to date have been able to uncover no specific biological role for the bioflavonoids, and there is no evidence of a specific dietary need for them. The bioflavonoids can chelate copper and they have an antioxidant activity. Specifically, research has proven them able to preserve the life of adrenalin by preventing its oxidation. Also, there are strong indications that the bioflavonoids may prevent the development of excess fragility in the blood capillaries.

These substances do exhibit some noticeable effects in the body with respect to enhancing the utilization of ascorbic acid. In some manner the bioflavonoids appear to assist in the proper absorption and use of vitamin C. The exact way in which they work is unknown. The popular writings on nutrition list many health improvements resulting from increased dietary intakes of the bioflavonoids, but all of these seem to be the same as reported for increased vitamin C intake. It also seems that in some cases supplementation of either vitamin C or the bioflavonoids alone is largely ineffective, but together they accomplish the needed result. Obviously, a large amount of serious research is still required on the bioflavonoids. I can find no information on the bioflavonoids with specific reference to avian nutrition.

ENZYMES

Though most of the sections in this book contain some information on individual enzymes, this section will cover enzymes in a more general way. A rather heated debate has raged for years over the subject of enzymes in the food supply. Some authorities, particularly in the health food industry, maintain that enzymes must be present in the food eaten. Other authorities hold that any enzyme entering the digestive system is broken down and utilized for its parts, and the body manufactures any enzymes that are required. I suspect that the whole truth lies somewhere in between these opposing views.

Enzymes are protein compounds that control all body processes. They function as catalysts in the body for all biochemical processes. Though they are probably synthesized by most body cells, the liver and the pancreas are truly enzyme factories. The cells of these two organs produce a variety of enzymes that are necessary for the digestion and utilization of nutrients within the body.

The body contains and requires an untold number of different enzymes. The only figure available to me indicates over 700 different enzymes have been identified, and there are probably thousands of them required by the body. Some of these work in an acid medium, such as pepsin in the stomach at a pH of 1.8, which is extremely acid. Others work in an alkaline medium, such as trypsin from the pancreas, at a pH of 8.2. For this reason, the actions of many enzymes may be hindered or stopped if the body's tissues become too acid or too alkaline. One drop of blood contains over 100,000 enzyme molecules, in addition to all of the other blood cells and nutrient items. Over one-fourth of the enzymes active in the body also contain a metal ion. The sections on minerals go into greater detail on many of these metal-based enzymes.

All living tissues are rich in enzymes. Once the tissue dies, the enzymes gradually decompose. Whether they are totally digested when eaten, or absorbed and utilized without change, one primary fact must be paramount in your knowledge. Any amount of cooking destroys all enzymes. At temperatures of 125° Fahrenheit, all enzymes have been destroyed or rendered inactive. The ramifications of this fact are as yet almost totally unknown.

OROTIC ACID

This substance is popularly considered as a vitamin and is referred to in a number of publications as vitamin B-13. Nevertheless, I can discover no scientific source in this country that yet accepts this view. It has been synthesized and is used as a treatment for multiple sclerosis in Europe. The supplement form of this substance is calcium orotate.

Orotic acid has been reported to be necessary for a number of reactions within the body. The body metabolism of folic acid and cobalamin is said to require orotic acid, and it is reported to be essential for the biosynthesis of nucleic acid. Its presumed necessity for the regeneration of the body's cells is the basis for its use in the treatment of multiple sclerosis. There are known human hereditary diseases in which overproduction of orotic acid occurs and the substance then appears in the urine. This is found primarily in the oriental races of humanity.

The best known sources of orotic acid are root vegetables and whey. There are no known specific deficiency symptoms for this substance, but a deficiency may cause liver disorders, cell degeneration, premature aging, and overall degeneration, as in multiple sclerosis. Obviously, a great deal of additional research is necessary to determine the exact body requirement and nutritional effects of this substance. At least, at the state of current knowledge, there is no known toxicity of orotic acid. I have as yet uncovered no information regarding the possible need of orotic acid in avian nutrition.

PANGAMIC ACID

Pangamic acid is referred to in many places as vitamin B-15, but its nature and composition are still in doubt.

It has not yet been proven definitely to be a vitamin. Most of the research to date on pangamic acid has been done in the Soviet Union, but again we do not have an exact description of the chemical compound on which their experimentation has been done. The Soviets took an early interest in B-15 because of its reported powers to increase oxygenation of the cells for greater stamina and to retard the aging process at the cell level. Perhaps the advanced age of the Politburo members had something to do with this interest. This compound is widely used now in health care in the Soviet Union and some other countries. Their research has been translated into English, and it is readily available. The Soviets definitely regard pangamic acid as a vitamin and claim that it is of vital importance in maintaining health and full activity into old age.

Whether pangamic acid will be classified unconditionally as a vitamin at some future date is open to question at this time. Based upon Russian research into its use in the body, it seems quite probable that pangamic acid will be listed as a vitamin. Brewer's yeast, pumpkin seeds, sesame seeds, nuts, and whole grains are good sources of pangamic acid, if you desire to insure that there is a sufficient supply in the nutrition of your birds.

RNA and DNA

The formal names for these complicated substances are ribonucleic acid and deoxyribonucleic acid. They are not nutrients, but cell components. Since any nutritional study will encounter them frequently, they are covered here only in very basic form to answer any question that the beginning student might have. Nucleic acids are structural components of the cells, and living cells produce them. A detailed, scientific examination of these substances is available in the *Review of Physiological Chemistry* listed in the bibliography. For reasons of brevity, all publications refer to these substances as RNA and DNA.

RNA is a single-stranded molecule built on a base of ribose, one of the simple saccharides. There are three different classes of RNA which differ in size, function, and stability. These are messenger RNA, shortened to mRNA; transfer RNA, written tRNA; and ribosomal RNA, written rRNA.

Messenger RNA shows the most variation in form of the RNA's in size and stability. The mRNA transfers information from the gene which carries the genetic material to the cell's machinery for making proteins. The tRNA serves as an adaptor for the translation of information from mRNA into the specific amino acid being produced. The rRNA acts as the machinery for the synthesis of proteins from the mRNA patterns. As you might suspect from the complexity of this process, the rRNA is very complex, and its molecules are groups of at least four other RNA molecules plus nearly 100 specific protein molecules.

RNA is the user of the genetic information, and the DNA is the storage house of that information. The primary function of DNA is to provide the progeny with the genetic information possessed by the parent. This holds true from the simplest bacterium to the human being, though a human cell will contain about 1000 times more DNA than the bacterial cell. The complete set of chromosomes contains enough DNA to code for one million pairs of genes.

DNA is a very long, complex, double-stranded molecule. In construction, it looks much like a spiral staircase with no center pole. The two outside strands run in opposite directions, and each side seems to contain all of the stored genetic information. These strands unwind and separate, apparently in small sections, when the cell begins to divide, which is only at very specific times. When the cell divides, both halves of the DNA rebuild the sides lost into a once again complete DNA molecule.

Somehow, it seems very hard to conceive of all of this incredible complexity and organization in such a small package occurring without the guidance of a supremely wise Intelligence.

UBIQUINONE

The discovery of ubiquinone, perhaps more commonly called coenzyme Q, is one of the more recent nutritional advances. This discovery took place only in 1961. The structure of ubiquinone is very similar to that of vitamin E and vitamin K. Still, since it is synthesized within the body, it is not technically considered as a vitamin. Coenzyme Q serves as an essential link in the respiratory chain in which energy is released from the energy-yielding nutrients. Without this link in the metabolic chain, the release of energy would be incomplete.

Ubiquinone is found in nearly all living cells. Vitamin C and selenium function to maintain high tissue concentrations of this substance, and any excess can be excreted in the urine. Synthesis of ubiquinone depends on the presence of two amino acids — tyrosine and phenylalanine, and five vitamins — niacin, folacin, cobalamin, pyridoxine, and pantothenic acid. A pantothenic acid deficiency will depress the synthesis of coenzyme Q by 50%.

PART THREE

THE MINERALS

CHAPTER 10

INTRODUCTION TO MINERALS

Minerals exist in the avian body in both organic and inorganic combinations. About five percent of the body weight is in the form of minerals. Analysis of the residual ash of living things reveals twenty to thirty minerals present, over and above the minerals that are known to be essential. These additional minerals may be simply body contaminants, or they may have an as yet unestablished role in nutrition.

The body has mechanisms for controlling the absorption and excretion of essential minerals, and all body tissues and internal fluids contain varying quantities of minerals. The controlling forces for the levels of these minerals within the body are called the body's homeostatic mechanisms. The homeostatic mechanisms for some minerals are very effective and exacting, but virtually nonexistent for others.

Minerals in nature exist as combinations of isotopes. The nature of the mineral is dictated by the number of protons in the nucleus, but the number of neutrons may differ. These different numbers of neutrons are the differ-

165

ent isotopes of the mineral. The body apparently cannot use all isotopes indiscriminately, as will be covered in the discussions of biological transmutations among the essential minerals.

Mineral elements in the body fluids occur primarily as salts. These salts in solution will separate into their component ions, or electrically charged particles, and they are called electrolytes. The positively charged ions are referred to as cations, while the negatively charged ions are called anions. Eight essential minerals exist as cations; calcium, sodium, potassium, magnesium, manganese, zinc, iron, and copper. Cations have a deficiency of electrons, and this accounts for their positive charge. Five of the essential minerals are anions or are found in anionic groupings: chloride, iodide, phosphate, molybdate, and selenite. Bicarbonates and sulfates are also anions. The anions and cations are exactly balanced in all body fluids to maintain osmotic pressure. The main cation of the intracellular fluids is potassium, while the main one of the extracellular fluids is sodium.

Minerals are vital to the overall physical and mental health of an organism. Though the term mineral is used for all of these elements, technically speaking, some are not metals, such as chlorine and fluorine. These elements serve many functions within the body, and for purposes of organization are divided into bulk essential minerals and trace essential minerals. In order of their quantity found within the body, the bulk minerals, or "macro-minerals," are calcium, phosphorus, potassium, sulfur, sodium, chlorine, and magnesium. These are present in relatively high amounts in body tissues. Silicon is on the borderline between essential bulk minerals and essential trace minerals. All others essential in nutrition are trace minerals. The bulk elements are measured in grams and milligrams, though it might be better to refer to the body contents of calcium and phosphorus in humans in terms of pounds. They are by far the two most abundant minerals in the body. Trace minerals are measured in milligrams or micrograms.

Four basic elements form the vast bulk of the body and most organic compounds contain at least three of them. These are carbon, hydrogen, oxygen, and nitrogen. Carbohydrates and fats are made up of carbon, hydrogen, and oxygen, and protein contains nitrogen, in addition. Water is a combination of hydrogen and oxygen. Oxygen is required as a gas to metabolize all food products and maintain life in most living things. These four elements form about 95% of the substance of the avian or human body. No physical life as we know it would be possible in their absence. These four elements are so basic to life that they are normally ignored in discussions of nutrition. Other than the obvious need for oxygen, I have encountered no reference to any specific need for any of the other three basic elements in the body in their basic, elemental form, except as pertains to biological transmutations.

The absorption of minerals in the digestive system is not completely understood, but it now appears that the chelates formed of minerals may be the most important factor in their absorption. When a mineral atom is attached to an amino acid or any other chelating agent, which are collectively called ligands, a chelate is formed. The chelates form because of the peculiarities in the electron shells of the transitional metals. Amino acids, particularly cysteine and histidine, are excellent chelating agents. Peptides, which are linkages of two or more amino acids, and whole proteins can also serve as ligands.

Chelates have two primary metabolic functions in the body and one deleterious effect. First, they transport and store the metal ions of the essential minerals. Second, they can be essential in such functions as the formation of heme, the iron chelate portion of the hemoglobin molecule. This essential function is also evident in the formation of cobalamin around the cobalt molecule as a cobalt chelate. Chelates can be so stable that the metal ion becomes nutritionally unavailable. These have an unfortunate effect on nutritional requirements, since they tie up an essential mineral completely and prevent its utilization. This occurs with phytic acid, which attaches itself to zinc so securely that it is rendered unabsorbable. Oxalic acid will do the same to calcium, rendering it insoluble as calcium oxalate. This will be covered fully in the sections on the individual minerals.

One of the primary body functions of minerals is in the maintenance of the acid-base balance in the body. Those minerals which form an acid medium in solution are chlorine, sulfur, and phosphorus. The acid-forming minerals are found mainly in protein foods from animal sources and in cereal grains. Take care not to confuse this acid reaction in the body with the acid taste of foods. These acids in foods are broken down in the digestive cycles with no effect on the acid-base balance. The minerals that form a basic or alkaline medium in solution are calcium, sodium, potassium, and magnesium. These occur predominantly in fruits, nuts and vegetables.

If foods contain acids that the body cannot metabolize, such as benzoic acid, oxalic acid, and tannic acid, the acid potential of these overbalances the alkalinity of their base-forming mineral constituents. These non-metabolizable acids occur in such foods as cranberries, rhubarb, cocoa, and tea. Milk, pure carbohydrates, and fats will have no effect on the acid-base balance of the body. Should the balance begin to shift in either direction, the body has a variety of ways to bring the balance back to the required level. Since excess acidity is more often the danger, both the excretion of carbon dioxide through the lungs and the slight acidity of the urine excreted through the kidneys will rid the body of excess acidity under normal conditions. When normal excretion is insufficient, the body can neutralize either acids or bases by use of the carbonates, phosphates, and proteins that act as buffers in the blood. Even the bones can release phosphates to act as buffers and remove hydrogen ions, which are the basis of acidity, from the body fluids. If these buffers are not sufficient to handle excess alkalinity, the body can combine water and carbon dioxide which are normally excreted into carbonic acid. This carbonic acid will neutralize the excess alkali-forming elements.

In the same manner, the body can form a base from a nitrogen-hydrogen compound formed during protein breakdown to prevent excess acid from forming and causing a problem. In addition, the body can break down carbonic acid through the action of a zinc-containing enzyme called carbonic anhydrase. With this variety of means for neutralizing both excess acidity and excess alkalinity, it is rare to encounter any excess caused by dietary intake.

When feeding any type of birds, take care not to offer them exclusively animal products, such as eggs, and cereal grains. This will eventually cause an excess of body acidity. Likewise, if the birds are fed exclusively fruits, nuts, and vegetables, they will soon show an excess of body alkalinity. All wild birds instinctively will vary their diet to include both animal and plant sources to forestall any body imbalance. You must do the same when feeding birds in captivity. This also explains one reason besides nutritional deficiencies why birds maintained strictly on diets of cereal grains soon sicken and die.

Minerals in general perform a very wide range of functions in the body. They act as catalysts for many reactions in the body. In this function, they are not a part of the initial compounds nor of the end products, but they must be present for a reaction to take place. At least nine different minerals are required to catalyze the breakdown of fatty acids to energy, carbon dioxide, and water. The minerals are components of essential body compounds as parts of hormones, enzymes, and other compounds, and they are an essential part of several vitamins. Minerals are important in the maintenance of water balance in the body, with water movement governed by the concentration of minerals on either side of the cell membrane as electrolytes. Minerals are also required for the transmission of nerve impulses, the regulation of muscle contraction, and the growth of body tissue.

Though minerals are not destroyed in food preparation, processing, or storage, the refining of food products removes substantial quantities of both the bulk elements and the trace minerals from the food. This aspect will be covered fully with the discussion of each individual mineral. As previously mentioned, minerals can be rendered insoluble by a variety of factors.

Other elements in the same periodic group act as antagonists to the essential minerals and will displace them in a biological reaction. The best description I have seen of this is in describing the minerals as keys. Those in the same periodic group will all fit the same biological lock. But the displacing mineral can neither perform the required function nor get out, so it is similar to the wrong key in a lock. The antagonistic mineral will not work, but it prevents the right mineral from getting in to do the job. Consequently, the necessary biological job simply doesn't get done.

This general introduction to the minerals has laid the foundation for a better understanding of the biological functioning of each mineral. All of the essential minerals have unique functions to perform, and all are necessary

for life and health. I have also included a short section of
the additional minerals that may be proven essential in the
future and those that are found consistently within the
body.

CHAPTER 11

THE ESSENTIAL BULK MINERALS

CALCIUM

Calcium is the most abundant mineral in the body with as much as two percent of the body weight consisting of calcium. Calcium is usually associated with phosphorus in its biological functioning, and 99% of the calcium in the human body is in the bones and teeth. The percentage of body calcium found in the bones of birds is less, but still represents over 90% of the body's content. Obviously, calcium is an essential bulk element in nutrition, and much more remains to be learned about it, as the remainder of this section will reveal. The earth's crust contains calcium in the amount of about 36,300 parts per million, and it is present in sea water at the rate of around 400 parts per million. These are average amounts, taking the entire planet into consideration.

Food sources of calcium are irregular, and most foods of plant origin are low in calcium. For human consumption, milk is one of the very best sources for those who can digest it properly. Substantial portions of our black and oriental populations cannot digest it because of the lactose content. Fortunately, processing of the milk does not reduce the availability of calcium. The calcium content of the food is only a part of the body's calcium sources, as will be detailed in the subsequent discussion.

Though its function in bone structure is the biggest calcium use in the body, the remaining amount performs a wide variety of functions. The parathyroid hormone controls the calcium in the bloodstream to maintain a normal saturation level. Calcium, along with sodium and potassium, controls the contraction and relaxation of the heart muscle, or more plainly stated, calcium functions to control the heartbeat. It is also essential for the clotting of the blood, for the maintenance of acid-base equilibrium, for contraction and relaxation of muscle fibers, permeability of the cell membranes to fluid passage, and for the activation of many enzymes involved in the release of energy from carbohydrates, fats, and proteins. Calcium is also necessary for the formation and breakdown of a substance called acetylcholine, which is necessary for the transmission of nerve impulses from one nerve fiber to the next. Irritability of the nerves increases when the amount of calcium in the blood is below normal, and all of these functions will be maintained at the expense of calcium in the skeleton.

The skeleton is by any estimation an engineering marvel. Without its function in the bodies of birds, animals. and humans, we would be forced to move and exist as amoebas, or develop an exterior skeleton as have the lobsters and kindred creatures. Calcium in a complex compound with phosphorus gives rigidity and hardness to the bones and teeth. The bones are composed of complex crystals of calcium and phosphorus in a honeycomb structure, set around a framework of softer protein material, called the organic matrix. About two parts calcium to one part phosphorus are incorporated into this structure. This honeycomb structure gives strength and at the same time a huge surface area. Connecting canals of blood, lymph, nerves, and marrow pass throughout this structure, though in birds the bones are mostly hollow. The fluids surrounding these bone crystals supply the materials needed for growth and repair, and they withdraw material as necessary. The basic structure changes constantly in response to body changes. Bone tissue is not permanent, and about 20% of bone calcium is replaced every year.

Calcium and phosphorus occur together, circulate together, and work together in the body. When discussing bones, in particular, it is impossible to discuss one without the companion function of the other entering in. Decalcification, for example, involves the removal of both calcium and phosphorus from the bones. Bones can accumulate a reserve supply of both calcium and phosphorus. If this available reserve is used up, the minerals will be removed from the structure of the bone itself. This removal usually occurs first from the spine and pelvic bones. Normally, 30% or more of this structure can be withdrawn before the loss will even show up on an x-ray. The bones will also lose calcium from inactivity of the body.

Of course, vitamins are necessary for the proper utilization of calcium within the body, as are a variety of enzymes. Vitamin D is of particular importance, and its functioning with calcium was fully covered in the section on vitamin D. Vitamin A is of crucial importance in depositing the minerals within the bones. Vitamin C is required for formation of the connecting material between the cells and the walls of the vessels in the bones.

A variety of factors affect calcium absorption in the digestive system. Calcium dissolves best in an acid solution, such as the stomach contents, and it is absorbed as it moves into the small intestine. When the intestinal contents become alkaline, absorption is poor. Though the affinity of strontium, particularly radioactive strontium-90, for the bones is well known, the body preferentially will absorb calcium at a nine to one ratio over strontium, providing the calcium is available. Strontium is also excreted preferentially over calcium. Calcium must be separated from the food mass and ionized before it can be absorbed, and still only 40% to 60% is absorbed. Though rats usually absorb 100% of their dietary calcium, humans may absorb as little as 10%.

The best dietary ratio to promote the highest rate of absorption is one part calcium to one part phosphorus. Lactose is an excellent promoter of calcium absorption in humans, so the calcium in milk is very well absorbed. An increased bodily need for calcium will increase the level of absorption, also, as will an adequate amount of vitamin D. Anything that speeds the movement of the food mass through the intestine will decrease the calcium absorption rate. Laxatives will have this effect in humans, and a high fiber diet will also decrease calcium absorption. For this reason, the calcium from vegetables with their high fiber content is more slowly absorbed than that from animal sources. The presence of dietary fat also lowers calcium absorption. The more stress is experienced. the less calcium will be absorbed. Also, calcium ions are needed for the proper absorption of cobalamin, also called vitamin B-12.

Two naturally occurring acids are detrimental to calcium absorption, in addition. Cereal grains, such as wheat, contain a substance called phytic acid, which combines with phosphorus to form phytates. These phytates inhibit calcium absorption in humans, though some other species possess phytase, the enzyme needed to break this compound apart and utilize it. Nutritionists state that the body seems to be able to adapt to high phytic acid intake and still absorb calcium. (I question this assumption for reasons detailed later in this section.) Oxalic acid is present in spinach, beet greens, chard, and rhubarb, and this combines with calcium to make calcium oxalate. This compound cannot be absorbed in the intestinal fluids, and it is eliminated.

Calcium is so easily excreted that there is no evidence of bad effects from even excessive calcium intake. Any excess is excreted through the kidneys, though other factors do enter in. If vitamin D is in excessive supply, for example, too much calcium can accumulate in the blood. This will cause accumulation of calcium in the kidneys. If too much phosphorus is in the blood with too little calcium, the result will be muscular twitching. In addition, excess calcium in the diet decreases the absorption of zinc.

There is rather intense controversy among nutritionists as to what level minimal daily requirements should be set. This controversy seems to an outside observer to be an exercise in futility, for a variety of reasons. First, even in areas where calcium intakes are low, calcium deficiency does not occur. There is no evidence of adverse effect from low calcium intake on any human diet. Second, there is now strong evidence that no relationship exists between calcium intake and bone loss as in osteoporosis. Also, there is no evidence that low calcium intake is a deterrent to growth. And finally, no clinical condition can be classified as a calcium deficiency. This is remarkable when considering that the United States Department of Agriculture reports 30% of American diets to be calcium deficient. These are strong statements, all based on thorough research.

Calcium deficiency, by these known facts, seems nonexistent. For the answer to what is really going on within the body with relation to calcium, I had to turn to the new science of biological transmutation. This clearly, simply, and effectively outlines the biological origins of calcium, as opposed to the conventionally accepted dietary origins. If there is any question as to where my present views lie after several years of nutritional reading and research, the concluding comments will spell out my position quite effectively.

Calcium is obviously a very important and basic necessity for life. As such, nature has devised an almost bewildering number of ways to assure that no living thing goes without its vital calcium. The living body seems able to transmute three minerals into calcium: potassium, magnesium, and silicon. This knowledge is not a recent development, since as far back as 1880 Von Herzeele established beyond doubt that germinating seeds with no source of calcium contained calcium after germinating. Von Herzeele was the first to conclude that there was an actual transmutation of the elements in living things. However, as with so many other initial discoveries, this information has been largely ignored for the last hundred years.

The periodic charts of the elements deal with atoms as a whole and elements as a mixture of isotopes, while biological changes are accomplished at the level of the atomic nucleus. Each element may have one or more isotopes, having the same number of protons in the nucleus, but differing numbers of neutrons. Only certain of these isotopes can be used by the body in biological transmutations, and organisms seem to succeed better in transmutation with the heavier isotopes. Naturally occurring elements are mixtures of isotopes, and as outlined in the periodic charts have no biological value for transmutations. How living creatures, apparently by enzymatic action, can move particles from one atomic nucleus to another is at present a complete mystery. Yet, there can be no doubt that these changes occur.

Potassium and silicon are two basic sources of calcium within the body. Two of the potassium isotopes can be transmuted into calcium: potassium-39 and potassium-41, as follows:

potassium-39 plus hydrogen-1 yields calcium-40
potassium-41 plus hydrogen-1 yields calcium-42

This transmutation is covered more thoroughly in the section on potassium. Three silicon isotopes are transmutable into calcium in the following four reactions:

silicon-28 plus carbon-12 yields calcium-40
silicon-30 plus carbon-12 yields calcium-42
silicon-29 plus carbon-13 yields calcium-42
silicon-30 plus carbon-13 yields calcium-43

The section on silicon contains more information in this regard.

The primary source of calcium seems to be magnesium, since there are six verified transmutations from magnesium to calcium:

magnesium-24 plus oxygen-16 yields calcium-40
magnesium-26 plus oxygen-16 yields calcium-42
magnesium-25 plus oxygen-17 yields calcium-42
magnesium-25 plus oxygen-18 yields calcium-43
magnesium-24 plus oxygen-18 yields calcium-42
magnesium-26 plus oxygen-18 yields calcium-44

Refer to the section on magnesium for further information on magnesium transmutations.

Note that in all of these potassium, silicon, and magnesium transmutations to calcium, calcium-44 can come only from magnesium. Since the shells of many sea animals are formed by such transmutations, and the creatures transmute only magnesium from sea water into calcium, there should be a larger portion of the calcium-44 isotope in their shells than occurs in land creatures. With chemical analysis of the shell, this proves to be true, further strengthening our basis of knowledge of these transmutations. For a complete review of the subject of biological transmutations, I highly recommend the book by Louis C. Kervran, *Biological Transmutations*, listed in the bibliography.

It is possible to induce a calcium deficiency in chickens and other animals by strictly controlling the diet. A severe deficiency of calcium and phosphorus can cause permanent stunting of size or malformations of bones, and also of the teeth in animals. The symptoms of deficiency are slowed growth, lower food consumption, abnormal posture and walking, and shortened life span. Adult chickens will produce thin eggshells, egg production will be reduced, and they will experience painful muscular spasms. The ratio of calcium to phosphorus in the diet is crucial, in addition, since a ratio of as much as 3.3 parts of calcium to one part phosphorus is sufficient to produce rickets and other leg abnormalities.

Where the nutrition of cage birds is concerned, calcium need not be of great concern. If direct calcium is not supplied in sufficient quantity in the diet, the avian body should be able to transmute other minerals into calcium to create whatever is necessary, as chickens do. I stress that such transmutation in cage birds is not confirmed, and some may not be able to accomplish this. Consequently, it is always wise to offer cuttlebone or mineral blocks to supply any amount of calcium that might be needed. I personally prefer to use crushed eggshells, since they are free and contain over 98% calcium in their mineral content.

PHOSPHORUS

Phosphorus is the second most abundant mineral in the body, making up about one percent of body weight.

This amounts to well over one pound of phosphorus in the human adult, and it is a part of every cell. It is an essential bulk element in nutrition, and about 22% of the body's mineral content is phosphorus. The egg's mineral contents are over 25% phosphorus, making this the most abundant mineral element in the egg. From 85% to 90% of the phosphorus content of the human body is as calcium phosphate to give rigidity to the bones and teeth. This function of phosphorus is discussed thoroughly in the section on calcium, since both minerals work together so closely in this function. The rest of the body's phosphorus content is distributed through all of the cells and fluids of the body. The earth's surface has a phosphorus content of about 1,180 parts per million, and sea water contains around 70 parts per billion.

Virtually all foods that are rich in protein are also rich in phosphorus. For avian nutrition, peanuts, eggs, black walnuts, some other nuts, and sunflower seeds are rich in phosphorus. Most fruits and vegetables, by contrast, are low in phosphorus.

Evidence of biological transmutation to create or transmute this mineral also exists. The living organism can combine magnesium and lithium to produce phosphorus, or in a reversible reaction combine phosphorus with hydrogen to produce sulfur. The first transmutation is further confirmed by giving a magnesium overdose to test animals. When this is done, both the calcium and phosphorus levels of the body will rise. It is also probable that carbon-12 plus fluorine-19 can be joined to produce phosphorus-31. Any test will clearly demonstrate that cows excrete and give daily in milk far more phosphorus than they ingest. Yet, a deficiency of phosphorus in either cows or humans is unknown. Phosphorus is far too important to life for nature to take a chance on deficiency which might result from a low phosphorus supply in dietary sources

alone. Thus, the natural development of life has assured
that a phosphorus deficiency cannot occur under any
normal conditions.

Many factors influence the absorption of phosphorus
in the digestive system. Though about 70% of dietary
phosphorus is absorbed, 100% of the phosphorus from
animal food sources is available, while only 30% of the
phosphorus from plant sources is available. Almost all of
this is absorbed as free phosphorus. An overabundance of
either calcium or phosphorus in the diet will interfere
with the absorption of the other in the digestive tract. For
chickens, a calcium:phosphorus ratio of from 1.5:1 to
2:1 seems best, while laying hens have a wider tolerance.
A similar ratio should be the best for cage birds, also.

Phosphorus occurs in whole grains as phytic acid. This
will bind calcium and make both the phosphorus and the
calcium completely unabsorbable. Phytic acid may
account for 86% of the phosphorus present in seeds.
About 80% of the phosphorus in corn exists as phytate, a
compound of phytic acid and phosphorus. Phytic acid
occurs in wheat, oats, flax, rye, rice, soybeans, and peanuts,
any of which may be used in the feeding of birds in captivity.

A number of other facts about phosphorus are of interest. The presence of beryllium in the diet prevents
phosphorus absorption, and this will cause rickets. Beryllium seems to form an insoluble compound with phosphorus called beryllium phosphate, which is not absorbable. Also, high levels of calcium phosphate in the diet
will aggravate a manganese deficiency, and high phosphate
levels also reduce iron absorption. In addition, phosphates
are used to remove excess fluoride from water supplies,
since fluorides have a strong affinity for phosphates.

Phosphorus has an essential role in virtually all body
processes. It is vital to any reaction that involves the

uptake or release of energy, and it is an important structural component in the skeletal system. In the form of phosphate, phosphorus is responsible for the controlled release of energy resulting from the oxidation of carbohydrates, fat, and protein. It is a part of the adenosine triphosphate which stores body heat energy in a high energy bond for slow release as necessary. Phosphate also attaches itself to many nutritional substances to facilitate their passage through the cell membranes. It transports fats and fatty acids in the bloodstream as phospholipids, since they are insoluble in the blood fluids in their basic forms. Phosphorus is an integral part of both DNA and RNA and is also a part of many coenzymes.

Any excess of phosphorus in the body is excreted through the kidneys, and needed supplies of phosphorus are resorbed through the kidneys. The presence of Vitamin D increases this rate of phosphorus resorption. Also, the parathyroid hormone affects the level of phosphorus in the bloodstream and its rate of kidney resorption. It is interesting to note that hens excrete phosphorus from the body at a much higher rate when they're laying. Even during starvation, there is a continuous loss of phosphorus from the body.

As previously mentioned, a dietary deficiency of phosphorus is unknown in humans. Deficiency symptoms have appeared in chickens on strictly controlled diets, however. Either a deficiency or a wide variance in the calcium: phosphorus ratio will cause rickets. Growth failure will always result from a phosphorus deficiency. A severe deficiency causes a loss of appetite, weakness, and death within ten to twelve days.

The aviculturist is safe from worry with regard to this nutrient. A natural phosphorus deficiency is unknown, and only a gross imbalance in the calcium:phosphorus ratio or a vitamin D deficiency in the diet is likely to cause any

problem with regard to phosphorus. If you supply one of
the foods with a high phosphorus content mentioned
previously, plus a good calcium source, such as eggshells,
cuttlebone, or mineral block, you are free from any problem of mineral balance. The birds will balance their own
intake with no conscious thought on your part.

POTASSIUM

Potassium is a vital bulk element in the nutrition of
birds, animals, and humans. Plants also require potassium
as a bulk mineral, and both plants and animals have high
potassium requirements. About five percent of the total
mineral content of the body is potassium, and it is the
third most abundant mineral in the body after calcium and
phosphorus. The human body can contain as much as 300
grams of potassium, well over half a pound. This amounts
to about 2,000 parts per million of the body contents, on
an average. Potassium is a bulk element in sea water, with
about 380 parts per million, and the earth's crust contains
potassium in great abundance with about 25,900 parts
per million. The chemical symbol for potassium is K,
derived from the Latin name for this mineral, Kalium.
Rubidium will displace potassium in metabolic functions.
The body uses potassium in a variety of ways. Since
it cannot be conserved or resorbed in the body, it is fortunate that the dietary supplies are so widely available.
Potassium is rapidly absorbed in the small intestine, and
humans need an intake of from two to six grams a day.
Any body excess is excreted through the kidneys. Within
the body, potassium acts as a catalyst and enzyme activator
within the cells in many reactions, especially in the release
of energy and in glycogen and protein synthesis. It is a

major factor in maintaining osmotic pressure within the cells. Though potassium is not so easily mobilized as sodium for the purpose, it is important in maintaining the cell's acid-base balance by offsetting excess acid-forming elements. It also seems to increase the permeability of the cell membranes. Potassium speeds up the intake of neutral amino acids such as glycine, and it is important in the breakdown of lysine. Radioactive potassium-40 can be used to determine the amount of body fat relative to lean tissues. In addition, potassium plays a role in the transmission of nerve impulses. Finally, this mineral is important in maintaining the body's electrolyte balance.

The body cells and tissues are very high in potassium, while the body fluids are contrastingly high in sodium. Muscle and nerve cells are especially high in potassium. Within the cell, there is one part of sodium to ten parts of potassium. Potassium works with sodium in the body fluids to regulate the blood and water balance, urinary acidification, nerve conduction, and muscle contraction. Sodium and potassium are antagonists and as such they regulate the necessary equilibrium between the fluids within and outside of the cells. An abnormal balance of these two nutritional elements will result in paralysis of the nerves of the heart and lungs. An increase in the sodium level within the cell can counteract the important effect of potassium as a catalyst and interfere with cellular metabolism, especially in protein synthesis.

Potassium also has a number of known relationships with magnesium and calcium in the normal functioning of the body's tissues. First, a magnesium deficiency can cause decreased retention of potassium. Potassium acts with magnesium as a muscle relaxant in opposition to calcium. Surprisingly, though a magnesium injection will cause an animal to fall asleep, a potassium injection will awaken it. An adequate supply of magnesium is needed to retain the correct amounts of calcium in the cells. Potassium is required for normal heart activity and acts in a manner opposite to calcium. Potassium favors the relaxation of the heart muscle, while calcium favors its contraction. Therapeutic doses of potassium have even been used to slow the heartbeat in cases of serious injury.

Much of the conventional knowledge of potassium activities in the body is flatly contradictory. Though it is a vital bulk element, there is little information on minimal needs — researchers are rarely able to induce a deficiency state. Also, deficiencies seldom occur from inadequate dietary intakes. Even in low protein and low potassium diets, even to starvation, animals may grow slowly, but do not show a potassium deficiency. The kidneys continue to secrete potassium in large amounts even when test diets deficient in potassium are fed for several weeks. Since potassium has been proven to be neither retained nor resorbed in the body, this contradiction taxes the average person's credulity.

Only Louis C. Kervran's explanations of the biological transmutations involving potassium can adequately explain what is occurring within the body. The body creates potassium-39 by combining sodium-23 and oxygen-16. For this reason, the amounts of sodium and oxygen available are at least as critical to potassium metabolism as is the dietary content of potassium. The presence of potassium depends upon the availability of oxygen. This transmutation is an endothermal reaction in that it absorbs heat. This enables the body to exist in reasonable health and comfort in dry climates where the air temperatures are consistently well above the body temperature, when perspiration alone could not lower the body temperature sufficiently. The requirement then is for a bountiful supply of sodium and oxygen to be transmuted into potassium, thus soaking up a large amount of excess heat. One only needs to review the importance placed on salt in the Bible to realize that sodium chloride is vastly more than a food flavoring or preservative. Fresh sodium injected into the body will be transmuted immediately into potassium.

Should potassium become too abundant in the body, it can be transmuted into calcium. Potassium-39 plus hydrogen-1 will yield calcium-40. This reaction can occur with other isotopes, also, as with the following reaction:

potassium-41 plus hydrogen-1 will yield calcium-42

In this transmutation, potassium is the agent of equilibrium. By removing acidic hydrogen and creating alkaline calcium, potassium helps maintain the body's acid-alkaline balance. The body controls excess potassium so efficiently through kidney excretion and transmutation that there is no known potassium toxicity, even when kidney failure causes an excessive buildup.

If the dubious need further convincing evidence of the reality of this transmutation, we can turn to our feathered friends for a final example. Hens deprived of calcium to the point at which they are producing only soft-shelled eggs will begin producing calcium-rich eggshells only twenty hours after being fed mica. Mica is a potassium aluminum silicate. It contains no calcium, but it does contain potassium, which the hen's body transmutes into calcium very efficiently. The silicon in mica is also transmuted into calcium, as discussed in the section on silicon. In tests with guinea fowl under the same conditions, removing the mica from the diet resulted again in soft-shelled eggs. Keep in mind that available potassium is not stored in the body to any extent.

In transmuting potassium-39 plus hydrogen-1 into calcium-40, the body has a ready source of calcium whenever needed. This transmutation is also reversible with calcium-40 minus hydrogen-1 giving potassium-39. The study of biological transmutations helps to explain how a hen is able to produce calcium-rich eggshells continuously, even when no attention is paid to calcium in the diet. This also satisfactorily explains how my Society Finches on diets exclusively of whole white proso millet and shelled sunflower seed with water have been able to lay clutches of eggs with calcium-rich shells, far more than their diet or body reserves could provide, even though both of these foods contain only one one-hundredth of one percent calcium. Millet has 0.43% potassium, and sunflower seed is 0.06% potassium, an adequate amount to provide the calcium necessary for eggshells through transmutation.

Two of the nutritional books in my collection have stated that excess salt will deplete the body's potassium supplies. The problem with statements such as this is that no one explains what constitutes an excess. Is this a laboratory force-feeding which produces grossly distorted results? I cannot render a judgment on such limited information, particularly when I must also consider the body's ability to transmute excess sodium into potassium. The knowledge of potassium seems to become murkier with time rather than clearer.

Deficiencies of potassium can be induced in experimental animals, and diarrhea can cause a deficiency by hindering absorption of potassium. Symptoms of such a deficiency are overall muscle weakness, heart weakness, intestinal distension, and weakness and ultimate failure of the respiratory muscles. Humans will show mental apathy, fatigue, constipation, and muscle cramps in the calf muscles. Chicks that are deficient in potassium show high mortality rates and slow growth. Chicks seem to require about 0.4% of the diet as potassium, about the percentage contained in millet. Rabbits and turkeys seem to require more, at least 0.6% of the diet. In starvation, some potassium can be derived from metabolized tissue protein.

Kwashiorkor, the protein deficiency disease, cannot be cured by increased protein intake alone. Potassium must also be added to the diet.

Potassium is widely distributed in food sources, and plant material is especially rich in this mineral. All vegetable matter contains it, especially green leafy vegetables, whole grains, fruits, nuts, and dates. Potassium is the second most abundant mineral in the contents of the egg. Only phosphorus is more abundant. Refining whole wheat into white flour will remove about 77% of the potassium content. In addition, potassium in foods occurs in a very soluble form, and it can be lost in cooking with water.

Though the importance of potassium in the avian diet is undeniable, the bird breeder does not need to be overly concerned about the dietary content available to the birds. Any varied diet of plant products should provide a sufficient amount of potassium for even the most discriminating avian taste.

SULFUR

Sulfur is considered a major bulk mineral in the nutrition of plants, animals, and birds. It occurs in sea water at the rate of about 885 parts per million and in the earth's crust at the rate of about 5,200 parts per million. Sulfur is found in every cell of both plants and animals. It is the fourth most plentiful mineral in the body after calcium, phosphorus and potassium.

Sulfur is found virtually everywhere in nature and all food sources will contain some. For avian nutrition, the cereal grains, nuts, and eggs are among the highest sources. Eggs, in particular, are very rich in sulfur. The characteristic odor of rotten eggs is caused by the formation of hydrogen sulfide gas in the decaying process. Over 15% of the mineral content of an egg is sulfur, some of it in an unbound, inorganic form. It is the most abundant mineral in the albumen of the egg and one of the four most abundant in the total contents of the egg, excluding the shell. The inorganic sulfur in the egg is the reason for the formation of the dark stains of silver sulfide on silverware used for eggs.

Keratin is the primary protein that forms feathers, hair, claws, nails, and beaks. It has a very high sulfur content, which produces the odor of sulfur dioxide gas when feathers are burned. The amino acid cysteine, one of the sulfur-containing amino acids, is found in abundance in keratin. The wool of sheep is also extremely rich in sulfur, with a sulfur content of five percent. Many of the strong odors in nature are caused by sulfur-containing compounds.

Half of the sulfur in the body is in the muscles. Most of this sulfur content is in the amino acids cystine, cysteine, taurine, and methionine. The body is capable of synthesizing the first three if it has a sufficient supply of sulfur. Methionine is an essential amino acid that must come from the diet. Since sulfur is a part of these amino acids, it is a necessary part of any protein containing them.

Sulfur also serves a variety of other functions in the body. There are at least four vitamins which have been proven to contain sulfur. These are all within the B complex — thiamin, pantothenic acid, biotin, and lipoic acid. Sulfur is required for the formation of melanin pigment, which forms in the presence of sunlight from sulfur and two amino acids. Several hormones contain sulfur, including insulin, the hormone that regulates carbohydrate metabolism. Sulfur also appears to be necessary for the synthesis of collagen, the protein that forms such an integral part of the cell structure. Also, there is a possible sulfur antagonism by vanadium.

In his review of biological transmutations, Louis Kervran states that plants, animals, and bacteria can all create sulfur by merging two oxygen atoms into one sulfur atom. He refers to sulfur as a condensate of oxygen. In addition, phosphorus plus hydrogen will yield sulfur in a reversible reaction. It is interesting to note that no sulfur deficiency has ever been noted in plants, though some soils contain none. The only sulfur source for these plants is biological transmutation. Sulfur is continually being removed from the land as a constituent of the amino acids in crops, so the only conceivable source for all of this sulfur is through transmutation. Fortunately, oxygen is always available to plants through the air for the transmutational formation of sulfur as needed.

With biological creation as necessary within the body and as a result of its wide and abundant distribution in virtually all living things, there is almost no chance of any deficiency ever developing in cage birds. No deficiency symptoms as such are known, since it is impossible to formulate a diet devoid of sulfur. It is certain, however, that such a diet would cause almost immediate death from lack of the amino acids, vitamins, and hormones previously mentioned. No sulfur supplementation should ever be necessary in the diets of cage birds.

SODIUM

Though salt has been important in human life since the dawn of time, it was only in 1937 that research indicated the role of sodium as a dietary essential. Salt is a compound of sodium and chlorine, called sodium chloride. Sodium occurs in sea water at the rate of 10,500 parts per million, and the earth's surface contains about 28,300 parts per million. All living things require sodium, but most do not get their dietary sodium in the form of salt.

Sodium is present in the body mainly in the fluids outside of the cells. About 50% of the body's sodium content is in these fluids where sodium serves as a cation. However, up to 10% of the body's sodium is in the cells. The remainder, which will range from 30% to 45% of the body content, is in the skeleton in humans. Some mammals carry a much higher amount of body sodium in the bones with as much as 55% located there. About half of this skeletal sodium is present as a body reserve. The body can draw upon this reserve when less sodium is available in the diet or when body losses are high. The absorption of sodium is mostly in the small intestine, with a small amount absorbed in the stomach. This absorption is an active, energy-requiring process.

The kidneys filter the blood constantly to maintain normal blood levels of sodium. Aldosterone, a hormone secreted by the adrenal glands, controls the regulation of blood sodium. The kidneys can either resorb or excrete sodium, as the body's needs demand. If the need for sodium increases, the secretion of aldosterone will increase. This increase in the aldosterone level will stimulate both absorption and resorption of sodium. If the intake of sodium is high, the secretion of aldosterone decreases, and less sodium is retained. When the dietary intake of sodium exceeds the kidneys' ability to excrete it, the blood and fluid levels of sodium will rise. This rise in blood sodium stimulates thirst, and the increased water intake enables the kidneys to excrete more sodium.

Loss of sodium from the body can occur in ways besides urinary excretion with a number of effects. Any kidney damage or adrenal damage can cause excessive losses of sodium through the urine. The urinary level frequently reflects the dietary intake of sodium. Excessive amounts of sodium can be lost in sweating, and this will cause muscle cramps. In cases of diarrhea, there is a major sodium loss through the intestines. In addition, large losses of sodium may cause excessive vomiting. A low level of sodium in the fluids causes potassium and water to leave the cells. This cell dehydration causes the feeling of fatigue that goes along with sodium depletion.

Sodium serves a variety of functions within the body. Since sodium accounts for 90% of the basic or alkaline ions in the fluids outside of the cells, it counteracts the acid-forming elements to maintain body neutrality. It is essential for the absorption of glucose and for the transportation of other nutrients across the cell membranes. Sodium is involved in the contraction and relaxation of muscles, and it both stimulates the nerves and enables the transmission of nerve impulses. Also, sodium is very important in the maintenance of the body's fluid volume. As a part of bile, pancreatic, and intestinal juices, about twenty grams of sodium per day are secreted into the digestive system. However, most of this is resorbed.

Sodium in the body appears to come primarily from dietary sources. Its role in biological transmutations is discussed in the section on potassium. In hot weather, sodium or salt is not excreted, but is transmuted into potassium in a heat-absorbing reaction. The largest amounts of sodium in the diet are found in animal products, rather than in foods of plant origin. For cage bird nutrition, eggs, kale, spinach, celery, carrots, and Swiss chard contain appreciable amounts of sodium. Over 14% of the mineral contents of an egg are taken up by sodium. Most other grains, vegetables, fruits, legumes, and nuts are low in sodium. Oils contain no sodium at all.

Deficiencies of sodium have been caused in chickens and other animals for experimental purposes. In a deficiency, the bones will soften, growth failure shows up with a variety of internal disorders, and utilization of protein and energy is greatly reduced. A sodium deficiency also interferes with reproduction. A deficiency in chickens will cause reduced egg production, poor growth, and cannibalism.

An excess of sodium is also possible, but extremely unlikely, since such a large amount of sodium or salt is absolutely unpalatable. If sodium concentrations in the cells rise too fast for the cells to pump it out, the result is water taken in to dilute it, and the cells become swollen. Less than one percent salt in the diet of chicks will cause watery droppings, decreased growth, loss of appetite, and some mortality. Extended wings, poor feathering, constant drinking, and dehydration are among other symptoms of excess salt. Chicks are not seriously affected, however, and there is no mortality increase until salt becomes 7.5% of the diet. This amount exceeds the ability of chicks to consume enough water to flush out the excess salt.

No dietary supplementation with any sodium compound should ever be necessary for cage bird diets that contain a small amount of salt. Many of the commercially available vitamin-mineral supplements do contain salt. Vionate, for example, contains from 0.5% to 1.5% salt. In cage birds, too much salt is as great a danger as too little, since they cannot excrete excess sodium through sweat. There is little danger of either a deficiency or an excess on any normal cage bird diet, however.

CHLORINE

Chlorine is classified as a major mineral in nutrition. In the amount contained within the body, it ranks sixth after calcium, phosphorus, potassium, sulfur, and sodium.

Elemental chlorine is a greenish-yellow gas which is extremely poisonous. In sufficient concentration in the air, chlorine is deadly. In its inorganic form, chlorine will destroy vitamin E on contact. It occurs in sea water at the abundant rate of about 19,000 parts per million and in the earth's crust at the rate of about 200 parts per million. Bromine will replace chlorine in chemical reactions within the body. Since chlorine is highly reactive, it forms compounds readily and occurs primarily as chlorides in nature.

The commonest form of chlorine is in the compound sodium chloride, common salt. Without sodium chloride, animal life is not possible. However, an excess of salt can be as deadly as a lack of it. For this reason, all birds and animals are able to excrete excess salt to a certain extent. Many sea birds and fish have special organs for eliminating excess salt that they ingest. This sodium chloride content of the body is found in the extracellular fluids, the fluids found circulating outside of the cells. It controls the volume and pressure of those fluids.

The primary function of chlorides in the body seems to be in the regulation of the body's acid-alkaline balance. Since sodium is alkaline and chlorine is acidic, the kidneys can excrete sodium to increase body acidity and chlorine to increase body alkalinity. Also, chlorine is a highly important and necessary ingredient for the formation of hydrochloric acid for digestion in the stomach. Though chlorine also occurs in the body as calcium chloride, these seem to be the only functions of chlorine in the body. No other role for chlorine in nutrition has yet been discovered.

Though the infant science of biological transmutation has not yet delved deeply into the study of chlorine, Louis C. Kervran, the most noted specialist in the field, feels that chlorine can be formed within the body by the combination of sodium and carbon to achieve the nuclear structure of chlorine. Two other possibilities exist, also.

First, the formation of chlorine from carbon plus lithium and oxygen should be possible, or alternately, as a second possibility, silicon and lithium might be combined to create chlorine. No biological confirmation of these possible transmutations has come to light yet.

Chlorine is one of the four most abundant minerals in the contents of a chicken egg. Over 16% of the mineral content of an egg is chlorine. In any state of chloride deficiency, chicks will show a specific nervous reaction. With any sharp noise, scare, or handling, the chicks will fall forward with legs stretched out behind them in a state of paralysis. They will recover after a couple of minutes and it will be a while before this characteristic symptom can be repeated.

Sufficient chloride content should be present in most common cage bird food items to prevent any deficiency or deficiency symptom. In addition, any commercially prepared food or vitamin-mineral supplement will contain supplementary sodium chloride. Any deficiency of this nutrient in cage bird maintenance is highly unlikely.

MAGNESIUM

Magnesium is an essential bulk mineral in nutrition. All birds, animals, and plants, including algae, fungi, and bacteria, require magnesium for life. Magnesium is abundant in the earth with 20,900 parts per million in the crust on the average and 1,350 parts per million in sea water. The human body can contain as much as 28 grams of magnesium. It is found in all of the cells of the body. In plants, magnesium is an essential part of chlorophyll. This green compound is similar to the hemoglobin in animal blood, but magnesium replaces iron in the structure of the chlorophyll molecule.

The presence of magnesium in living organisms has been known since 1859. It was identified as a dietary essential for mice in 1926 and for rats in 1932. Nevertheless, most information on magnesium's biological functioning has been learned since 1950. Between 50% and 60% of the body content in humans is in the bones. The balance is concentrated within the cells, including the red blood cells, and magnesium is alkaline in cell solution. The body can mobilize magnesium from the bones to maintain normal blood and tissue levels. The body's ability to absorb and excrete this mineral as necessary to maintain a correct balance is quite well developed. The kidneys resorb magnesium as necessary to prevent the body loss of excessive amounts in the urine. Any actual excess to body needs is excreted either by way of the urine or through the bile and the intestine.

Absorption of the dietary intake of magnesium occurs primarily in the small intestine. Normally, about 43% of the intake is absorbed. In low dietary levels, as much as 75% of the magnesium may be absorbed. If the dietary level is high, only 25% may be absorbed. Absorption will also increase as the levels of protein and calcium in the diet increase. Raising either the calcium or phosphorus content of the diet will increase the magnesium requirement of chicks. It appears that a common carrier transports both calcium and magnesium across the intestinal wall. Absorption will be reduced in diets high in phytic acid, found in abundance in cereal grains.

One of the primary functions of magnesium in biological activity seems to be in the functioning of the muscles and nerves. Increased blood levels of magnesium have a definite anesthetic effect. Low blood levels will cause irritability and nervousness with convulsions in severe cases. This is caused by increased transmission of nerve impulses and increased muscular contraction. In the nerve cell fluids, magnesium is involved in the conduction of nerve impulses. In the functioning of the muscles, calcium and magnesium are strong antagonists. Calcium will stimulate muscular action, and magnesium acting with potassium will relax muscular action. Because of its anesthetizing effect, a magnesium injection can be used to cause animals to fall asleep. At the highest levels in the blood, magnesium will cause coma and eventual death.

Hundreds of enzymes have been found to be activated by magnesium. Because of this biological effect, magnesium is important in almost all of the functions of the body. It is needed for the synthesis, breakdown, and stability of DNA. Magnesium is necessary for the activation of amino acids so they can be incorporated into the protein molecules. It is important in cellular respiration and is vital to cell metabolism by its function of catalyzing several reactions involving the release of energy, synthesis of body compounds, absorption and transportation of nutrients, and any muscular physical activity.

The magnesium content of eggs and the rate of egg production are important results of the content of this mineral in the diet of chickens and other birds. The mineral contents of the egg are 5% magnesium, and eggshell contains about 1% magnesium. By far the largest part of magnesium in the egg is in the shell and shell membrane. In laying hens, magnesium may be drawn from the bone at times of dietary deficiency. Egg size, magnesium content of the egg, and weight of the shell will all decrease due to deficiency of magnesium in the diet. Any increase in calcium at the same time will make the effects of a magnesium deficiency even more pronounced.

Magnesium is the only bulk element which plays an active role in the enzyme systems involved in the metabolism of foods. For this reason, the dietary need for magnesium is greater whenever the diet is rich in carbohydrates. About 300 to 350 milligrams of magnesium per day are required for human health, and beryllium will replace magnesium in its biological functions.

The transmutation of calcium into magnesium within the living body is now proven beyond doubt. Though plants use vast quantities of magnesium in the manufacture of chlorophyll, magnesium deficiency is never found unless a calcium deficiency also exists. Plants that are cultured in magnesium-free water form chlorophyll normally as they grow, indicating an adequate supply of magnesium. The transmutation involved is one atom of calcium minus one atom of oxygen to yield one atom of magnesium. The more calcium added for the plants' absorption, the more magnesium will be found in the plant tissues. If magnesium is missing in the living plant tissues, calcium can replace it and be transmuted to magnesium, but the reverse does not hold true in plants.

In the animal kingdom, the transmutation of magnesium and oxygen into calcium does occur regularly. Both animals and birds secrete more calcium than they ingest. This indicates a reverse transmutation in these groups from that existing in plants. Shellfish, for example, can make calcium-rich shells with no calcium resources available, only an abundant supply of magnesium, as occurs in sea water. The transmutation involved here is the combination of magnesium plus oxygen to yield calcium. Refer to the section on calcium for the exact isotopes involved in this transmutation. In addition, in some germinating seeds the magnesium content decreases while the calcium content increases, indicating a similar transmutation within these seeds.

Kervran states that the sodium in blood plasma is the source of magnesium production by transmutation in animals. The transmutation involved is sodium plus hydrogen to yield magnesium. Experiments with men in the Sahara Desert proved conclusively that during great dry heat a living organism secretes 80% more magnesium than it ingests. Kervran further estimates that at this rate, the body would have exhausted all of the magnesium that could be mobilized from tissue storage in only eight days. Yet, the subjects remained in fine health over the eight month period of the experiment. Since more sodium was ingested than excreted during the same period with no sodium accumulation observed, the conclusion is inescapable. The living body is able to transmute sodium into magnesium.

The best sources of magnesium in the diet for cage birds are in nuts and whole grains. Soybeans are also rich in magnesium, and green, especially leafy, vegetables with a high chlorophyll content are rich in magnesium. Any refining, processing, or cooking will reduce the magnesium content of the food. From one-half to three-quarters of the magnesium content is lost in vegetables cooked in water. As much as 80% of the magnesium content is removed in the refining of whole wheat into white flour.

In a severe dietary deficiency of magnesium, muscle control will be lost. This uncontrolled neuromuscular activity will result in tremors first and then convulsive seizures. There will be calcification of the soft tissues as more calcium is absorbed. Newly hatched chicks fed a diet with no magnesium will live only a few days. Low magnesium levels will cause slow growth, lethargy, panting, and gasping. When disturbed, the chicks will have brief convulsions and go into a comatose state which is sometimes temporary, but often fatal. Even a marginal magnesium deficiency with nearly normal growth will result in a high rate of mortality. Severe deficiencies of this type are not a danger on any normal avian diet.

An excess of magnesium will not occur in any normal diet, but has been deliberately caused in nutritional experimentation. A rate higher than one percent in the diet will cause some reduction in egg production and a decrease in eggshell thickness in laying hens. In growing chicks, a one percent dietary magnesium content slightly depresses growth and causes very wet droppings.

The chance of a deficiency of magnesium occurring in cage birds is minimal. This mineral occurs widely in food sources and is unlikely to be in short supply in any diet of whole foods. A diet high in refined food products, however, would probably be less than adequate in magnesium content.

SILICON

Silicon is the second most abundant element in the earth. Over one-fourth of the known earth surface is composed of silicon, and only oxygen is found in greater abundance. Even in sea water, silicon occurs at the rate of about four parts per million. The body contains fairly large amounts of silicon and research has proven it to be an essential mineral in the maintenance of life. It is on the borderline between trace minerals and bulk elements in nutrition, since it seems to be required in daily amounts of up to one gram. It is most unfortunate that many standard nutritional sources fail even to list silicon as a necessary nutrient.

The likelihood of any silicon deficiency developing is negligible, since silicon is so plentiful on the earth's surface. Researchers feeding purified diets to determine silicon necessity and deficiency symptoms have proven that silicon is essential for growth and skeletal development in rats and chicks. Supplementation has resulted in significant increases in the growth rate of these test animals. Symptoms of a deficiency in chicks were a reduced growth rate, atrophied organs, and very pale legs and comb with no wattles. Skeletal development was significantly retarded.

Silicon is an integral component of both cartilage and collagen, and any deficiency will show up in abnormal cartilage and connective tissues. These connective tissues have a high silicon content, as it is a part of the essential structure of these tissues. In the collagen molecule, there seem to be from three to six atoms of silicon for each protein chain.

With respect to silicon's importance in bone formation, I have encountered two completely different theories as to its functions. Either, both, or neither may be correct, and I present both as well-documented possibilities. Both theories agree on the fact that silicon is of vital use to the body.

First, the research of Eric J. Underwood, as reported in *Trace Elements in Human and Animal Nutrition*, indicates that silicon is needed as the bone material is formed and hastens the rate of bone mineralization. This need slacks off as mineralization proceeds to the point at which very little is needed for the completion of bone mineralization. It seems probable that silicon is involved with phosphorus in some manner in the formation of bone.

The second explanation comes from Louis C. Kervran in *Biological Transmutations*. This explanation of silicon's use in bone formation involves the transmutation of silicon plus carbon to make calcium. There are three isotopes of silicon that the body uses in this transmutation. These yield three different calcium isotopes, as follows:

silicon-28 plus carbon-12 yields calcium-40
silicon-30 plus carbon-12 yields calcium-42
silicon-29 plus carbon-13 yields calcium-42

silicon-30 plus carbon-13 yields calcium-43

Since ancient times the knowledge of horsetail (Equisetum) for recalcification has been a part of medical knowledge and folklore. This plant is extremely high in organic silica, a silicon and oxygen compound. Fractures are repaired and healed much faster with organic silica extracts than with the administration of calcium. Experimentation and x-ray examination of bone healing have proven that organic silica is a vastly more successful healing agent for bones than is calcium. However, for reasons not yet understood, mineral silica will decalcify the bones.

The phenomenon of biological transmutation also explains why at hatching a chick contains four times more calcium than the yolk and white of the egg together will contain. The fact that this increase in calcium is not coming from the shell has been conclusively proven, despite the claim by Romanoff and Romanoff in *The Avian Egg* that it originates in the calcium bicarbonate of the shell. However, the shell membrane contains 0.5% organic silica. This silica is transmuted by the growing embryo into calcium as it matures. A chicken egg will contain slightly more than half a milligram of silicon, which makes it the eighth most abundant mineral in the chicken egg.

Foods from plant sources are usually much richer in silicon than those from animal sources. Whole cereal grains are an excellent source, and the high fiber grains, such as oats, are much higher in silicon than the low fiber grains, such as wheat and corn. As might be expected, there are substantial losses of silicon in any refining process. Cage bird diets that contain cereal grains, fruits, or greens should supply an adequate amount of silicon for any avian needs.

CHAPTER 12

THE ESSENTIAL TRACE MINERALS

ARSENIC

Arsenic is one word calculated to strike terror into the heart of the wife-beater. Yet, arsenic is not nearly so poisonous as its reputation would suggest. As of this writing, enough good effects have been reported from its supplementation in trace amounts that there seems no doubt that it is an essential trace mineral.

Arsenic occurs naturally in sea water at the rate of about three parts per billion. The earth's crust contains it in the amount of two parts per million. Some shales are especially rich in arsenic. The source of arsenic in air pollution is coal burning. There are relatively large amounts of arsenic in sea foods, and it seems to be completely non-poisonous as found in the natural foods. Arsenic is found throughout the human body in low concentrations with higher concentrations in the skin and nails and the highest amounts in the hair.

Organically bound arsenic is readily absorbed in the body and rapidly eliminated, primarily in the urine. As

far as positive effects of arsenic research are concerned, in
the days before antibiotics, arsenic was a common treatment for syphilis and yaws, a tropical skin disease characterized by multiple red pimples. In research on chickens,
arsenic compounds added to the diet have caused improvements in growth and market grades. Arsenic supplementation promotes the longevity of rats, and it can alter the
sex ratios of the offspring of both mice and rats. In an
experimental deficiency, rats will exhibit rough coats,
significantly lower growth rates, and enlarged, blackened
spleens.

An excess of arsenic in the diet has caused a reduction
of egg laying in chickens, and decreases in body weight
gains in turkeys. Also, arsenic is toxic to mice at the continued dosage rate of five parts per million in their drinking water. Some compounds, such as arsenic trioxide, are
definite poisons, since they are readily absorbed and retained in the body. As little as thirty milligrams is deadly
to a human being. Arsenic can replace phosphorus in biological reactions, and it can also cause skin lesions in
people.

At present, supplementation with arsenic in any form
would seem to be unnecessary. The traces needed should
be provided easily by a normal avicultural feeding pro-
gram, since arsenic occurs in the necessary trace amounts
in fruits, cereal grains, and most other common food
items in the cage bird diet.

CHROMIUM

Research on chromium is a relatively new development
in the field of nutrition. Virtually all nutritional knowledge of this essential trace mineral dates from 1959 to

the present. I can find no mention of chromium in any book on the subject of nutrition before that date. Obviously, research work has far to go with respect to the importance of chromium in nutrition. However, at this point, there can be no doubt that chromium is an essential trace nutrient in nutrition.

Chromium occurs naturally in sea water at the average rate of two parts per billion and in the earth's crust at the rate of about 200 parts per million. The amount locked up in the crust is insoluble, however. It is present in air pollution as a by-product of coal burning, and can accumulate in the lungs in insoluble forms. One form of chromium has been proven to cause cancer in metal workers. Otherwise, toxicity is unknown. Inorganic chromium is only one percent absorbable, but inorganic compounds are effective in treating the protein deficiency disease called kwashiorkor.

Modern refining methods are a disaster for the chromium content of our foods. Refining whole wheat into white flour removes 40% of the chromium content. Sugar refining is far more destructive, removing 92% of the chromium content in the transition from raw sugar to white sugar. In addition, 75% of the chromium content is lost in polishing rice.

Chromium plays a vital role in the body's glucose metabolism. An adequate supply of chromium is essential to the effective use of insulin. In its known body use, chromium is bound into an organic compound referred to as the Glucose Tolerance Factor, called GTF for short. See the section on vitamins for a more thorough discussion of the GTF. Chromium seems to be the basis of the Glucose Tolerance Factor, just as cobalt is the basis of vitamin B-12. Chromium in the GTF form works so closely with insulin in glucose metabolism that either one is almost completely ineffective without the other.

Feeding glucose after a complete fast causes three

changes in the blood. First, blood sugar levels will rise. Second, insulin levels will rise, and third, chromium levels in the blood will rise as chromium is drawn from tissue storage. The chromium level of the blood always rises with the glucose level. This increased blood level causes a resulting significant increase in chromium excretion in the urine. Initial credit for this series of recent discoveries goes to Klaus Schwarz and Walter Mertz. In 1959 they discovered that chromium was the deficient factor in reduced glucose tolerance, also called mild diabetes.

In western countries, the chromium content of the human body decreases with age, but this does not occur in eastern countries. The most probable cause for this difference is the far higher consumption of refined carbohydrates, in particular white sugar and white flour, in the western countries. Chromium accumulates in the body in the liver, corneas and skin. It has been shown to increase growth, to stimulate the formation of cholesterol and fatty acids, and to be necessary for the maintenance of normal cholesterol and sugar metabolism. The bile contains chromium, and vanadium can antagonize and replace it in the body. An acute infection will cause a decrease in the amount of chromium in circulation. A supplement of chromium has been reported authoritatively to cure both hypoglycemia (low blood sugar) and hyperglycemia (high blood sugar) overnight.

Tests with rats and mice prove that two to five parts per million of chromium as a drinking water supplement will result in significantly better growth in male mice and rats, but curiously, no change in females. Any deficiency is characterized by impaired growth and reduced longevity, plus disturbances in the glucose, lipid, and protein metabolism. Chromium has proven very important to eye health in rats, also, with a deficiency causing opacity of the corneas which is not reversible upon chromium supplementation. In experiments conducted by Dr. Henry A. Schroeder, rats grew faster, survived longer, and at death showed no atherosclerotic plaques in their aortas. In a low chromium diet, elevated blood cholesterol and sugar levels were evident, while chromium supplementation resulted in low blood cholesterol and sugar levels. Though old rats developed corneal opacity under low chromium diets, the significant finding was that chromium deficiency is an instrumental factor in atherosclerosis.

At present, there is no evidence of any natural chromium deficiency in man or animal. As previously stated, the low chromium levels in the human life of western nations are attributable to the high degree of food refining in those countries. It now seems certain that a deficiency will contribute materially to the development of atherosclerosis and arteriosclerosis over the long term. A deficiency can also inhibit protein synthesis in the body. A severe deficiency will cause immediate hyperglycemia or hypoglycemia, as soon as body chromium reserves are exhausted. It is highly significant that a fully developed deficiency of this type can be completely cured by one adequate dosage of an absorbable chromium supplement.

The two best sources of organically bound chromium in the diet are not common in cage bird feeding. They are brewer's yeast and sugar beet molasses. Beef liver is an ideal source with 1,000 parts per million of chromium. Nuts and cereal grains are good sources, in addition. Whole wheat is a particularly good source of biologically active chromium. Vegetable oils have some chromium, but animal meats and fat have several times as much as any of the plant sources. Surprisingly, seafoods are not a good source of chromium. Eggs have a high chromium content, but unfortunately, it occurs in a form that is predominantly not absorbable. Though inorganic chromium compounds are poorly absorbed, the natural organic complexes, such as occur in brewer's yeast, are much better absorbed.

The content of chromium in food is dependent upon its existence in the soil upon which that food is grown. Research in several European countries has shown the extreme value of a chromium addition on deficient soils. As little as 100 grams per acre on deficient soils has increased the crop yield on those soils by more than forty percent!

Nutritional authorities state that the nutritional significance of chromium in birds is not yet established. Though this may be technically true, I can't imagine any future research proving it non-essential. The unity of all nature dictates that all animal metabolism will depend upon the same systems and nutrients, albeit in differing ways and in different quantities. Since chromium has been proven an essential nutrient in humans and rats, it would be shortsighted in the extreme to suppose the same will not prove true in birds.

The best sources of chromium in cage bird nutrition will be the whole cereal grains. Any whole seed, fruit, or vegetable grown in a soil with adequate chromium content will contain a sufficient amount for its metabolism. Insects will also contain a sufficient amount. As previously stated, no natural chromium deficiency has been noted anywhere.

COBALT

Cobalt is present in the earth's crust at the relatively abundant average rate of 23 parts per million, yet soils deficient in cobalt occur in wide areas. It occurs in sea water at the rate of about one part per ten billion. As early as 1935, researchers had listed cobalt as a vital trace mineral in human and animal metabolism. Though little research is available to me on birds at this time, the functions of cobalt indicate that it is also an essential trace mineral for all cage birds, as a component of cobalamin, vitamin B-12.

I find diametrically opposed views as to cobalt's use in plant nutrition. Some claim a vital role, while others claim that though cobalt is found in many plant sources, there is no evidence that it plays any part in plant metabolism.

Cobalt forms an integral part of cobalamin, which in pure form is a red, crystalline compound. Approximately four percent of the dry weight of cobalamin is cobalt. No other function of cobalt in animal or man is yet known. Other possible functions are suspected, but are as yet unproven. Cobalt does exist in the body separately from cobalamin, but its possible functions are as yet unknown.

Unrefined foods seem to contain adequate amounts of cobalt. However, refining foods removes very substantial portions of the cobalt in their composition. Cooking alone causes losses from one-third to 90% in many raw vegetables. Polished white rice has lost about 38% of its cobalt content. Up to 98% of the cobalt is removed in refining raw brown sugar to white sugar. Only a maximum of 12% of the cobalt is left in white sugar.

Good sources for dietary cobalt are cereal grains, oils, fats, oily seeds, and nuts. Whole wheat is an especially good source if it is grown on soil that is adequate in cobalt content, but milling whole wheat into white flour removes up to 89% of the cobalt. The best sources for human consumption are the seafoods. Eggs are also an appreciable source, with the yolk containing twice the cobalt of the egg white. Any excess is excreted primarily in the urine.

Deficiencies of cobalt have occurred only in experimental or domestic animals. Ruminants on pasture deficient in cobalt suffer from wasting disease, also called by the name "salt sick." This disease is characterized by loss of weight and appetite, anemia, and general wasting away. The symptoms are similar to starvation, with the additional symptoms of pale skin, and blanched mucous membranes. The ruminants seem to have a higher cobalt requirement than other animals, probably because it is less well absorbed in this group of animals. Too little cobalt inhibits the synthesis of vitamin B-12. Cobalt is fairly well absorbed in the digestive system, but it is not readily stored in the liver nor elsewhere in the body.

Human research has proven that cobalt deficiency results in vitamin B-12 deficiency and pernicious anemia. Never fear, however; plenty of raw liver in your diet will protect you completely from pernicious anemia. Folic acid, another of the B complex vitamins, can also mask a cobalt deficiency. In addition, rhodium, in the same periodic group of the elements, can displace cobalt in its metabolic functions.

Too much cobalt is definitely toxic. Deliberate administration of a large excess has caused polycythemia in mammals and birds, a condition resulting from too many red blood cells in the blood. Yet, people have taken continually one thousand times over the amount of cobalt necessary for health without ill effect. An excess in beer to maintain the foamy head has caused heart failure in heavy beer drinkers at the intake rate of about 1.2 parts per million. Though cobalt chloride can stimulate red blood cell production in cases of anemia, the large twenty to thirty milligram doses necessary often prove toxic. A high quality protein diet has proven to offer considerable protection against cobalt toxicity.

If your birds are eating a diet of whole grains, any oily seeds and nuts, or eggs, no supplementation with cobalt should ever be necessary.

COPPER

The human race has known of and used copper for untold thousands of years, but it was not until 1833 that Boutigny demonstrated the presence of copper in mammals. In 1928 copper's true importance was recognized when it was discovered to be an essential trace mineral. Sea water contains about ten parts of copper per billion, and the earth's crust has a content of around 45 parts per million. This copper-rich ground is unevenly distributed, however, and many areas are seriously deficient in copper.

So far as can be determined, all living things require copper. All plant life requires it, including bacteria, fungi, and algae, as do animals, insects, and birds. In some sea life, such as mollusks, copper serves as the oxygen carrier, though it has only one-half the carrying capacity of iron, which serves this function in birds and the other higher vertebrates. The National Research Council recommends two milligrams daily for human needs. Absorption of copper in the diet is normally only about thirty percent of the amount ingested. The copper is absorbed in the stomach and the first part of the intestine. Only here is the food mass acid enough to allow absorption. Copper eaten will show up in the bloodstream in fifteen minutes after being consumed. A high ascorbic acid content in the diet seems to reduce intestinal absorption, and it will increase the severity of a copper deficiency in chicks.

One of copper's most important functions appears to be in the prevention of anemia. Copper assists in the formation of hemoglobin, the oxygen-carrying blood protein found in the red blood cells, facilitating iron absorption in some manner. It is not a part of the hemoglobin molecule, but is vital to the formation of that molecule by influencing the iron in the synthesis of the hemoglobin.

Though the final decision is not in, most research indicates that copper aids in the release of iron from the liver. At any rate, anemia cannot be prevented or cured by iron alone. Copper must be present in addition to the iron.

Copper also performs a vital function with ascorbic acid in the synthesis of elastin. This is the connective tissue of the blood vessel walls. If copper is insufficient, the tensile strength of the elastin and the blood vessels will be flawed. This vascular weakness will cause a variety of circulatory problems.

Copper serves a variety of other functions in the body in its primary actions as a catalyst. Copper is necessary for the maintenance of normal nervous functioning, and it is required for the formation of the phospholipids which form the myelin sheath for the protection of nerve tissue. Copper is necessary for the production of ribonucleic acid, commonly called RNA, and it is involved in protein metabolism and healing. It is present in many enzymes performing these varied functions within the body, and copper is necessary for proper bone formation and maintenance. Many other metabolic functions of copper have been identified, but these cannot be adequately judged because of the complex interactions of copper with other trace minerals.

Copper is required for the formation of the dark pigment called melanin. It is a part of the enzyme tyrosinase. This enzyme is needed for the conversion of the amino acid tyrosine into melanin. The absence of this necessary enzyme has been associated with albinism. Copper is responsible for the black wool on sheep, and with inadequate copper in the diet, even a black sheep will produce white wool.

An unusual pigment in one of the turacos (Turacus corythaix) is called turacin. This pigment contains a copper salt whose color depends upon the amount of moisture present in the feather. As a consequence, the normal feather color of this bird is purple-red, but in a rain, the bird assumes a blue color. Turacin is a unique pigment, since it is unlike either the melanin pigments or the lipochrome pigments.

The copper content of the soil will affect the content in any products coming from that soil, but it is difficult to create a copper deficiency on a varied diet. The mineral is too abundant and widespread not to be in adequate supply in most diets. Nuts, fats, meats, cereal grains, and seafoods are notably good sources, but all living things will contain some copper. By far the most abundant source of copper seems to be oysters, with the relatively huge content of 137 parts per million. The copper content of a hen's egg according to one authority is about 30 milligrams, and less than one percent of that amount according to another authority. I am unable to resolve the contradiction. Common sense says .3 milligrams is right.

Unrefined foods will contain sufficient copper for all normal health needs, but refining removes a great deal of the copper content. Around 68% of the copper is removed from whole wheat in processing it into white flour. Significant amounts of copper are dissolved from copper pipes, particularly if the water is acid.

A natural deficiency of copper is unknown in humans, but has been documented in livestock grazed on pastures deficient in copper with no outside food source. Many Florida soils fall into this category. Still, deficiencies are very unlikely and will occur only in experimental or domestic animals, as far as is known. Lest that statement be lost on your consciousness, I must stress that cage birds classify as domestic animals. In livestock, a copper deficiency will cause diarrhea, loss of appetite, and anemia. There is a wide range of possible symptoms, depending on the species, but the symptom common to all species is anemia. Depressed growth, bone disorders, depigmentation of wool or fur, or abnormal fur growth are also possible symptoms. Chicks will become lame after two to four weeks on a deficient diet. Bones will be fragile and easily broken. Adult birds will show depigmentation of feathers with abnormal feather growth, and hens will show reduced egg production.

There is some body storage of copper and this will also make a deficiency highly unlikely on a varied diet. The highest concentrations of copper in the body will be in the liver and brain primarily, with large amounts also found in the kidneys and heart. The bones and muscles have lower concentrations of copper, but their content totals from 50% to 75% of the total body copper content. Ceruloplasmin is a copper-containing protein that stores copper in the blood. Any excess intake of copper to a certain point can be excreted by the liver through the bile into the intestine.

Several other minerals are antagonists of copper in the body. For example, copper occurring with large amounts of sulfur, as it does in eggs, may be partly or totally unabsorbable. The sulfur combines with the copper in the inactive and relatively insoluble form of copper sulfide. An overabundance of molybdenum will create a deficiency of copper, since molybdenum inactivates the copper for biological functioning. There is also a biological antagonism between copper and zinc, but in this instance, copper will make the zinc unavailable for biological activity. Finally, it has been reported that silver in the diet antagonizes copper, and an excess of silver will result in copper deficiency symptoms.

Copper in excess of the amount the body can use or excrete has a definite toxic effect. Copper in inorganic form acts as an enzyme inhibitor. Ingestion of ten times the amount normally found in the diet will cause nausea and vomiting. Many deaths have been reported from copper poisoning, but only one is known from a great excess of copper in the drinking water, that of an infant in Australia. Chronic, long term toxicity occurs only in a recessive hereditary condition known as Wilson's disease.

For cage bird nutrition, the copper content of the food variety normally offered will be sufficient to prevent any deficiency from developing. A diet of predominantly refined foods might be low in copper, but even the purified diets used in nutritional research usually contain enough copper impurity to prevent any deficiency symptom from developing. The greater concern with respect to this mineral should be in the possibility of an excess from the amount dissolved from copper pipes in acid water. This source can be intense in extreme cases, particularly where water sits overnight in the pipes accumulating an ever greater quantity of dissolved copper. In general, however, copper is not a nutrient about which the aviculturist need have any concern.

FLUORINE

The necessity of writing about this trace element does not fill me with the greatest of joy. No other nutrient is surrounded by so much emotion and uncompromising attitude. Its value in nutrition is controversial, and the available literature on fluorine is contradictory.

Nevertheless, a number of definite statements can be made safely about this nutrient. Fluorine occurs in all body tissues at the rate of about 37 parts per million as fluoride compounds, with a very high proportion of the body's content found in the skeleton. The earth's crust contains a relative abundance of fluorine with about 700 parts per million. Sea water contains it at the rate of 1.3

parts per million. All known life seems to have evolved from sea water containing fluorine in this amount, so such a concentration cannot possibly be of any danger to any living species.

Elemental fluorine is a greenish-yellow, highly poisonous gas. It is an extremely reactive element and will instantly form a compound with a wide variety of other elements. Fluorine gas is so active that it will etch glass. Air pollution contains fluorine as a by-product of coal burning.

Fluorine in nutrition is invariably in the form of a compound with other elements, usually as a fluoride, so that term will be used freely in the subsequent discussion. Most of the fluorine in sea water is in the form of sodium fluoride. Much fluorine in the body is as calcium fluoride or magnesium fluoride.

In nutrition, fluorides have never been proven to be essential for life. However, though they are not vital, their absence will result in ill health. Up to ten parts per million have resulted in substantial increases in the growth rate of rats. Fluorine is also important for normal reproduction. Fluorides are important in bone and tooth structure in mammals, but in human nutrition, as little as two parts per million in the food and water supply over a twenty year period will produce symptoms of toxicity. Fluorine is cumulative in the body at any level of intake. The fluoride content of eggs from hens on a high fluoride diet will be much higher than normal. However, without adequate fluoride content in the diet, bones and teeth will be soft and brittle. Consequently, if your birds have soft teeth, be sure their diet carries sufficient fluorine!

An excess of fluoride is as bad as a deficiency. An excess during tooth formation will make teeth so soft they will wear away. Fluorides in excess act as enzyme inhibitors. Fluorine readily binds magnesium into a relatively insoluble form which occurs with calcium fluoride as a constituent of bone. Excess fluorides are excreted primarily in the urine. Also, vitamin C will nullify fluoride toxicity and carry excess fluorides from the body via the urine. With an adequate ascorbic acid intake or synthesis internally, a noticeable fluoride toxicity is highly unlikely.

Organically bound fluorine occurs in many whole foods. Fish, cheese, and meat are all good sources. Seafoods are also good sources, but by far the richest source is tea, with up to 398 parts per million. Heavy tea drinkers should be especially careful of the cumulative effects of the high fluoride content. Molybdenum is another trace mineral which will increase fluorine absorption and retention in the body, especially in the muscles and brain.

With particular reference to birds, feeds from a variety of geographical areas should contain sufficient fluoride content for good health. Since a deficiency is possible, however, keep in mind the dietary necessity for fluorine, particularly in any problem involving weakness of the bone structure. Except on diets from the most deficient soils, no fluoride supplementation should ever be necessary. This is not a nutrient that should cause the aviculturist any concern.

IODINE

Whether or not a severe iodine deficiency will cause death is debatable, but the effects can be worse than death. Iodine is an essential trace nutrient. The mineral itself was first discovered in Napoleon's time, though written knowledge of the treatment of goiter by foods rich in iodine goes back to about 2700 years before Christ, to the reign of the Chinese emperor Shen-nung. He mentions seaweed as an effective remedy for goiter, and we now know seaweed to be rich in iodine. In 1820 the Swiss physician Coindet recommended iodine specifically as a remedy for goiter. This was periodically rediscovered by physicians for the next 100 years, but only in the 1920's was this treatment widely accepted. People never seem to be able to learn from the discoveries of others the first time around.

Though iodine occurs in the earth's crust at the average rate of about three parts per ten million, wide areas of the land have soils with little or no iodine. Near the coastlines, rains carry enough iodine inland for trace needs, since it occurs in sea water at the rate of about 50 parts per billion. Soils in the United States Great Lake Basin are especially deficient in iodine. In addition, in Switzerland the iodine available naturally is locked up in rock formations and is unavailable for nutritional purposes. This has made Switzerland a notable area for the study of iodine deficiencies over the years.

Iodine has a very worthwhile use in relation to the unsaturated fatty acids in research work. Each available double bond in these fatty acids will take up two atoms of iodine. Iodine can be used in this way to measure the degree of unsaturation in mixed fats. The highest iodine values are the most highly unsaturated fats. This type of test provides no information on the specific type or arrangement of the unsaturated fatty acids, however.

Iodine occurs in foods mostly as inorganic iodide. Any uncombined iodine in the diet must be changed to iodide, which is iodine joined to another atom or group of atoms, before absorption. Iodide is freely absorbed at all levels of the digestive tract. The primary organ of storage is the thyroid gland, but small amounts are also found in the kidneys, salivary glands, skin, hair, and female reproductive system. A chicken's body stores iodine extensively enough that a full year's deficiency after an abundant supply causes no strong deficiency symptoms. Any excess is excreted, primarily in the urine.

Once the iodide absorbed into the blood from the intestine reaches the thyroid gland, it is oxidized and converted to organic iodine in the form of the hormone thyroxine by combining with the amino acid tyrosine. This is the only known function of iodine in the body. Each thyroxine molecule contains four atoms of iodine, and it controls a wide variety of body functions. Chief among its functions are control of the rate of metabolism, control of growth, muscular control, and mental capacity.

A deficiency of iodine in the diet will cause first an enlargement of the thyroid gland, as it attempts to keep up the production of its hormones with an insufficient supply of iodine. The resulting swelling is called a goiter, and it is extremely rare with the current wide knowledge of iodine requirements in nutrition. In chickens and probably in all cage birds, an iodine deficiency will cause a reduction in the iodine content of the egg, decreased hatchability, and prolonged hatching time. Embryonic thyroid glands will also increase in size. Lack of thyroid activity will cause hens to become very fat and to cease laying.

In order to give an idea of the extremely fine line between iodine sufficiency and deficiency, I quote the last paragraph from Chapter 9 of Dr. Lionel James Picton's book, *Nutrition and the Soil*.

"A notable example of the narrowness of the margin between just enough and only a little less but disastrously too little was disclosed in 1927 in Switzerland. In view of the European menace, a review of the manpower of the country was undertaken, and it was found that goitre occurred much more often in the cantons speaking German than in those that speak French or Italian. Though the speech was different, the race was the same. No differences in the hygiene or sanitation of the different districts nor in the mineral content and purity of their water supplies could be found; the suggestion that the mere articulation of the gutteral language might be responsible was quite untenable — there was no similar frequency of goitre in Germany. At last the true explanation dawned on the investigators: the cooking customs went with the language. The German-speakers threw away the water in which their vegetables had been boiled, and with it went the iodine-containing salts which the boiling water had extracted from them; but the French- and Italian-speakers were fond of soup for which they used all the vegetable water. Thus they commonly got enough iodine to protect them against the development of goitre."

A deficiency in mammals interferes with conception and reproduction. Young will be born weak or dead. Pigs will be born hairless and bloated, with thick skins and puffy necks. Much as iodine is needed in nutrition, crystalline iodine is extremely toxic — it is poisonous in any quantity.

After iodine supplementation to correct a deficiency, sufficient Vitamin E must also be in the diet to promote healing of the scar tissue in the thyroid gland. Without a sufficiently nutritious diet, healing of the damaged thyroid will be slow and incomplete. Remaining scar tissue will prevent its return to full function until that scar tissue is dissolved and replaced by healthy thyroid tissue.

A large excess of iodine in the diet can be toxic and will also cause goiter. In chickens with a severe excess, over about 300 parts per million, egg laying will cease, early embryonic death will be evident, and eggs will show reduced hatchability and delayed hatching. These adverse effects are only temporary in nature, and will revert to normal when the excess intake of iodine ceases. Laying by the hens will resume within seven days of stopping the dietary excess. You will note that the symptoms of excess are substantially similar to the symptoms of deficiency.

A really severe deficiency in humans results in myxedema, a disease characterized by greatly decreased thyroid activity, dry skin, swelling around the nose and lips, and mental deterioration. At its worst, iodine deficiency in child development results in cretinism. Symptoms of this are arrested physical and mental development and complete idiocy. To get an idea of the curse of cretinism and the heart-rending disasters caused by acute iodine deficiency, you need only read chapter 9 of Dr. Picton's book in full.

For the nutrition of cage birds, supplies of iodine are adequate in a varied diet of seeds, greens, fruit, nuts, eggs, and other whole, unprocessed foods that come from a variety of geographical areas. In addition, all standard vitamin-mineral supplements have iodine added to insure the minimum needs in cage bird nutrition.

IRON

The knowledge of iron as an essential trace mineral reaches back farther than the specific knowledge of any other known nutrient. The ancient Greeks knew of iron as a treatment for anemia over 2,000 years ago. As early as 1746, Manghinis discovered that iron is a constituent of the blood. Iron is vital to all plants and animals, and is a necessary ingredient in the process of photosynthesis. Mollusks, such as snails, which live out of water, need iron, as do all insects. Most life forms on earth would cease to exist without iron.

Fortunately, the earth's crust has a relative superabundance of iron, with about 50,000 parts per million. Most soils have an adequate iron content, and iron occurs in sea water at the average rate of 3.4 parts per billion.

Iron occurs in most foods, and a deficiency is the next thing to impossible on a diet of unrefined foods. Meats; dark green, leafy vegetables; eggs; and whole grains are all good sources. For avian nutrition, the whole grains, greens, fruits, and nuts should provide an adequate amount of iron in the diet. Egg yolk, in particular, is an excellent source, and one average egg will contain about one milligram of iron. Refining removes much of the iron from foods. 76% is removed in the milling of whole wheat into white flour.

Assimilation is the major roadblock to adequate iron content in the body. Generally, 10% or less of the iron in foods is absorbed through the intestinal wall. The stomach's hydrochloric acid dissolves iron to make it available for absorption. The presence of ascorbic acid, vitamin C, or other acids greatly increases the percentage of absorption. Nickel also seems to aid in the absorption of iron. Vitamin E, by contrast, is reported to be a strong antagonist of iron in some sources. Other sources say that there is no foundation for this belief. At any rate, any excess build-up of iron in the tissues is prevented in the intestinal wall as the saturated cells slow down the iron absorption.

The function of iron is to carry and exchange oxygen in the blood. The human body contains 60 parts per million of iron, and the relative body content of a bird will be similar. The red blood cells contain 57% of the body's iron in the protein compound called hemoglobin. Female mammals need far larger amounts of iron than males because of three exclusively female functions: menstruation, gestation, and lactation. Female birds will need much more than males to supply the iron necessary for egg production. Iron is absolutely vital to the life of all higher species. Death will result without it.

A number of other functions of iron in the body are

known. For example, a number of necessary enzymes in the body's metabolism contain iron. Another essential use of iron in the body is in the formation of myoglobin. This is a muscle protein which carries oxygen in the muscle cells. The body cannot form myoglobin without iron, and this is why an iron deficiency will cause such chronic fatigue. Seven percent of the body iron in a dog is in the myoglobin, compared with about 3% in an adult man.

Iron is of special interest in its relationship to feathers. The turacos or plantain-eaters of Africa use iron in the formation of turacoverdin. This iron-containing pigment is the basis for the green coloring of the feathers of turacos. The turacoverdin pigment is unique to this family of birds. Also, in an acute iron deficiency, feathers produced by New Hampshire Red Chickens will contain no red pigment.

The utilization and control of iron levels in the body are a key to health. Copper has been proven to be necessary to the proper utilization of iron. Pyridoxine, vitamin B-6, appears to be essential in the regulation of iron levels in the body. If the control mechanisms fail, iron toxicity can be the result. Iron salts, such as ferrous sulfate, are toxic, and have been fatal in overdose many times.

Iron is stored in the liver primarily. A brown protein called ferritin is one storage form, and a brownish-yellow phosphate called hemosiderin is another. If the body's control mechanisms have failed, excess iron can overwhelm the capacity of the liver. Siderosis is one disease caused by the toxic nature of excess iron in the body. In siderosis, up to 18 times the normal body storage of iron is maintained with toxic effects.

Iron and manganese have a very close biological relationship. An excess of manganese will impede the assimilation of iron. Experimentation in biological transmutation has left no doubt that iron can be transmuted into manganese by microorganisms. Actinomycetes and some bacteria perform this function. Isotope 56 of iron can lose one proton in a biological transmutation and become manganese. Louis Kervran states that one of the best sources of iron for humans is in the manganese content of whole wheat, rice, and other cereal grains. The human body will transmute this manganese into iron by the withdrawal of one atom of hydrogen. With sufficient organically bound manganese in the diet, iron deficiency will never occur. Whether this transmutation is performed by intestinal bacteria or by one of the body's organs is unsure at this time.

Iron need not be of concern to the bird breeder and aviculturist, since it is so widely distributed in nature. Any varied diet of natural, unprocessed foods should supply a sufficient amount of iron for any avian need. Only on diets with a high percentage of refined foods is there a possibility of iron deficiency.

MANGANESE

Manganese was one of the earliest trace minerals to be proven essential in nutrition. That discovery took place in the year 1931, and since that date research has proven it to be essential to all life forms, both plant and animal. Every living thing from the lowest bacteria and fungi to birds and human beings requires trace amounts of manganese for life. Manganese is found in sea water at the rate of only about one part per billion, but the earth's crust contains a relatively abundant supply of manganese, with about 4,000 parts per million. The bodies of primitive man contained far more manganese than does the body of modern man, and wild animals also retain in their bodies far more manganese than humans retain in their tissues.

This may be the result of our high degree of food processing and the fact that so many soils have been depleted of manganese. Should these possible causes of low manganese levels prove true with future research, then modern man is suffering from a constant deficiency of this vital trace mineral.

Absorption of dietary manganese seems to be very poor. As little as one percent of the amount ingested may be absorbed, and absorption appears to depend on the formation of natural chelates. The effect of other dietary metals on the absorption of manganese does not appear to be severe, except in the case of iron. A high iron content in the diet will reduce manganese absorption, and a high manganese content will cause a decrease in iron absorption in test animals. A high calcium and phosphorus intake also will interfere with manganese absorption and aggravate any existing deficiency. Fortunately, absorption of manganese takes place throughout the small intestine, and changes in the acid-base balance do not affect absorption of the manganese in the diet.

Though manganese is widely distributed on the earth's surface, plant deficiencies of this mineral may occur even though the soil is not deficient. This plant deficiency happens when the soil is too alkaline. Alkaline soil causes the oxidation of manganese into a form that the plant roots cannot absorb. This results in a bleaching or chlorosis of the leaves, a symptom of manganese deficiency in plants. Merely returning the soil to a more acid state is sufficient to cure any deficiency in such plants. In areas of highly alkaline soils, a favorite trick to make the soil compatible with acid loving plants, such as azaleas, camellias, and gardenias, is to pour diluted pickle juice or vinegar around them every few months.

In spite of the many years of research on the metabolic functions of manganese, its actions within the body are

still not well known. Even the proven effects of a manganese deficiency frequently cannot be related to a specific
function of manganese in the body. Manganese takes part
in many known enzyme reactions, and it is essential for
the activation of several enzymes. In this capacity, it stimulates the formation of cholesterol and fatty acids in the
liver, and is essential for the release of energy within the
cells. Manganese is also important in the formation of the
thyroid compound, thyroxine, and it is required for both
lipid and glucose metabolism. Manganese functions closely
with vitamin K in that vitamin's blood clotting function,
and vitamin K alone will not act without adequate manganese in the body at the same time.

Several other functions of manganese are known, but
again the exact basis for these actions has not yet been
discovered. Manganese is essential for the development of
the organic matrix for bone tissue, though it does not seem
to be directly involved in bone calcification. Perhaps the
most puzzling function of manganese is in the contribution
it makes to motherly love in mammals. Female rats deficient in manganese will abandon their offspring, and
whereas adoption of orphaned babies is usually almost
automatic, healthy females will refuse to adopt babies that
are suffering from a manganese deficiency in over 90%
of the cases studied. The physiological basis for such
actions at this point is totally unknown. Diabetics have
been shown to have very low manganese levels which may
be a contributing cause of this human disease. Also, symptoms of multiple sclerosis have been induced in rats from
a manganese deficient diet.

Manganese is found throughout the body, but the
bones, liver, kidneys, and pancreas contain higher concentrations of body manganese. The pancreas seems to rely
particularly heavily on an abundant supply of manganese.
A deficient female animal will produce young with an

abnormal pancreas, or occasionally with no pancreas at all. At any rate, it is somewhat comforting to learn that such deficiencies, severe enough to cause noticeable symptoms, have occurred only in experimental or domestic animals. Yet, the aviculturist should never forget that cage birds are also domestic animals and may be subject to a manganese deficiency, as is described later in this section.

Manganese deficiency will destroy the reproductive process. Male rats reared on a manganese deficient diet will be sterile. In the first stage of such an induced deficiency, females will give birth to living young, some or all of which will show a lack of muscular control. In a more serious deficiency of manganese, the young will be born dead or will die shortly after birth. Poor lactation will also become prevalent in females. In the most severe deficiency, animals will not mate and will also be sterile, with testicular degeneration in the males. There will be a high rate of mortality by the time this stage of deficiency is reached.

Severe manganese deficiency will show up in both chickens and mammals with similar symptoms in some areas. In chicks the main symptom of severe manganese deficiency is perosis, a deformity characterized by great enlargement of the tibiometatarsal joint. This is accompanied by twisting, thickening, and shortening of the bones. The tendon will slip from its proper position, which gives the common name "slipped tendon" to this deformity. Mammals will exhibit reduced bone mineralization and defective bone structure, along with reduced growth.

Hens suffering from a manganese deficiency will have reduced egg production, decreased hatchability, and an increase in eggs with thin shells or no shells at all. The embryos from eggs laid by deficient hens will have a deformed appearance referred to as chondrodystrophy.

Among the symptoms of this deficiency disease are shortened and thickened legs and shortened wings. The embryos
will have a shortened lower mandible, giving them a beak
resembling a parrot's. The abdomen will protrude and the
growth of the down and the body will be retarded.

With a less severe deficiency, chicks that have hatched
will be deformed in that the head and beak will point
straight up, a posture referred to as star-gazing. This is a
sure symptom of manganese deficiency, which also occurs
in mammals. The condition is also apparently irreversible.
Research has indicated that this particular deformity is
probably caused by a structural defect in the inner ear.

Several years ago I noted this symptom of star-gazing
in my Society Finch fledglings. Unfortunately, at that time
my library did not contain the specific nutritional information that is now available for my research. At that time
I presumed this was merely a genetic defect, since it occurred only in two or three of my eighty breeding pairs,
and only in a minority of their offspring. Now, of course, I
can be certain that this problem was the result of the
biochemical individuality of these few birds, each of which
had a higher manganese requirement than my diet could
provide. Though the star-gazing posture is also a symptom
of thiamin deficiency, the particular characteristics dis-
played in my finches pointed more towards a manganese
deficiency. Experience is obviously the best teacher in
such cases, but it is a merciless master, unforgiving of
ignorance. Perhaps the information in this volume will help
you spot similar deficiencies in your own breeding stock
and recognize them as such, allowing at least an oppor-
tunity for correction.

Chickens seem to require about 50 parts per million
of manganese in their diet. The manganese levels in the
eggs of chickens and other birds vary greatly, depending
upon the amount consumed in the diet. The concentration

in the egg yolk is four to five times as high as that in the egg white. The 50 parts per million needed by chickens is only one part in 20,000 of the food that needs to be manganese for an adequate dietary supply. Nuts are probably the best source, along with green, leafy vegetables. Whole grains, especially wheat and buckwheat, are excellent sources. Human specialities, such as tea and spices, are especially rich in manganese, with cloves probably the highest available source.

As discussed in the section on iron, manganese can be biologically transmuted into iron, and the opposite transmutation also occurs. Actinomycetes and bacteria can transmute iron, Fe-56, into manganese, Mn-55, by withdrawing one proton, in effect one hydrogen atom. This process occurs in the ruins of ancient temples in Cambodia, where surface microorganisms transmute the iron content of the rock into a dark coating which contains 5% manganese. In controlled testing, these bacteria can be cultured on ferrous sulfate and will produce manganese by transmuting the iron in the ferrous sulfate. During seed germination, the opposite transmutation occurs; manganese will disappear while an equal amount of iron appears. Neither transmutation has yet been observed in birds, to the best of my knowledge.

As previously mentioned, refining removes a great deal of the manganese in whole foods. In the processing of whole wheat into white flour, 80% or more of the manganese is removed. Whole wheat with an average value of 31 parts per million of manganese may have 160 parts per million in the germ, 119 parts per million in the bran, but only 5 parts per million in the white flour. Refining raw sugar into white sugar removes around 89% of the manganese.

Up to certain point, an excess intake can be excreted through the bile into the intestinal tract. Manganese can then be resorbed, excreted again, and resorbed several times before finally being eliminated. However, the body's ability to excrete an excess of manganese can be overwhelmed. A toxic excess occurs only rarely in miners and metal workers in the manganese industry from inhaling a toxic excess of manganese dust. This results in a form of severe pneumonia and a nervous disease similar to Parkinsonism.

Though a deficiency in cage bird diets is a definite possibility, as proven by my own experience with Society Finches, it is not likely. Every aviculturist should be aware of the symptoms described herein to be able to spot any such problem in its early stages. Supplementation, if necessary, is simple, and there is little likelihood of feeding your birds a toxic excess. Fortunately, manganese is among the least toxic of the trace minerals to birds. Hens in experimentation will tolerate as much as 1,000 parts per million with no toxicity. Levels higher than this may be toxic, especially to chicks, so a degree of caution is advisable. Just because one part per thousand is good in the diet definitely does not mean that ten parts per thousand is better! That would constitute a sufficient amount to be deadly in its toxicity.

MOLYBDENUM

Molybdenum is a silvery gray metal which looks something like lead in its pure metallic form. There is a relative shortage of molybdenum in the earth's crust in comparison with the known quantities of other nutritionally important metals, only one part per million. It occurs in sea water at the rate of about fourteen parts per billion.

Molybdenum is an essential trace mineral in nutrition. Research has proven it essential to all mammals, and further research with chickens indicates molybdenum as also essential in the nutrition of birds. Molybdenum is found in low concentrations in all tissues and fluids of the body. It is a proven constituent of several necessary enzymes required in the body's metabolism. One of these enzymes is xanthine oxidase. This enzyme is an essential catalyst for the oxidation of a number of substances in the body's metabolism. Aldehyde oxidase performs similar catalytic functions within the body, as another molybdenum-containing enzyme. Much research remains to be completed to determine the true functions of these enzymes in the avian body, however. These may be somewhat different from the uses in the body of a mammal.

Molybdenum is readily absorbed in the digestive tract, and a higher dietary intake will result in higher concentrations in the body. Tungsten can replace the molybdenum in some enzymes in mammals, which will result in weak biological activity in those enzymes. When more molybdenum is absorbed than the body needs, the excess is filtered out by the kidneys and excreted in the urine. Sweat is also a route for excretion of excess molybdenum in those animals having this excretory function.

Both deficiency and toxicity symptoms are known in birds and animals. A deficiency of molybdenum will cause a reduction in growth in chickens, but little is known about any other effect of a deficiency. Supplementation of the diet of chicks with trace amounts will result in an increased growth rate, and all species seem to have an extremely small requirement for this nutrient. Researchers have proven that an overload from excess molybdenum is possible. An excess in the diet at the rate of 2,000 parts per million will decrease growth severely in chicks, and anemia will also develop at dietary levels of 4,000 parts per million. Though toxicity shows up at levels below 200 parts per million, no confirmed cases of molybdenum poisoning have ever been reported on natural diets. Nevertheless, toxicity symptoms will occur regularly on pastures overly abundant in molybdenum. Cattle are affected first and seem to be the most sensitive domestic animal to excess molybdenum in the diet. Horses are not affected at all, even at much higher levels of dietary intake. Whole liver in the diet has been reported to counteract any molybdenum toxicity in humans.

Plants cannot take up molybdenum from the soil if the acidity is too high. Most plant deficiencies, characterized by dead leaf edges, occur in soil with a pH lower than 5.2. Simply raising the soil pH to 7 with the addition of lime is usually sufficient to alleviate any deficiency symptom in plants. Still, plants take up molybdenum in the least amounts of any trace mineral.

Molybdenum is vital to legume plants in particular. The nitrogen-fixing bacteria associated with these plants must use molybdenum as a catalyst for synthesizing the absorbable nitrates that plants absorb and use in their building of proteins. Vanadium can substitute for molybdenum in some of these nitrogen-fixing bacteria. One writer has flatly stated that any soil lacking all molybdenum will be completely barren. Obviously, any molybdenum deficiency in the soil will cause a corresponding deficiency in the plants grown in that soil and consequently also in the animals consuming those plants.

Molybdenum strongly antagonizes copper absorption. Since copper is the vital mineral for the production of the black wool of a black sheep, the addition of molybdenum to the diet of black sheep will cause them to produce white wool. Alternating a high molybdenum intake with a high copper intake in black sheep will cause the production of wool that is banded black and white. Sulfur is also involved in this process, but the molybdenum is the decisive factor. A copper excess can be corrected by the simple addition of molybdenum to the diet. Likewise, a molybdenum excess can be alleviated by additional copper in the diet.

The best sources of molybdenum for the nutrition of the seed-eating cage birds are the whole cereal grains. Milling wheat to make white flour will remove about 48% of the molybdenum in it. Dark green, leafy vegetables are also a good source, as is liver. Dairy products, fruit, and eggs also contain a respectable amount of molybdenum. There is a tremendous variation, frequently over a hundred-fold, in the molybdenum content of vegetables, depending upon the molybdenum content of the soil on which they were grown. Fortunately, this mineral is widely enough distributed in the natural food supply that there is very little likelihood of a deficiency developing in a varied diet. It is not a mineral that you need to be particularly conscious of in avian nutrition, as long as you feed a variety of whole, natural foods.

NICKEL

Nickel is relatively abundant in the earth's crust, which has a content of around 80 parts per million. Sea water also contains nickel in the amount of about three parts per billion. Nickel is widely distributed in human and animal tissues and only seems to be in any concentration in the pancreas. Within the individual cells, however, there are significant concentrations of nickel in both RNA and DNA. Human tissues contain nickel at the rate of about one part per ten million.

Very recent research in the field of nutrition indicates that nickel is an essential trace mineral in chicks, rats, and pigs. The future research into the requirements for this mineral will very likely indicate its vital necessity for humans and all birds as well. The need for nickel in metabolism is extremely small. It is truly a trace mineral, and it has been difficult to formulate diets for testing that are sufficiently low in nickel to cause symptoms of deficiency. With respect to human nickel metabolism, it is puzzling that the levels of nickel in the blood double after an acute heart attack and are also abnormally high after an acute stroke or severe burns. The reason for this increase and the source of the additional nickel are still unknown. This sudden increase in nickel definitely does not come from the heart itself, however, since reserves in that organ are simply not that extensive.

Nickel is poorly absorbed in the body, and less than 10% of the dietary content will be absorbed. Retention in the body is also poor, as the body has efficient mechanisms for excreting excess nickel. This is a further indication of the extremely small amounts of nickel necessary for optimal nutrition. Human sweat will contain about twenty times as much nickel as is found in normal concentration in the blood.

Though concentrated amounts of nickel can be toxic, this metal is fairly safe at quite high levels. Chicks are unable to tolerate a dietary intake of 700 parts per million in the food supply, however, without exhibiting symptoms of toxicity. These will take the form of a lower growth rate, reduced food consumption, reduced energy metabolism, and a large reduction in retention of nitrogen. However, rats fed 1,000 parts per million showed no ill effects even after several months of continuous feeding. This would indicate that the excretion process for excess nickel in mammals is more efficient than that of chickens and probably most other birds. Air pollution contains considerable amounts of nickel, the by-product of burning coal and petroleum. Breathing nickel dust will cause cancer in the nose, sinuses, and lungs of humans, with skin irritation appearing in sensitive individuals.

Though the need for nickel is extremely small, all species tested will show similar deficiency symptoms. Chicks will show a number of deficiency symptoms within three to five weeks on a deficient diet. They will exhibit color changes in the skin and skin eruptions in certain areas, thicker legs, and swelling in the hocks. There will also be both structural changes and a change in appearance of the liver, along with biochemical changes within the body. Rats will show similar symptoms with impaired growth and reproduction. Fetal death, less active offspring during the suckling period, rougher fur, and less weight at weaning will also be evident. Pigs will suffer from the same symptoms with higher mortality in the piglets.

Any deficiency in nickel in rats will have a very adverse effect on iron absorption which will result in severe anemia and greatly reduced storage of iron in the tissues. Even a doubling of the iron content of the diet will not restore normal iron levels in the tissues or completely cure the anemia. The exact role that nickel plays in these changes is not yet understood.

The best dietary sources for nickel have not been determined, since research on this mineral in its biological functions is so recent. Green, leafy vegetables contain considerable amounts of nickel, and a varied diet of whole seeds, greens, fruit or nuts should contain sufficient nickel content for any avian need. The likelihood of any serious nickel deficiency occurring in cage birds is nearly zero, and should not be a source of concern for any aviculturist.

SELENIUM

Selenium as an element was discovered by Berzilius over a hundred years ago. The earth's crust contains it at the rate of about nine parts per 100 million, but it is very unevenly distributed. The soils of South Dakota are very high in selenium, while Ohio soils are very low. Sea water contains selenium at the rate of four parts per billion, on the average. Selenium is also a component of air pollution as a by-product of coal burning.

Any mention of selenium before 1950 was in relation to its toxicity. Only its poisonous aspect was known before that date. Cattle grazed on land with an overabundance of selenium showed typical toxicity symptoms — brittle hair, hooves that were brittle and fell off, and serious wasting disease. In humans, when the ability of the body to excrete selenium via the urine is exceeded, it is excreted through the lungs as a gas, giving a characteristic garlic breath. Elemental selenium has little toxicity, but selenium oxides are very toxic. An intake level of 10 to 20 parts per million will produce toxicity, and selenium can cause cancer if consumed in excess over a lifetime.

The properties of selenium are similar to those of sulfur and tellurium. For this reason, selenium will displace sulfur in the body's metabolism. This displacement of sulfur is the cause of the wasting disease noted in cattle. An excess of selenium will also cause malformation in bird embryos.

A revolution in our knowledge of selenium occurred in the 1950's through the work of Klaus Schwarz. In 1957 his efforts resulted in selenium's reclassification as an essential trace mineral. The level needed varies from 0.05 to 0.2 parts per million. The optimal intake seems to be about 0.2 parts per million, and this is the level of content in the human body. Apparently, death will not result from a serious deficiency of selenium, though impairment of health will be severe. A total lack of selenium will cause death from destruction of the pancreas. Selenium works very closely with vitamin E in its metabolic functions.

Selenium deficiency has been studied extensively in chickens at this point, and the resulting information should apply to all cage birds. First, a deficiency is unlikely in birds fed a varied diet of whole, unrefined foods. It is widely available in foods, and the amounts required are very small. Selenium deficiency has been directly related to muscular dystrophy, atrophy of the pancreas, liver necrosis, and infertility.

The spontaneous swelling and hemorrhage disease of chickens called exudative diathesis is caused by selenium deficiency. Though either selenium or vitamin E will cure most deficiency symptoms in other diseases, selenium alone completely prevents exudative diathesis.

Degeneration of the pancreas is the most serious effect of selenium deficiency. The lack of pancreatic enzymes in the digestive system will result in inability to absorb vitamin E from the intestinal tract. In cases of severe selenium deficiency and resulting emaciation, supplementary selenium will cause the pancreas to return to normal within ten to seventeen days. Normal growth will also resume. The effect of selenium supplementation alone on growth is greater than the effect of vitamin E alone, and it is equal to that of vitamin E and selenium given together.

Reproductive failure is certain in selenium deficient birds. Selenium is especially abundant in the male reproductive system, and males seem to have a higher selenium requirement than females. Hatchability of eggs will drop to zero by the 17th week in chickens suffering from selenium deficiency. With supplementation, hatchability will return to over 90%.

A selenium deficiency can be partly relieved by additional vitamin E intake. These two nutrients have a strong interactive role in nutrition. There are at least three ways in which selenium spares vitamin E in the body. First, selenium preserves and protects the activity of the pancreas, thus allowing for normal absorption of vitamin E in the intestinal tract. Second, selenium is an integral part of the enzyme glutathione peroxidase, which destroys peroxides by converting them to harmless alcohols. This reduces the amount of vitamin E required to maintain the cells' lipid membranes from destruction by the peroxides. Third, selenium aids in an as yet unknown way in the retention of vitamin E in blood plasma. See the section on vitamin E for more information regarding this nutritional interrelationship.

A number of other nutritional functions of selenium have been discovered recently. It can reduce the toxicity of arsenic, mercury, silver, and copper. Selenium also protects against cadmium toxicity, and it is an antioxidant in the body. Selenium is necessary for protein synthesis in the body. Also, selenium may be required for normal growth. A trace selenium supplement will prevent stillbirths and wasting of the young that survive in livestock.

With specific reference to human nutrition, we may require more selenium than other mammals or birds. Human milk contains up to six times as much selenium as a cow's milk. Cancer rates among people are significantly lower in areas where selenium occurrence rates are higher.

Good sources of selenium are brewer's yeast, eggs, liver, and garlic. Animal sources are generally higher in selenium than plant sources. Nuts are also a good source. Again, a variety of whole seeds, fruits, insects, etc., should supply all of the selenium needed in avian nutrition, providing they do not all come from an area that is known for selenium deficient soils. All foods lose selenium in processing. Whole brown rice, for example, has fifteen times the selenium content of milled white rice. Selenium is stored in all body organs to some extent, but the primary area seems to be in the liver. No supplementation should be necessary in a varied cage bird diet of whole, raw foods.

TIN

Information on the nutritional aspects of tin is extremely hard to find. Very little research has been done on tin as an essential trace mineral, and the available material is very recent. Until the late 1960's, tin was considered strictly as a relatively harmless contaminant in the food supply. It is found in large amounts in many processed foods as a by-product of the canning and processing. Asparagus packaged in glass has traces of tin added to make it taste like the product from a metal can. Tin occurs in sea water at the rate of three parts per billion.

Tin has been proven an essential nutrient for the growth of rats, but its exact biochemical functions within the body are not yet known. In experimental dietary testing with rats, their growth rate improved by nearly 60% when one to two parts per million of tin were added to their highly purified diet. This successful demonstration was achieved with the use of stannic sulfate and several other tin compounds as the source of the dietary tin. Other than the slower growth, no other deficiency symptoms were noted. The latest information I have been able to find indicates that no research with any birds or other animals other than mice has yet occurred to expand the knowledge of this essential trace mineral.

Tin is found in most human and animal tissues. It is poorly absorbed from the digestive tract and poorly retained within the body. This would account for tin's low degree of toxicity. Any excesses are excreted through the colon. Considering the large amounts of tin occurring in many diets, it is fortunate that this metal has only a low level of toxicity. Five parts per million of tin in the diet for life produced completely normal mice and male rats. Female rats did show a shorter life span with fatty degeneration of the liver at this dietary concentration. This would indicate a greater sensitivity on the part of females to dietary tin. In higher concentrations in the diet, these animals will exhibit slackened growth and reduced hemoglobin synthesis.

Though no information seems to be available on tin in avian nutrition, any trace requirement should easily be supplied from cereal grains, fruits, nuts, and vegetables. At this point, there is no need to consider any supplementation of tin in the diet. Cage birds will get any traces of tin needed in any regular, varied diet.

VANADIUM

Vanadium is a proven essential trace mineral for humans, rats, and chickens. It is therefore logical to presume that it is also an essential nutrient for cage birds, though any research in this regard is unavailable to me at this time. The earth's crust contains a relative abundance of vanadium at an average rate of 110 parts per million. Sea water is a carrier of vanadium in the amount of about five parts per billion, and it is detectable in most body tissues. All other elements with the same properties as vanadium, such as zinc, have been found to be essential to nutrition, in addition.

Almost all nutritional knowledge of vanadium seems to

be a product of research in the 1970's. I have found only
one nutritional reference to vanadium before 1970, that
from 1962, though surely research work was in progress
before that date with presumable published research
papers in the periodical literature. Future research and
experimentation undoubtedly will increase our knowledge
of this mineral's nutritional value tremendously.

Vanadium serves the same purpose in sea squirts that
iron serves in the blood of higher vertebrates. Up to four
percent of the blood cell material of a sea squirt is vanadium. It serves to transport oxygen for the life processes
of creatures in this family. It is an effective substitute for
iron in this organism, though not a very efficient substitute.
The most unusual feature to human eyes is that this vanadium base gives the sea squirt green blood.

The food items with the largest levels of vanadium are
not normally used in avian nutrition. They are black
pepper, soybean oil, corn oil, olives, and gelatin. Vanadium
is more highly concentrated in fats and vegetable oils.

Nuts contain a good quantity of vanadium within their
fat content. In the body, this mineral is stored in the fatty
tissues. Marine life is the most consistently reliable source
of vanadium. At a maximum possible intake from both
dietary sources and from air pollution, there is no known
toxicity of vanadium. Any excess over body needs is excreted in the urine. The source of vanadium in air pollution is from burning coal and the Venezuelan and Iranian
low-sulfur petroleums.

Researchers have established a definite correlation
between vanadium deficiency and heart disease. Vanadium
is abundant in the drinking water supplies of those United
States areas where heart disease is lowest. Relatively high
levels of vanadium help to lower serum cholesterol levels.
It acts similarly to chromium and zinc in this regard. Other
research results indicate that vanadium also speeds the de-

struction of existing cholesterol. Changes in vanadium levels in any given area are proven to show up in the hair, and presumably also will be detected in the feathers of birds.

Animal research has brought forth a number of facts about dietary vanadium that may be of interest to the aviculturist. Deliberately generated deficiencies of vanadium in young chickens cause a significant decrease in feather growth. Deficiency also decreases the reproduction rate in rats and increases mortality in their offspring. Vanadium has been proven essential to the growth of rats in laboratory experimentation. Also, vanadium deficient diets have resulted in increased triglyceride levels in chickens. Chromium has been demonstrated to be an antagonist of vanadium in chickens. Sulfur may also be such an antagonist, counteracting or neutralizing the effect of the vanadium present. Also, niobium can displace vanadium, since both are in the same periodic group.

Vanadium poisoning is possible, but has been reported only in petroleum workers inhaling vanadium-laden dust directly into the lungs. Other workers in the vanadium industry who absorb considerable amounts of the metal will get green tongues and little more. This is the same effect the tongue shows from a synthetic creme de menthe the morning after.

In many areas, vanadium deficiency may be a problem, as evidenced by the research on heart disease reported in this section. I doubt that it should be a major concern of aviculturists, since whole, unprocessed fatty seeds should contain vanadium in sufficient quantity. Nevertheless, research on vanadium needs in living organisms is too recent and incomplete to allow even a preliminary judgment at this time. As with all other aspects of nutritional study, keep an open mind with regard to vanadium. Be prepared to change your views and expand your knowledge with every new research development.

If you feel the necessity to supplement your birds' diet with vanadium, kelp is a readily available source of it and of all other necessary trace minerals. Supplementation with purified sea water is another possible source for all of the essential trace minerals. Mix it one part to ten parts with regular drinking water. In my personal experience, this is a perfectly safe method of supplementation, and it is of considerable value for long term supplementation.

ZINC

The importance of zinc in nutrition cannot be overstressed. Zinc is vital to life, and it is more abundant in the cells than any other trace element. All birds and animals, as well as all plants, including algae, fungi, and bacteria, require zinc for life. Zinc has been recognized as an essential nutrient for fungi for over a hundred years. It is found in the earth's crust at the rate of about 65 parts per million, and sea water contains it at the rate of around fifteen parts per billion. Zinc will be found in human tissues at an average rate of 33 parts per million and in animal tissues at the average rate of about 30 parts per million.

In 1934 zinc was discovered to be a trace essential mineral in the nutrition of rats and mice. Additional information has been accumulating since that year regarding its importance in nutrition, and the future undoubtedly holds more information yet to be discovered. Absorption occurs in the proventriculus and in the small intestine of birds. Pyridoxine must also be present in the body for the utilization of zinc. The colostrum of all mammalian species is three to four times richer in zinc than the later milk.

Zinc occurs in higher accumulations in several parts of

the body. Twenty percent of the zinc in the human body is present in the skin. Because of this high skin content, large quantities of zinc can be lost in the sweat, especially in the tropics. The hair, nails, and eyes also contain high concentrations of zinc. The skin and fur of rats combined contain 38% of the zinc in the body. The protein keratin contains zinc as one of its constituents, which accounts for the high zinc content in hair and feathers. Copper, nickel, and zinc are all proven to be involved in taste, but zinc is the main factor. This is one specific area where zinc works very closely with pyridoxine. A severe zinc deficiency will cause anemia among other symptoms to be discussed later, and it is required for the synthesis of nucleic acids and the protein portions of some vital enzymes. Stress depletes body tissues of zinc and will greatly increase the zinc requirement. Approximately 85% of the zinc in the blood is in the red blood cells.

Zinc apparently plays a very important role in the health and proper functioning of the eye, since the retina of the eye is very high in zinc content. The visual parts of the eye can contain up to 4% zinc. In dogs and foxes, these zinc values can rise as high as 85,000 parts per million, or 8.5% of the choroid tissues. The function of these extremely high zinc levels is unknown. Nevertheless, they occur in the eyes of all species tested, including fish. The fluorescent reaction of many animals' eyes to light at night depends upon zinc-containing enzymes.

A substance called phytic acid exists in cereal grains which will bind zinc in an unusable form. Diets exclusively of cereal grains will bind so much of the zinc content that severe deficiency will result. If the zinc is in a chelated form, however, the phytic acid cannot bind the zinc, and it will be available for absorption and use in the body's metabolism. Also, the zinc requirement in the diet is partly dependent upon the calcium content of the diet. An increase in dietary calcium will increase the zinc requirement.

The first obvious symptoms of a zinc deficiency in humans are fortunately highly noticeable and relatively harmless. A borderline deficiency will cause white spots or lines on the fingernails or sometimes a milky, opaque appearance on the whole fingernail. This will be accompanied by poor growth in both the hair and nails. White spots will occur most frequently on the index finger and little finger of the dominant hand, that is, on the right hand for right-handed people. Brittleness will accompany this discoloration, and the spots will not disappear with zinc supplementation. They must grow out over a period of months. A deficiency is also noticeable by the development of stretch marks in the skin from exercise or rapid growth.

In 1961 zinc deficiency was definitely linked to retarded growth, delayed sexual maturity, and delayed wound healing. These effects are not surprising when you consider that zinc is a constituent of at least 25 different enzymes in the body involved in digestion and metabolism. One of these zinc-containing enzymes plays an important role in the calcification of bone tissue and in the formation of eggshells. Calcium will displace zinc in many of its metabolic functions and will inactivate many of these zinc-containing enzymes. The major organ involved in zinc metabolism is the liver. Supplementary zinc in the dietary intake will increase the efficiency of feed utilization up to 25%. Healing is speeded by an adequate dietary intake of zinc, and in a severe deficiency healing will not occur until the zinc content of the body is increased.

A zinc deficiency in chicks will cause poor growth, abnormal bone development with shortening and thickening of the leg bones in proportion to the degree of zinc deficiency, and enlargement of the hock joint. Changes and disproportionate growth will occur in other bones, also, with resulting spine curvature and fusing of vertebrae. Skin will show scaling, especially on the feet. Very poor feathering will be evident with loss of appetite and death. Chicks hatched from hens that have been fed a deficient diet will be weak and will not stand up, eat, or drink. An accelerated respiratory rate and labored breathing are other deficiency symptoms. If the chicks are disturbed, the symptoms are aggravated and the chicks often die.

Embryos will exhibit grossly impaired skeletal development. Toes often will be missing, and in extreme cases there will be no lower skeleton or limbs. The eyes occasionally will be absent or underdeveloped. In any zinc deficiency there are changes in both carbohydrate and fat metabolism. Any deficiency during the critical period of brain growth will permanently affect brain function with reduced brain size and a reduction in the total number of brain cells.

Zinc deficiencies will be most likely to show up in humans consuming foods grown on soils that have been depleted of their zinc content. This is particularly true in areas such as Egypt, Iran, and Iraq, where agriculture for thousands of years has completely depleted the soil of this mineral. Zinc deficiency has been studied intensively in both Egypt and Iran, where soils and the foods grown on those soils are severely deficient in zinc. The symptoms are dwarfism, rough and hyper-pigmented skin, underdeveloped sexual organs, and a lack of secondary sexual characteristics. These deficiency-related malformations respond well to treatment with supplementary dietary zinc, if caught in time. One might also note that the fragility of the red blood cells increases in any period of zinc deficiency.

The section on iron covered the unique female requirements for iron, and in this section we must turn to zinc as the mineral with unique functions in the male reproductive system. The highest concentrations of zinc in the male body occur in the reproductive system, and any sexual activity causes great body losses of zinc which must be replaced in the diet. These concentrations of zinc obviously serve a vital purpose in the male, but this has not yet been pinned down to specifics. The prostate gland, seminal fluid, and spermatozoa are all very high in zinc, and any prostate problem invariably shows a subnormal level of zinc concentration. Men should be aware of this constant zinc loss and the need for its continual replacement. This is as important to the life and health of the male as an abundance of iron is to the female. Fortunately, any zinc deficiency in the male reproductive system does not result in permanent damage. Complete recovery will occur with the resumption of adequate zinc intake. All stages of reproduction in both male and female will be harmed by any zinc deficiency.

Zinc is available in a wide variety of foods, but in general the zinc content of plant protein is less than that in animal protein. By far the richest known source of zinc is oysters, with herring in second place, far behind. Oysters may contain as much as 1,000 parts per million of zinc. Other seafoods, meats, maple syrup, liver, wheat, buckwheat, oats and other cereal grains, nuts, and eggs have appreciable amounts of zinc. Nuts are a better source than meat. One chicken egg will contain up to one milligram of zinc, most of which will be found in the yolk. Sunflower seeds and pumpkin seeds are also excellent sources. Refining of foods removes a great deal of the zinc content, and at least 78% of the zinc is removed in the processing of whole wheat into white flour.

Of all of the trace minerals, zinc is the least likely to produce toxic effects. Though it is relatively non-toxic, a consistent intake of over 1,000 parts per million can cause depressed growth and appetite, arthritis, and internal hemorrhages. No known diet could possibly provide zinc in this concentration. An excessive intake at one time can cause diarrhea at first, followed by nausea and vomiting. Yet, one recorded instance of a deliberate ingestion of 12 grams of elemental zinc, a little less than half an ounce, produced only intense difficulty in staying awake, with constant falling asleep even over meals for several days, but no other noticeable effects. An excess of zinc will also cause a large loss of iron from the liver and a later loss of copper from the liver, both of which will cause anemia.

Zinc is a mineral that must be of primary concern to the aviculturist. Research has indicated that even the widely varied American diets are frequently quite deficient in zinc. If you doubt this, look around at the number of individuals with white spots on their fingernails, a dead giveaway of zinc deficiency (not a sign of frequent lies, as old wives tales would have you believe). I can recall that my own fingernails showed this symptom back when I was a teenage sex maniac, as well as a nutritional illiterate.

All of this means simply that the limited variety of the average cage bird diet is more likely than not to be deficient in this mineral. It is the rare aviculturist that feeds his charges oysters, herring, or pumpkin seeds, probably the three richest sources of zinc. Much of the zinc in cereal grains will be rendered unavailable by the phytates contained in these foods. This leaves sunflower seeds, eggs, and nuts as the only likely sources of zinc in any quantity in most cage bird diets. The result is every likelihood of a deficiency and resulting breeding failure caused by the concentrated needs for zinc in normal sexual functioning. In any suspected mineral deficiency, zinc is the first mineral that should be supplemented in the dietary intake, since it will be the most likely to be deficient.

OTHER MINERALS FOUND CONSISTENTLY
IN THE BODY

BARIUM

Barium is abundant in the earth, and the human body contains .3 parts per million of this element. Barium occurs in sea water at the rate of about six parts per billion. About 93% of the barium in the human body is found in the bones with the remainder distributed throughout the body. Barium is detectable in the body tissues of all newborn infants. Brazil nuts are very rich in barium, and there is apparently no toxicity at any normal level of intake.

Though evidence exists of a possible body requirement for barium, there is no conclusive evidence as yet that it performs any essential biological function in birds or other living things.

BORON

Boron occurs in sea water at the relatively huge rate of 4,600 parts per billion. Many soils are deficient in it, particularly along the Atlantic Coastal Plain, in Wisconsin, and in the northwestern Pacific Coast States. Boron occurs in air pollution as the result of coal burning.

Research many years ago proved boron to be an essential trace mineral for plants. Many specific deficiency symptoms have been noted and verified in a variety of crops. However, no research has proven yet that boron is essential for either birds or animals. This may be because boron seems to be required only for flavonoid synthesis. These compounds are found only in the higher plants. Nevertheless, boron is found throughout the bodies of birds and animals, and it is stored primarily in the bones. It is almost completely absorbed from the food and is excreted in the urine. Boron is toxic to mice and rats at the rate of ten parts per million in continuous dosage.

Eggs contain consistent traces of boron, at the rate of about 40 micrograms for one chicken egg. This is an indication that in the future boron may be proven necessary to the development of embryonic birds.

Until such time as boron is definitely found to be essential in animal and bird nutrition, no concern or supplementation seems warranted. Any plant material will have much higher concentrations of boron than animal products, should any breeder be interested in assuring a supply in the event of possible need. The trace amounts that might possibly be necessary should be found in a varied diet of seed, greens, fruits, and other foods that the average aviculturist supplies.

BROMINE

Bromine seems at this point a likely element to be proven essential in trace amounts at some time in the future. Experiments with chicks have shown that bromine can substitute for part of their chloride requirement. The addition of trace amounts of bromine to purified diets for chicks results in a small, but significant, increase in growth. All animal tissues except thyroid contain from 50 to 100 times more bromine than iodine. Those proportions are reversed in the thyroid tissue. There is no large accumulation of bromine in any part of the body.

Bromine occurs in sea water at the substantial rate of about 65 parts per million. Whereas the body content of primitive peoples is only one part per million, the body of modern man contains about 2.9 parts per million. An increase in the dietary intake of bromine will result in an increase in tissue levels of this mineral. Any excess in the body is filtered out by the kidneys and excreted in the urine.

CADMIUM

Cadmium is a serious pollutant in modern life and is extremely toxic in excess amounts. However, research has shown indications that cadmium may be essential in trace amounts. I stress that no need for this element has yet been proven, but that possibility does exist. Cadmium occurs in sea water at the rate of about .03 parts per billion. Most intake comes from the food supply, but sizable amounts enter the human body from smoking. Fortunately, cadmium is poorly absorbed, with only 3% to 8% of the ingested amount entering the bloodstream. Excretion of excesses is very slow. Oysters are a very rich source of cadmium with a content of three to four parts per million.

Cadmium toxicity has been reported many times. The toxic effect of an excess will affect all parts of the body and will cause reproductive failure. Part of its toxicity is caused by antagonism to copper, iron, and zinc. At the current state of our nutritional knowledge, cadmium is not considered a necessary trace mineral in the nutrition of cage birds.

RUBIDIUM

Though there is currently no information that proves rubidium to be necessary to biological functioning, there

are some indications that it might one day be classified as
an essential trace mineral. Rubidum is closely related to
potassium, and it is found in living tissue in higher concentrations than in the environment. Rubidium is abundant in the earth with sea water containing about 120
parts per billion. The human body contains about 4.6 parts
per million. Meats are high in rubidium content, as are
soybeans. Grains, fruits, and vegetables also have appreciable amounts.

All plant and animal cells freely allow the passage of
rubidium through the cell membranes. Also, rubidium can
replace potassium as a nutrient for the growth of yeast.
The body does not accumulate rubidium in any particular
organ or tissue, and no cases of rubidium poisoning are
known. As much as 200 parts per million of rubidium in
the diet are not toxic, but a quantity of 1,000 parts per
million causes a decrease in growth, reproduction, and
lifespan. There is no confirmed information on any dietary
requirement for rubidium in finches or other cage birds.

STRONTIUM

Strontium has received a very bad press over the years
because of its wayward isotope, strontium-90. This
element is not always such a villain, however. Strontium
is common in sea water at the rate of about 8 parts per
million. The human body contains over four parts per
million of strontium, and there is strong evidence that it
is required by the body in trace amounts. Since this evidence is not yet conclusive, strontium has not yet been
classified as an essential trace element. It seems likely that
its designation as essential will occur in time with further
research. Plant sources are generally richer in strontium
than animal sources, except for bone.

There is no evidence of strontium accumulation in any particular tissue other than bone, and strontium does seem to have an affinity for the bone tissue. Absorption of strontium ranges from 5% to 25% of the dietary content. Absorption is reduced with age. The amount of calcium in the body strongly influences the effects of strontium. The less calcium is present, the more toxic will be the strontium. Any excess of strontium will cause incoordination, weakness, posterior paralysis and bone deformation. I have encountered no information with relation to strontium in cage bird nutrition.

OTHER MINERALS

A fairly large number of elements occur in trace amounts in all human tissues. No biological function is known nor suspected for any of them in either humans or birds. The fact that they occur consistently in the body, however, means that there is the possibility they may one day be proven essential in trace amounts. Of this list, lead in particular is a highly toxic pollutant. It would be a great surprise to discover that lead is necessary for nutrition, even in trace amounts. These are the elements found in the body consistently:

Aluminum	Germanium	Radium
Antimony	Gold	Silver
Bismuth	Lead	Titanium
Cesium	Lithium	Uranium
Gallium	Niobium	Zirconium

Of the minerals in this list, germanium is the one most likely to eventually be classified as essential, since it has the chemical structure necessary for such functioning.

TISSUE SALTS

In any extensive nutritional research, sooner or later you will encounter the tissue salts. These are also called cell salts or biochemic tissue salts. A virtual cult has been built up around the use and curative powers of these twelve mineral salts. Yet, if you have learned anything from the previous sections on vitamins and minerals, you now know that there is no such thing as a panacea in nutrition. The bodies of birds and animals are simply too complex in their structure and nutritional needs to permit us to believe that these twelve salts are a cure-all. Without the vitamins and trace minerals, nutrition is not complete, and death will result from malnutrition. Though all of these salts are found in the living body, nothing in my research has yet indicated that the body's cells do not synthesize all of these in adequate quantity, with the exception of sodium chloride, if provided with the necessary raw materials. The twelve tissue salts and their reported functions are listed below. Only sodium chloride, common salt, is dealt with in detail in the sections on sodium, potassium, and chlorine.

Calcium fluoride   — gives elasticity to body tissues
Calcium phosphate   — promotes health and nutrition of cells
Calcium sulfate   — serves as the blood purifier
Iron phosphate   — serves as the oxygen carrier
Magnesium phosphate —   acts as anti-spasmodic and supplements potassium phosphate
Potassium chloride   — cures sluggish conditions
Potassium phosphate   — serves as a nerve nutrient
Potassium sulfate   — acts with iron phosphate as an oxygen carrier

Sodium chloride   — serves as the body's water dis-
                            tributor
Sodium phosphate   — acts as an acid neutralizer
Sodium sulfate   — maintains proper density of
                            intercellular fluids
Silicic Oxide   — acts as a cleanser and eliminator

There may be more value in this knowledge than meets the eye or the mind at this point, however. You may have noted in the sections on minerals that every element that is a part of this list is also involved in a proven biological transmutation. As I mentioned in the foreword, our current knowledge of nutrition is very limited, and it is advantageous to keep a completely open mind regarding any items that may be of value in biological functioning.

CHAPTER 13

CONCLUDING COMMENTS

Anyone who has waded through the nutritional quagmire up to this point deserves a word of commendation. Yet, with all that has been outlined already, there are still a number of loose ends that need to be covered. Some of these should serve to open the mind and feed the imagination. Much remains to be discovered in nutrition, and not all that remains is in the realm of the five physical senses. This chapter will present a number of interesting developments that have a bearing on nutrition. A number of the items presented here are from my general knowledge and are not traceable to the books listed in the bibliography.

Much of our knowledge of nutrition is a by-product of the nuclear age. By tagging the nutrients with a radioactive element, researchers can trace them through digestion, absorption, circulation, and eventual utilization. This tool of research has been of inestimable value in piecing together the nutritional puzzle. Both fortunately for research and unfortunately for long term health, the body does not seem to discriminate between a natural isotope and a radioactive isotope. For this reason, radioactive isotopes are ideally suited to the task of following nutrients to their eventual utilization point within the body.

Still within the field of radioactivity, we are well aware of the damage that the emissions of radioactive substances can do to living bodies. The study of biochemical individuality shows that individuals within a species show a wide variance in their ability to withstand radioactive bombardment without significant physical damage or illness. This dosage has been measured in roentgens, and a dose of 500 roentgens in the older radioactivity measurement is generally considered to be fatal for humans. However, in 1958 a species of happy, proliferating bacteria was discovered within the water of a nuclear reactor at Los Alamos. It lived and reproduced every twenty minutes in an environment that was thought to be instantly deadly to any living species. These bacteria of the pseudomonas family were tested extensively and found able to tolerate for eight hours a dose of 20,000,000 roentgens. That is twenty million roentgens, when 500 roentgens is deadly to a human. What more can I say except hooray for the tenacity of life?

As you read further into the known information on nutrition, you will encounter the research terms "in vivo" and "in vitro" in your reading. These terms describe the conditions under which an experiment was conducted. An experiment in vivo was conducted within a living body, on a living bird or animal. An experiment in vitro was conducted in an artificial environment, such as in a test tube or other laboratory apparatus.

Many avicultural works warn of the danger of genetic faults in a strain of birds and the danger of perpetuating such faults by injudicious inbreeding. I have called this into question before, and though there be no doubt that something is being reinforced, it does not always seem to be a genetic fault for physical deformity. Rather, the problem seems frequently to lie with the reinforcement of high genetic requirements for particular nutrients, the lack of which is bound to result in the physical deformity symptoms of deficiency. Though physical defects may well be a result of inheritance, never discount the possibility of deficiency symptoms caused by a high nutrient requirement.

The enrichment of refined foods has become common practice in the United States. This undoubtedly helps in providing the minimum nutrients necessary for health, but it certainly does not replace all that are lost in processing. Enrichment does not even replace one-quarter of what has been lost. Too many have looked upon the enrichment of refined foods as a panacea. It is not. If anything, this process has lulled everyone into a false sense of security while nutritional disaster overwhelms us. Review the introduction to vitamins for a recap of the vitamin losses from processing. The mineral losses are as bad or worse, and are covered in the sections on minerals.

If the diet for either birds or people contains a large amount of processed or cooked foods, supplementation with vitamins and minerals that are in short supply is the only way to assure freedom from deficiency symptoms. There are a variety of vitamin-mineral supplements on the market, but I do not recommend mixing them with either seed or water for reasons listed in the introduction to vitamins. A full range supplement can be a great convenience and reassuring comfort to the aviculturist trying to make sure that the birds are getting all of the nutrients necessary. Supplements are not a substitute for good, basic feeding, however. Nothing will replace nature's perfect balances as found in seeds, fruits, nuts, insects, and fresh greens.

Though it should be obvious, I must forcefully point out that any cooked food is a dead food. The living fruits, vegetables, and nuts are totally killed by cooking, down to the last cell. Most people never stop to think that what they eat is dead matter, if it has been cooked in any way. If this is not in the mind for human nutrition, it certainly will not be in the mind where the nutrition of cage birds is concerned. No other creature cooks food before eating it, and few bother to kill their food first. If the total organism, such as an insect, is killed, the cells making up that organism still live for a considerable time.

The fact that astounds most observers is that an invisible part of the total organism remains alive and well even after the physical part is completely removed. This used to be an esoteric teaching exclusively, but now it is physically proven every day through the new development called Kirlian photography. Actually, this process is not that new, since the technique dates back to the 1880's and the early days of photography. But it was the dedicated work of Semyon D. and Valentina Kh. Kirlian of Alma-Ata, Kazakstan, that will be remembered as long as scientific study exists. Their perfection of this process of photography earned them the highest honor mankind can bestow — the process was named after them and today is known throughout the world as Kirlian photography.

The exact force that this process is photographing is still in doubt, but the technique is solid and the results are inspiring. When a portion of a leaf is removed and the electrophotograph still shows the forces emanating from the missing area as well as from the intact leaf, the ramifications are interesting, to say the least. As mentioned in the foreword, only the Rosicrucian philosophy, as outlined in the Rosicrucian Cosmo-Conception by Max Heindel has explained such phenomena to my satisfaction.

The point to be made is that cooking will completely destroy these unidentified life forces. What role they may play in the nutrition and the maintenance of life in both birds and humans is completely unknown at this time. Nevertheless, I can safely assume that such strong life emanations cannot be without effect on the receiving body when eaten. I anxiously await further information and developments in this field.

A basic law of nature is that perfect nutrition means perfect health and total immunity from all disease. Very gradually, the realization is growing that germs are only part of the problem of disease. There is no way any microbe can get a foothold in the body if nutrition and health are in top shape. This might be called the toxemia theory, for it holds that germs can cause disease only where toxic waste products accumulate for them to live on. The accumulation of toxic wastes implies a state of less than perfect health. Experiments with human volunteers have proven that the healthy body is completely unaffected by the injection of living cancer cells. The cancer cells are almost instantly overwhelmed by the body's normal defenses. The same will apply to all other foreign life entering the body.

The human body contains a hidden electrical system. Ages ago, the Chinese tapped this system and designed a science called acupuncture to use it to medical advantage. A German doctor has now used this system as a basis and devised an electronic machine that can monitor these micro-volts of power coursing through the body. The reading produced by this new electronic device will pinpoint the location of body dysfunction, and when mated to a properly programmed computer, it will dictate the exact cure. This is similar in principle to the automotive diagnostic machines used in most large garages in this country. However, only a handful of medical doctors are yet using it. Presumably, of course, the same sort of system exists in the avian body.

If you are an average or skeptical reader, by now

you're ready to exhibit your disbelief of this new invention in the strongest of terms. Only the few will be open-minded and inquisitive enough to accept the possibility of such a diagnostic revolution. Such is human nature. However, it appears now that this will be the wave of the future, much as the first orbited satellite was the wave of the future. This system of diagnosis is used at the Nevada Clinic of Preventive Medicine, 6105 W. Tropicana Avenue, Las Vegas, Nevada. Perhaps one day in the future the office of every medical doctor will be equipped with this new blessing of technology. Only time will tell.

An interesting controversy has been in evidence in the avicultural field for some years. This concerns the use of sunflower seed in the avian diet. Opponents of its use claim a narcotic effect resulting from the content of a substance called papaverine in the sunflower seed. Papaverine is defined as a non-addictive antispasmodic and nerve relaxant. It is a salt of a lesser alkaloid of opium. Opium has among its contents one percent papaverine. At this point, it is still doubtful whether it is papaverine that actually exists in sunflower seeds, or just a similar compound. Personally, I do not feel that this substance, even if it exists in sunflower seeds, is a problem in avian nutrition. The outstanding nutritional value of sunflower seeds far outweighs any slight disadvantage that such a substance might cause.

Another field that has great promise for the future is that of biological transmutation. Through several years of study and observation of nutrition, I have become firmly convinced of the solid foundation upon which this knowledge rests. The impossible contradictions that fill standard nutritional texts where minerals are concerned are fully cleared up by the information on biological transmutation. Obviously, such a radically different view of life and science will require many more years to be fully accepted.

But the precedent is already established. Naturally radio-active minerals are continuously and naturally transmuted, as radium into lead, for example. Living organisms routinely combine nitrogen with oxygen at room temperature, while the same process in a laboratory takes electric arc temperature or a very high temperature and pressure to accomplish the same end. The discoveries of Louis Pasteur required many years for full acceptance, and the work of Louis C. Kervran will take no less time. Nevertheless, I feel certain that the future will regard Kervran in the same manner that we now regard Newton, Mendeleev, and Pasteur. When confronted with this possibility, Kervran stated, "I simply point out what has always existed." How true, and what more has any other scientist in history ever done?

In natural environments, birds and animals have a number of protections against any nutritional deficiency. The sheer variety of their natural diets is the most basic of these protections. In addition, the birds can transmute a number of elements within their own bodies. The mechanism of craving is yet another means for assuring an ample supply of nutritional substances. The body instinctively craves certain foods that are rich in the nutrients needed. This replenishes the supply of any nutrient that is approaching a deficiency state. In addition, to assure species survival, biochemical individuality is the emergency mechanism.

Finches and other small birds with their high rate of metabolism will show symptoms of any deficiency far faster than human beings. A severe deficiency of any nutrient will cause physical symptoms in a small bird within days or weeks, at most. In humans this same deficiency may take months or years to manifest itself as definite, physical symptoms. For this reason alone, all aviculturists must pay close attention to the birds in their care and to the nutritional content of their diets.

When maintaining and breeding any finches or other birds in captivity, two factors are vital. These are nutrition and environment. The most ideal plan for achieving perfection in both areas is worthless if the materials used are poor. The best materials available are useless without a good plan for their logical, efficient use. Success with birds involves a sincere desire and a plan. The last item required is knowledge, and I hope that this book has given you a part of that knowledge.

GLOSSARY

Abdominal — Concerning that portion of the body between the ribs and pelvis which contains the intestines.

Absorption — The process of absorbing or soaking up a substance.

Acetylcholine — A white, alkaloid, crystalline compound necessary for the transmission of nerve impulses from one nerve fiber to the next.

Acid — A compound capable of acting with a base to form a salt.

Actinomycetes — A family of microorganisms resembling both bacteria and fungi.

Adenosine triphosphate — A high energy compound that serves to soak up excess heat energy from glucose and fat breakdown and stores this energy.

Adipose tissues — The body cell groups that contain the stored cellular fat.

Adrenal glands — A pair of small glands, one located above each kidney.

Adrenalin — A hormone secretion of the adrenal glands, also called epinephrine. It stimulates rapid breakdown of glycogen in the liver.

Alanine — One of the non-essential amino acids, a part of the pantothenic acid molecule.

Albinism — The total absence of normal color in any bird or animal.

Albumin — Any of a group of water soluble proteins found in many animal and plant sources.

Alcohol — Any of a large group of compounds which contains a hydroxyl group.

Aldehyde oxidase — An enzyme which contains molybdenum and is an essential catalyst for the oxidation of a number of substances in the body.

Aldosterone — A hormone secreted by the adrenal glands which controls the regulation of sodium in the blood.

Algae — Primitive, one-celled or multi-celled plants that lack true roots, stems, and leaves, but usually contain chlorophyll.

Alkali — A substance which is basic as opposed to acidic.

Alkaloid — An organic basic substance derived from plants, such as nicotine, quinine, atropine, and morphine.

All-rac-alpha-tocopherol — A new designation for dl-alpha-tocopherol, the synthetic form of vitamin E.

Alpha tocopherol — The chemical name for vitamin E which has been used to designate both the natural and synthetic forms.

Aluminum — A metallic element, atomic number 13, symbol Al, found consistently in body tissues, but with no known nor suspected nutritional function.

Amines — Nitrogen containing substances.

Amino acid — Any organic compound containing both an amino group and a carboxylic acid group.

Amino group — A compound of hydrogen and nitrogen that is a characteristic component of amino acids.

Amygdalin — A substance that is claimed to be a vitamin, alternately called vitamin B-17 or Laetrile.

Anemia — Any disease characterized by a deficiency of the oxygen-carrying material of the blood.

Aneurin — An old name for thiamin, vitamin B-1.

Angina pectoris — The severe chest pain caused by insufficient blood supply and characterized by feelings of apprehension and suffocation.

Animal starch — Another name for glycogen, the storage form of carbohydrate within the body.

Anions — Negatively charged ions.

Anorexia — Loss of appetite.

Antagonist — In nutrition, any substance that competes with a necessary nutrient for the same space.

Antibodies — Any proteins in the blood that are formed in reaction to foreign proteins, neutralize them, and by this action produce immunity against foreign microbes or their poisons.

Antihistamine — A substance that is used to reduce the effects on the body associated with histamine production.

Antimony — A metallic element, atomic number 51, symbol Sb, found consistently in the body with no known nor suspected biological function.

Antioxidant — Any chemical compound that prevents the combination of oxygen with a third substance.

Antirachitic factor — An outdated designation for vitamin D.

Antispasmodic — A substance which will ease or prevent a muscle spasm.

Aorta — The main artery leading from the heart.

Arachidonic acid — A polyunsaturated essential fatty acid with 20 carbon atoms in its chain.

Arginine — An essential amino acid.

Ariboflavinosis — A deficiency of riboflavin in the body.

Arsenic — A non-metallic element, atomic number 33, symbol As, an essential trace element in nutrition.

Arsenic trioxide — A poisonous compound of arsenic and oxygen.

Artificial — Not natural, synthetic or man-made.

Arteriosclerosis — A chronic disease in which thickening and hardening of the arterial walls interferes with blood circulation.

Ascorbic acid — The chemical name for vitamin C.

Aspartic acid — One of the non-essential amino acids.

Ataxia — loss of muscular coordination.

Atherosclerosis — The deposit of lipid-containing materials, usually on the walls of the arteries.

Atom — The smallest unit of an element, consisting of a nucleus of protons and neutrons, surrounded by a system of electrons.

Atomic — Concerning the basic, elemental structure of any substance and its component atoms.

Atrophy — The wasting away of the body or its tissues and organs.

Aureomycin — A trademark for chlortetracycline, an antibiotic.

Aviculture — The science, hobby, and profession of maintaining and raising birds in captivity.

Aviculturist — A person who maintains and raises birds.

Avidin — A protein substance found in raw egg white which binds biotin and makes it nutritionally unavailable. Avidin is inactivated by the heat of cooking.

Bacteria — Any one of the one-celled organisms living either free or as parasites, found everywhere in nature.

Barium — A metallic element, atomic number 56, symbol Ba, found consistently in the body, but not known nor suspected to be essential in nutrition.

Base — Any compound that is alkaline in nature as opposed to acidic.

Benzoic acid — An acid compound which the body cannot metabolize.

Beriberi — A severe deficiency disease caused by thiamin deficiency.

Beryllium — A metallic element, atomic number 4, symbol Be, with no known nor suspected nutritional function, but which will replace magnesium in its biological functions.

Beryllium Phosphate — An unabsorbable compound of beryllium and phosphorus.

Betaine — A compound formed by the oxidation of choline in the body, which acts as a methyl donor.

Beta-lipoic acid — a water soluble form of lipoic acid.

Bicarbonate — An anion group containing hydrogen, carbon and oxygen.

Bile — An alkaline liquid secreted by the liver, held in the gallbladder, and discharged into the intestine to aid in digestion.

Biochemic tissue salts — Twelve chemical compounds required for the proper functioning of the body, also called cell salts.

Biochemical individuality — The basic biological differences in nutrient requirement and body function among individuals within the same species.

Biochemistry — The study of the use and reactions of elements and compounds within the living body.

Bioflavonoid — A member of a group of biologically active substances found in plants, including hesperidin and rutin.

Biological — Concerning living things.

Biological transmutation — The ability of living things to change one basic element into another through internal, biochemical processes.

Biosynthesis — The production of complex compounds from more simple ones within the living body.

Biotin — One of the B complex vitamins.

Bismuth — A metallic element, atomic number 83, symbol Bi, found consistently in the body, but not suspected of any nutritional function.

Black tongue disease — The acute niacin deficiency disease in dogs, called pellagra in humans.

Boron — A non-metallic element, atomic number 5, symbol B, vital in the nutrition of plants, but with no known necessity in the nutrition of birds, animals, or humans.

Bromine — A non-metallic element, atomic number 35, symbol Br, found consistently in the living body, but not yet proven to be essential in nutrition.

Budgerigar — The formal and Australian name for the common grass parakeet.

Bulk elements — Those mineral nutrients needed in fairly large amounts daily, usually over one gram in humans.

Bulk minerals — Those mineral nutrients needed by the body usually in amounts of over one gram daily.

Butyric acid — A short-chain fatty acid with only four carbon atoms. It occurs in the butterfat of milk.

Cadmium — a toxic, heavy metallic element, atomic number 48, symbol Cd, poisonous in any quantity, but suspected of essential functions in trace amounts.

Calcification — Hardening of tissues by the deposition of calcium salts.

Calcium — A metallic element, atomic number 20, symbol Ca, an essential bulk element in nutrition.

Calcium bicarbonate — A white calcium, carbon, and oxygen compound that forms parts of bones, teeth, and shells. It is usually called calcium carbonate.

Calcium fluoride — One of the twelve tissue salts. One of the primary forms in which fluorine occurs in the body.

Calcium orotate — The supplement form of orotic acid.

Calcium oxalate — The insoluble combination of calcium and oxalic acid.

Calcium pantothenate — The calcium salt of pantothenic acid, still with biological activity as a vitamin.

Calcium phosphate — One of the twelve tissue salts. It accounts for up to 90% of the body's phosphorus content.

Calcium sulfate — One of the twelve tissue salts.

Calorie — The amount of heat needed to raise the temperature of one kilogram of water by one degree Centigrade at one atmosphere of pressure.

Canary seed — The seed of a grass native to Europe, Phalaris canariensis, widely used as a food for seed-eating birds.

Cannibalism — The act of feeding upon others of the same species.

Carbohydrate — A large group of carbon, hydrogen, and oxygen compounds used by the body for energy, including all sugars and starches.

Carbon — A non-metallic element, atomic number 6, symbol C, a basic component of all proteins, fats, and carbohydrates.

Carbon dioxide — A gaseous carbon and oxygen compound that is the waste product of complete combustion, along with water.

Carbon monoxide — A gaseous carbon and oxygen compound that is absorbed in the bloodstream much faster than oxygen and is fatal in excess.

Carbonate — A salt or ester of carbonic acid.

Carbonic acid — A weak, unstable acid that forms from carbon dioxide and water.

Carbonic anhydrase — a zinc-containing enzyme necessary for carbonic acid breakdown.

Carboxyl group — A carbon, hydrogen, and oxygen compound present in all organic acids.

Cardiac muscle — The muscles of the heart.

Carotene — A term used to designate the precursors of vitamin A.

Carotenoids — Vitamin A precursors found in plant sources, usually as yellow or orange pigments.

Carrion — Dead or decaying flesh.

Casein — A white, tasteless protein found in milk.

Catalyst — A compound which increases the rate of a chemical reaction or causes a reaction by its presence, but is not changed by this function.

Cataract — Opacity of the lens of the eye, causing partial or total blindness.

Cations — Positively charged ions.

Cell — The smallest structural unit of an organism that is able to function independently.

Cell salts — A group of twelve chemical compounds deemed vital to proper body functioning, also called tissue salts.

Cellulase — An enzyme which breaks down cellulose in the digestive system.

Cellulose — A carbohydrate compound which is the main constituent of all plant tissues and fibers.

Centigrade — Also referred to as Celsius, a temperature scale with the freezing point of water at a standard atmospheric pressure taking place at $0°$, and its boiling point at $100°$.

Cerebellum — The portion of the brain responsible for the regulation and coordination of voluntary muscular movement.

Cerebrum — The large, rounded portion of the brain taking up most of the cranial cavity.

Ceruloplasmin — A protein which contains copper and stores copper in the blood.

Cesium — A metallic element, atomic number 55, symbol Cs, found consistently in body tissues, but with no known nor suspected biological functions.

Chelate — To form a compound by joining an active substance to a metal ion, or the compound so formed.

Chelator — Any substance that attaches itself to a mineral to transport it in the body, also called a ligand.

Chemical energy — The energy stored in molecules of food.

Chemistry — The science which studies the structure, composition, properties, and reactions of matter, usually in its atomic or molecular forms.

Chitin — A semi-transparent, horny compound which forms the biggest part of crustacean shells and insect exoskeletons.

Chloride — A nutritionally essential anion of chlorine.

Chlorine — A non-metallic element, atomic number 17, symbol Cl, a vital bulk element in nutrition.

Chlorophyll — Any of a group of related green pigments containing carbon, hydrogen, oxygen, nitrogen, and magnesium, used by plants for photosynthesis.

Chlorosis — Bleaching, as of the leaves of plants deficient in manganese.

Cholecalciferol — vitamin D-3, found only in animal sources.

Cholesterol — A glistening white, soapy substance which acts as a precursor of vitamin D and is a constituent of all body tissues.

Choline — A compound generally considered as a member of the B vitamin complex, but required in such large amounts that it is often called a basic nutrient rather than a vitamin.

Chondrodystrophy — A deficiency disease resulting in a deformed embryo within the egg, caused by manganese deficiency.

Chromic acid — a corrosive, oxidizing acid which contains hydrogen, oxygen, and chromium.

Chromium — A metallic element, atomic number 24, symbol Cr, a vital trace element in nutrition.

Chromosomes — The DNA-containing portion of the cell nuclei in plants and animals, responsible for the determination and transmission of hereditary characteristics.

Cilia — Microscopic, hairlike growth extending from a cell's surface and often capable of rhythmic motion.

Cirrhosis — A chronic liver disease characterized by progressive destruction and regeneration of liver cells with an increase of connective tissue that eventually causes liver failure and death.

Cirruline — One of the non-essential amino acids.

Citrovorum factor — An alternate name for folinic acid, the biologically active form of folacin.

Clupanodonic acid — A non-essential, polyunsaturated fatty acid with 22 carbon atoms in its chain.

Coagulation — The change from a liquid into a soft, semi-solid or solid mass.

Cobalamin — An alternate name for vitamin B-12.

Cobalt — A transitional, metallic element, atomic number 27, symbol Co, a vital trace element as the base of the cobalamin molecule.

Cobalt chloride — A compound used therapeutically to stimulate red blood cell production. It is toxic in any quantity.

Coenzyme — An organic molecule that must be loosely associated with an enzyme for the enzyme to perform its function.

Coenzyme A — A substance containing pantothenic acid and several other compounds, the form in which pantothenic acid is used in most biological reactions.

Coenzyme Q — A compound synthesized in the body which is an essential link in the chain of events which releases energy from energy-yielding nutrients; also called ubiquinone.

Collagen — The fibrous material making up parts of bone, cartilage, and connective tissue.

Colostrum — The first milk produced after the birth of offspring, differing substantially in nutritional composition from later milk.

Comb — A fleshy, usually colorful crest or ridge growing on the top of the head, most prominently in the male.

Complete protein — A protein complex which contains all of the essential amino acids in adequate quantities.

Compound Lipid — A fat with a glycerol base, two fatty acids, and the third available position filled with another chemical group.

Congenital — Existing at birth, but not hereditary.

Constipation — Inability to expel waste products from the intestines.

Contaminant — A substance which makes another substance impure or corrupt, or anything what don't belong to be there.

Convulsive seizures — Intense involuntary muscular contractions caused by a variety of nutritional deficiencies and other factors.

Copper — A transitional metallic element, atomic number 29, symbol Cu, a vital trace element in nutrition.

Copper sulfide — A relatively insoluble compound of sulfur and copper.

Coprophagy — The eating of excreted waste material. In birds, the consumption of droppings.

Cornea — The transparent covering of the pupil and lens of the eye.

Craving — A longing or desire for a particular food item.

"Crazy chick disease" — A vitamin E deficiency disease in chicks, also called encephalomalacia.

Cretinism — An iodine deficiency syndrome with arrested physical and mental development and complete idiocy.

Crop — The widened area of the esophagus in birds which serves as a storage area for food, technically called the diverticulum.

Crude protein — All of the protein content of a substance, whether or not it is digestible.

Crystalline — Constructed of identically made up molecules repeated in a pattern.

Cyanide — A group of poisonous compounds which contain a cyanide group, consisting of carbon and nitrogen.

Cyanide group — A compound of carbon and nitrogen which is highly poisonous when combined with sodium or potassium.

Cyanocobalamin — A form of vitamin B-12 with an attached cyanide group.

Cysteine — One of the non-essential amino acids.

Cystine — One of the non-essential amino acids.

d-Alpha-tocopherol — The scientific name for vitamin E.

Death — The transfer of the higher spiritual forms from the physical body to the spiritual realms, with a resulting breakdown of the physical body into its component elements.

Decalcification — The removal of calcium and phosphorus from the bones.

Deficiency — An inadequate supply of a nutrient when referring to nutrition.

Deficient — Having an inadequate supply.

Degeneration — The deterioration of cells or tissues, causing a loss of the function of those tissues.

Dehydration — The loss of water from the tissues.

Dementia — Depression and mental imbalance, possibly caused by niacin deficiency.

Deoxyribonucleic acid — A long, spiral-appearing molecule that is the storage point for hereditary characteristics within the cell and its chromosomes.

Depigmentation — The loss of color.

Dermatitis — Inflammation of the skin.

Diabetes — One of a number of diseases characterized by an excessive discharge of urine and persistent thirst.

Diarrhea — In birds, the constant evacuation of very watery droppings.

Diffusion — The gradual scattering and mixing of one type of substance into another.

Digestion — The process of food breakdown in preparation for absorption which occurs in the crop, stomach, gizzard, and intestines of birds.

Diglyceride — A glycerol molecule with two fatty acids attached.

Disaccharide — A compound sugar consisting of two simple monosaccharide molecules.

Disease — Any condition of abnormality in the health of an organism brought on by malnutrition or invading microorganisms.

Diverticulum — Scientific name for the bird's crop.

dl-Alpha-tocopherol — Synthetic vitamin E.

DNA — deoxyribonucleic acid.

Double bond linkage — An open bond on two adjacent atoms that can be filled by other atoms, usually applied in nutrition to mean the open bonds on two adjacent carbon atoms, as in unsaturated fatty acids.

Duodenum — The first section of the small intestine.

Edema — Accumulation of fluids in the body tissues.

Eggbinding — A condition in which the hen cannot expel the egg from the oviduct and will die from the attempt, caused by nutritional deficiency.

Elastin — A connective tissue in the body found in blood vessel walls.

Electrolytes — The salts which in solution separate into their component electrically charged ions.

Electron shell — One of the paths around an atomic nucleus on which the negatively charged electron particles travel.

Electrophotograph — A photograph taken using Kirlian

photography to record the emanations of life forms that are invisible to normal human vision.

Element — A fundamental substance composed of atoms all having the same number of protons.

Emaciation — Thinness, leaness, and wasting away.

Embryo — An organism in its early stages of development, still within the seed, egg, or womb.

Encephalomalacia — A deficiency disease in chickens caused by vitamin E deficiency.

Enrichment — The addition of vital nutrients to food products that have lost them in the refining process.

Enzyme — A protein substance which functions as a biochemical catalyst in living organisms.

Epinephrine — A hormone secretion of the adrenal glands, also called adrenalin, which stimulates rapid breakdown of glycogen in the liver.

Epithelial cell — A cell on the surface.

Equisetum — Botanical name for horsetail, a common plant of the forest floor.

Ergocalciferol — vitamin D-2, found in plant sources.

Ergosterol — A provitamin used to form vitamin D-2, ergocalciferol, through irradiation.

Esophagus — The tube for passage of food from the mouth to the stomach.

Esoteric — Referring to a study that is not publicly known and is intended for and understood by only a small group.

Essential amino acid — An amino acid that cannot be synthesized by the body cells and must come from the diet.

Essential fatty acids — The fatty acids that cannot be synthesized by the body cells and must be taken in by way of the diet.

Ester — The combination of an alcohol and an acid.

Estrogen — A group of several female hormones produced mainly in the ovaries.

Extracellular — Outside of the cells.

Exudative diathesis — A deficiency disease in chickens

especially, caused by vitamin E and selenium deficiency. Selenium supplementation alone will cure this disease.

Factor R — An outdated designation for folacin.

Factor U — An outdated designation for folacin.

Fahrenheit — A temperature scale registering the freezing point of water at 32° and the boiling point at 212° under standard atmospheric pressure.

Fast — A period during which an organism ceases to eat any food.

Fat — Any glyceride ester of a fatty acid, including all animal or vegetable fats and oils.

Fat soluble vitamins — The vitamins which are not soluble in water — A, D, E, K, and F, which is also called the essential fatty acids.

Fatty acids — A large group of chemical compounds characterized by a chain of carbon atoms with a methyl group at one end and an acid or carboxyl group at the other end.

Fatty degeneration — The accumulation of excess deposits of fat in the liver or other organs which interferes with their functions.·

Ferritin — A brown protein which stores iron in the liver.

Ferrous sulfate — An iron salt which can be toxic and fatal in overdose.

Fertility — The capability of reproducing.

Flavonoid — Referring to any of a group of compounds found in the higher plants, many of them occurring as yellow pigments.

Flavoprotein — A compound of a protein and riboflavin found in the tissues.

Flax — Plants of the genus Linum that yield flaxeed, linseed oil, and linen fiber.

Fluorescent — Producing light by the emission of electromagnetic radiation.

Fluorescent bulb — A lamp that produces light by electromagnetic radiation which is stimulated by an electric current.

Fluorides — The compound forms in which fluorine occurs in the body.

Fluorine — A non-metallic element, atomic number 9, symbol F, an essential trace element in nutrition.

Folacin — A water soluble vitamin in the B complex.

Folates — A group of substances with folacin activity.

Folic acid — An alternate name for the vitamin folacin.

Folinic acid — Also called the citrovorum factor, it is the biologically active form of folacin.

Follicles — Groups of cells arranged in a circle, containing a cavity, such as that at the base of a feather or hair.

Fontanels — The soft spots in the skull of an infant.

Free radical — An atom or group of atoms having at least one unpaired electron.

Frijoles — The Spanish word for beans.

Fructose — A simple sugar or monosaccharide found primarily in fruits.

Fungus — Plural is fungi; any of the yeast-, mold-, smut-, or mushroom-type plants lacking chlorophyll.

Galactose — A simple sugar, or monosaccharide, found especially in the lactose of milk.

Gallinaceous — Any bird in the order Galliformes, including domestic fowl, pheasants, grouse, and quail, all having precocial young.

Gastrointestinal tract — The digestive tract, including the stomach and intestines.

Gelatin — A protein substance extracted from animal collagen by boiling it in water or acid.

Gene — A functioning hereditary unit that is located on a chromosome.

Germanium — A metallic element, atomic number 32, symbol Ge, found consistently in the body with no known nor suspected biological function.

Gizzard — The organ, especially in seed-eating birds, which grinds seeds together with grit to break down the seeds into digestible form.

Glucose — A monosaccharide, the most important sugar in nutrition.

Glucose Tolerance Factor — A compound with a chromium base which acts as a vitamin.

Glutamic acid — One of the non-essential amino acids.

Glutathione peroxidase — An enzyme containing selenium which destroys peroxides formed within the cells.

Glyceride — A lipid with a glycerol base and at least one fatty acid attached.

Glycerin — An alternate name for glycerol.

Glycerol — An alcohol which serves as the base for cell fats and oils.

Glycine — One of the non-essential amino acids.

Glycogen — The storage form of carbohydrate within the body.

Glycogen phosphorylase — A body enzyme that stores pyridoxine and aids the release of glycogen from the muscle tissues.

Goiter — The swelling in the throat produced by an expanding thyroid gland and caused by iodine deficiency.

Gold — A transitional metal, atomic number 79, symbol Au, found consistently in the body, with no known nor suspected biological function.

Gram — A unit of metric weight measurement, which is one one-thousandth of a kilogram or one thousand milligrams. There are 28.35 grams to the ounce.

Grit — Any small hard rock or shell ingested by seed-eating birds to assist the gizzard function in crushing and grinding of the food.

GTF — The Glucose Tolerance Factor.

Hatchability — The ability of an egg to reach full maturity of the embryo and hatch when placed in incubation.

Heme — The iron chelate portion of the hemoglobin molecule.

Hemoglobin — The iron-containing protein found in the red blood cells of the blood, giving the blood its characteristic color.

Hemorrhaging — Uncontrolled bleeding.

Hemosiderin — A brownish-yellow phosphate which stores iron in the body.

Hepatitis — A disease causing inflammation of the liver.

Heptoflavin — An outdated name for riboflavin.

Hereditary — Concerning the transferring of characteristics from parents to offspring.

Hesperidin — The most active of the bioflavonoids.

Histaminase — An enzyme in the digestive system which changes histidine into histamine.

Histamine — A compound formed from histidine, usually by bacterial or enzyme action.

Histidine — One of the essential amino acids.

Hocks — The main "knee" joints in the legs of birds.

Homeostatic Mechanisms — The body's methods of regulating the levels of minerals within the body.

Hormones — Secretions of one body gland or organ which are conveyed by the blood to stimulate another organ by means of their chemical activity.

Horsetail — A common forest plant, botanical name Equisetum, having a high content of organic silica.

Hydrochloric acid — A colorless, clear solution excreted by the stomach for the breakdown of proteins.

Hydrocortisone — A hormone secreted by the adrenal glands.

Hydrogen — A gaseous element, atomic number 1, symbol H, which is a basic component of all fats, proteins, and carbohydrates.

Hydrogenation — The act of combining with hydrogen.

Hydrogen sulfide — A foul-smelling, colorless gas formed by the combination of hydrogen and sulfur.

Hydrolize — To break down a chemical compound by reaction with water.

Hydrolysis — The breakdown of a chemical compound by reaction with water.

Hydrolytic rancidity — The action of microorganisms which causes fats to turn rancid. This does not interfere with their nutritional value.

Hydroxyglutamic acid — One of the non-essential amino acids.

Hyperglycemia — High blood sugar.

Hypervitaminosis A — A toxic excess of vitamin A.

Hypervitaminosis D — A toxic, excessive intake of vitamin D.

Hypoascorbemia — The inherited inability of an organism to manufacture its own ascorbic acid or vitamin C.

Hypoglycemia — Low blood sugar.

Hypothyroidism — Lowered activity of the thyroid gland.

Incandescent bulb — An electric light in which a filament is heated by the electric current to the point at which it gives off visible light.

Incomplete protein — A protein which lacks one or more of the essential amino acids in sufficient quantity.

Injection — The forcing of fluid into the skin, muscles, or blood by syringe or other similar means.

Inorganic — Consisting exclusively of mineral material, not composed of any organic matter.

Inositol — A vitamin in the B complex, sometimes considered as a nutrient rather than a vitamin, since it is required in such relatively large amounts.

Insulin — A hormone produced by the pancreas, which stimulates the entry of glucose into tissue cells.

International Units — A measurement of weight of vitamins A and D, with one unit equal to 0.3 micrograms of retinol, or .025 micrograms of vitamin D. One milligram contains 40,000 International Units.

Intestinal microbial synthesis — The manufacture of a substance by bacteria within the body's digestive tract.

Intestine — The portion of the digestive tract extending from the stomach to the anus.

Intrinsic factor — A secretion of the cells of the stomach wall which is necessary for intestinal absorption of cobalamin.

Invertase — An alternate name for sucrase.

In vitro — Refers to experimentation done in an artificial, test-tube environment.

In vivo — Refers to experimentation within the living body.

Iodide — A nutritionally essential anion, the form in which iodine usually occurs in foods.

Iodine — A non-metallic element, atomic number 53, symbol I, a vital trace element in nutrition.

Ion — An atom or group of atoms with a net electrical charge caused by the gain or loss of electrons.

Iris — The colored, muscular tissue surrounding the pupil of the eye, which controls the size of the pupil and the amount of light admitted.

Iron — A transitional metallic element, atomic number 26, symbol Fe, vital to nutrition in trace amounts.

Iron phosphate — One of the twelve tissue salts.

Irradiation — Exposure to bombardment by rays or particles.

Isoleucine — One of the essential amino acids.

Isotope — A form of a basic element which has a different amount of neutrons in the nucleus. Example — hydrogen has one proton and no neutrons; deuterium has one proton and one neutron; tritium has one proton and two neutrons. All have the physical characteristics of hydrogen.

IU — See International Units.

Kalium — The Latin word for potassium.

Keloids — Scar tissue which develops while an injury is healing.

Keratin — A strong, fibrous protein which forms hair, horns, hoofs, nails, scales, and feathers.

Ketones — Short-chain acids that are a by-product of incomplete fat oxidation.

Kidneys — A pair of organs located in back of the lower abdominal cavity, which maintain the body's water balance, regulate acid-base equilibrium, and excrete metabolic wastes as urine.

Kinetic energy — Active energy, as in the action of muscles.

Kirlian photography — A system of taking pictures under special conditions of electro-magnetic stimulation to show the life force emanations from any living thing.

Kwashiorkor — A severe malnutrition disease marked by anemia, edema, potbelly, depigmentation of the skin, and loss of hair or change in hair color.

Lactation — The formation and secretion of milk in humans and mammals.

Lactic acid — A compound formed in the muscles as a waste product of carbohydrate breakdown.

Lactoflavin — An original, now outdated, name for riboflavin, resulting from its isolation from milk.

Lactose — Milk sugar, a disaccharide composed of one glucose molecule and one galactose molecule.

Laetrile — The name for amygdalin in therapeutic doses, also called vitamin B-17.

Lauric acid — A non-essential saturated fatty acid with 12 carbon atoms in the chain.

Laxative — Any substance that stimulates the rapid movement of the food mass through the intestines.

Lead — A highly toxic metallic element, atomic number 82, symbol Pb, found consistently in body tissues, with no known nor suspected biological functions.

Lecithin — A compound lipid consisting of glycerol, two fatty acids, and choline linked with them through phosphoric acid.

Legumes — Any plant of the family Leguminosae, which bears pods of seeds, such as beans and peas.

Lens — The transparent organ of the eye behind the iris which focuses light rays entering through the pupil onto the retina.

Lesion — Any wound, injury, or sore.

Lesser mealworm — The larva of the beetle Alphitobius diaperinus, about one-half inch long when mature.

Leucine — An essential amino acid.

Ligand — A chelator.

Limiting amino acid — In an incomplete protein, the amino acid that is insufficient in supply and therefore makes that protein incomplete.

Linguistics — The study of the structure and theory of languages.

Linoleic acid — An essential polyunsaturated fatty acid with 18 carbon atoms in its chain.

Linolenic acid — An essential polyunsaturated fatty acid with 18 carbon atoms in its chain.

Lipochrome — An alternate, older name for carotenoid pigments.

Lipids — A term to indicate fats and oils as a unit.

Lipogenesis — The process by which the body makes fat from excess carbohydrates in the diet.

Lipoic acid — A vitamin of the B complex not yet proven essential for birds, animals, or humans, and possibly supplied by body synthesis.

Lipoprotein — The combination of a fat and a protein.

Lipositol — The phospholipid form of inositol in animal cells.

Lithium — A metallic element, atomic number 3, symbol Li, found consistently in body tissues with no known nor suspected biological function, other than in biological transmutations.

Liver — The largest gland in the body, which is the body's chemical factory. It performs a wide variety of chemical functions.

Lungs — The body organs that inhale air, extract oxygen from it, and exhale carbon dioxide gas and other waste products.

Lysine — One of the essential amino acids.

Macrocytic anemia — A deficiency disease caused by folacin deficiency.

Macro-minerals — Those mineral nutrients needed in large amounts; in the human body, those needed in amounts of over one gram daily.

Magnesium — A metallic element, atomic number 12, symbol Mg, an essential bulk element in nutrition.

Magnesium fluoride — A fluorine and magnesium compound, one of the primary compounds in which fluorine occurs in the body.

Magnesium phosphate — One of the twelve tissue salts.

Mal de la Rosa — The Spanish name for pellagra.

Maltase — An enzyme that catalyzes the splitting of maltose into two glucose molecules.

Maltose — A disaccharide composed of two joined molecules of glucose.

Mammary glands — The milk-producing glands in mammals.

Manganese — A transitional metallic element, atomic number 25, symbol Mn, an essential trace element in nutrition.

Mango — A tropical, leafy, evergreen tree native to Asia, or its sweet, juicy, yellow-orange fruit.

Mannose — A simple sugar or monosaccharide.

Mealworm — A larva of any of several beetles of the genus Tenebrio.

Megaloblastic anemia — A deficiency disease caused by folacin deficiency.

Melanin — A dark pigment found in skin, hair, and feathers.

Membrane — A thin, elastic layer of tissue that covers, separates, or connects the organs of the body.

Menadione — A synthetic vitamin K compound in the K-3 group, also called menaquinone.

Menaquinone — A synthetic vitamin K compound in the K-3 group, also called menadione.

Mercury — A metallic element, atomic number 80, symbol Hg, with no known nor suspected nutritional function.

Messenger RNA — A form of ribonucleic acid which transfers information from the gene to the cell's protein-making machinery, also written mRNA.

Metabolism — The physical and chemical processes involved in the maintenance of life.

Metabolize — To change and utilize for the maintenance of life.

Methionine — One of the essential amino acids.

Methyl donor — A molecule that contains a loosely bound methyl group that can be detached to perform necessary functions in the body.

Methyl group — A group of one carbon atom and three hydrogen atoms, loosely bound to a larger molecule.

Metric system — A decimal system of weights and measures based on the meter as a unit of length and the gram as a unit of weight.

Mica — Any of a group of complex silicates that crystallize in translucent or transparent layers.

Microbial synthesis — Manufacture by one-celled organisms.

Microgram — In metric weight, one one-thousandth of a milligram.

Microorganism — Any small, one-celled creature too small to be seen without magnification.

Microscopic — Invisible to the naked eye and able to be seen only with the use of a microscope.

Millet — Any of the seeds of the grass varieties called Panicum.

Milligram — In metric weight, one one-thousandth of a gram.

Mineral — A naturally occurring inorganic element with a crystalline structure, or a compound of such substances.

Mineral oil — A clear, liquid, petroleum by-product.

Mineralization — The deposit of mineral elements into a tissue in the body.

Molecular energy — The conversion of chemical energy stored in the molecules of food into kinetic energy for muscle action.

Molecule — The combination of atoms of different elements to form the smallest possible unit of a compound.

Mollusk — Any of a large group of marine invertebrates, such as shellfish.

Molt — The gradual shedding of old feathers and regrowth of new feathers in birds.

Molybdate — A nutritionally essential anion, with a molybdenum base.

Molybdenum — A transitional metallic element, atomic number 42, symbol Mo, an essential trace element in nutrition.

Money — A powerful force used in the human sphere,

which is designed to serve as both a medium of exchange and a store of value.

Monoglyceride — A glycerol molecule with only one fatty acid attached.

Monosaccharide — A simple sugar, such as glucose, which cannot be broken down into any smaller form of sugar.

Monounsaturated fatty acid — A fatty acid in which only one double bond linkage is unfilled.

Mucous membranes — The wet tissues lining all body channels which are exposed to the air.

Multiple sclerosis — A disease of the central nervous system characterized by hardening and degeneration of the tissues.

Muscular atrophy — A condition in which the muscles waste away.

Muscular dystrophy — A non-contagious deficiency disease in which muscles deteriorate and complete incapacitation is the end result. Vitamin E deficiency is closely linked with this disease.

Myelin — A white, fatty material which encloses the nerve fibers.

Myoglobin — A protein containing iron, found in the muscles, which carries oxygen in the muscle cells.

Myopathy — Any disease of a muscle.

Myristic acid — A non-essential saturated fatty acid with 14 carbon atoms in its chain.

Myxedema — A disease caused by severely decreased thyroid activity.

Nausea — The feeling of stomach upset and the need to vomit.

Necrosis — The death of living tissues.

Nestling — An immature altricial bird that is still being cared for by the parent birds in the nest.

Neuromuscular — Having to do with both nerve tissue and muscle tissue.

Neutrons — The particles in the nucleus of an atom with no electrical charge. Differing numbers of neutrons result in the different isotopes of the elements.

Niacin — A vitamin in the B complex, also called vitamin B-3.

Niacinamide — The animal tissue form of niacin, also called nicotinamide.

Nickel — A transitional metallic element, atomic number 28, symbol Ni, an essential trace element in nutrition.

Nicotinamide — The form of niacin present in animal tissues, also called niacinamide.

Nicotinic acid — The form in which niacin is present in plants.

Niobium — A transitional metallic element, atomic number 41, symbol Nb, with no known nor suspected biological functions. It can displace vanadium in biological reactions.

Nitrates — Compounds of nitrogen and oxygen.

Nitrogen — A gaseous element, atomic number 7, symbol N, most abundant gas in the air, and a component of proteins.

Nitrogen fixing bacteria — Any of numerous soil bacteria that are associated with legume plants and are able to change gaseous nitrogen into a form which plants can utilize.

Norleucine — A non-essential amino acid.

Nucleic acids — Any of two groups of complex compounds found in all living cells, necessary for the production of cell proteins and for cell reproduction.

Nucleus — (1) The central part of the atom, consisting of the protons and neutrons. (2) The central part of a cell which controls heredity, metabolism, and reproduction of the cell.

Nutrient — Any item from the food supply that the body needs for health, metabolism, or reproduction.

Nutrition — The nourishment or feeding of the body.

Nutritionist — A person who specializes in the study of the body's food and nutrient needs.

Nyoinositol — One of nine closely related six-carbon atoms, the only one biologically active as the vitamin inositol.

Obesity — Extreme fatness.

Oils — Any of a large group of substances that are slippery, combustible, viscous, liquid or liquifiable at room temperatures, and insoluble in water.

Oleic acid — A non-essential fatty acid, monounsaturated, with 18 carbon atoms in its chain.

Oligosaccharide — A complex sugar containing from three to six simple sugars or monosaccharides. The term polysaccharide usually replaces this term.

Ophthalmologist — A physician specializing in the treatment of the eyes.

Opsin — A protein in the eye which combines with retinal to form visual purple.

Optic nerve — A sensory nerve that connects the retina of the eye to the brain.

Organic acids — By-products of incomplete breakdown of glucose, other carbohydrates, and amino acids.

Organic matrix — The protein framework around which crystals of bone are formed.

Organism — A cell or group of cells functioning as an independent living unit.

Orotic acid — A substance that is claimed by some to be a vitamin with the designation vitamin B-13.

Osmosis — The passing of fluid through a membrane.

Osmotic pressure — The force that enables liquid substances to pass through a membrane until pressure on both sides of the membrane is equalized.

Osteoporosis — The abnormal removal of calcium and phosphorus from the bones resulting in very porous and weak bone structure.

Oviduct — A tube through which the egg travels during formation within the hen.

Ovoflavin — An old, outdated name for riboflavin, resulting from its isolation from eggs.

Oxalic acid — A substance found in spinach, rhubarb, and certain other vegetables, which binds calcium in an insoluble form.

Oxidation — Burning in any form. In nutrition, it is a very slow, controlled process.

Oxidative rancidity — The decomposition of fats caused by the addition of oxygen.

Oxygen — A gaseous element, the most common element on earth, atomic number 8, symbol O, which is a component of all water, proteins, fats, and carbohydrates.

Palmitic acid — A saturated, non-essential fatty acid with 16 carbon atoms in its chain.

Palmitoleic acid — A monounsaturated fatty acid with 16 carbon atoms in its chain.

Panacea — A cure-all, such as a nutritional substance or remedy that will cure all ills.

Pancreas — A gland behind the stomach which secretes digestive juices into the duodenum and also produces insulin.

Pangamic acid — A compound of uncertain composition that has been called vitamin B-15.

Pantoic acid — One of the two component parts of pantothenic acid. The other is alanine.

Pantothenic acid — One of the B complex vitamins, occasionally referred to as vitamin B-5.

Papaverine — A white, crystalline, non-addictive alkaloid found in opium, and used to relax muscle spasms and as a local anesthetic.

Para-aminobenzoic acid — Commonly called PABA, it is a part of folacin and was formerly considered as a separate vitamin.

Paralysis — Loss of the ability to move a part of the body voluntarily.

Paranoia — A baseless feeling characterized by delusions of persecution or grandeur.

Parathyroid — Any of four small glands located in the throat by the thyroid that secrete a hormone necessary for calcium and phosphorus metabolism.

Parkinsonism — A chronic nerve disease with tremors, muscular rigidity, and impaired motor control.

Passerine — Describing the perching birds and songbirds such as finches, warblers, jays, blackbirds, sparrows, etc.

Pasteurization — The process of heating to a certain temperature and holding that temperature for a certain period of time to destroy disease microorganisms.

Pellagra — The severe nutritional deficiency disease caused by niacin deficiency.

Pelvic bones — The bones making up that part of the skeleton between the lower limbs and the spinal column.

Penicillin — An antibiotic compound which inhibits the growth of disease-causing bacteria.

Pepsin — A digestive enzyme secreted by the stomach which catalyzes the breakdown of protein into peptides.

Peptide linkage — The primary chemical bond between amino acids that results in the formation of complex proteins.

Pericardium — The membrane tissue which surrounds the heart.

Periodic group — A group of elements with similar properties on the periodic chart.

Permeability — Ability to let something pass through, as water through a cell membrane.

Pernicious anemia — A nutritional deficiency disease caused by cobalamin deficiency.

Perosis — A disease, especially in chickens, characterized by pinpoint hemorrhages, slight puffiness around the hock joint, and leg bones twisting out of alignment, unable to support the weight of the bird.

Peroxide — A compound containing oxygen in which two atoms of oxygen are linked by a single bond.

pH — Potential hydrogen, a measure of the acidity or alkalinity of a solution.

Phenylalanine — One of the essential amino acids.

Phlebitis — Inflammation of a vein.

Phosphate — a compound of phosphorus and oxygen which occurs in combination with other elements, such as calcium, to form calcium phosphate.

Phospholipid — A compound of a fat or oil with phosphorus.

Phosphoric acid — A colorless liquid containing hydrogen, phosphorus, and oxygen.

Phosphorus — a non-metallic element, atomic number 15, symbol P, a vital bulk element in nutrition.

Photoreceptor — A nerve that is sensitive to light.

Photosynthesis — The process by which chlorophyll-containing plants produce carbohydrates and other organic compounds from inorganic elements and sunlight.

Phylloquinone — Any compound with vitamin K activity in the K-1 group.

Physiology — The vital processes of an organism, or the study of those processes.

Phytates — Compounds of phytic acid and phosphorus which inhibit calcium absorption.

Phytic acid — A substance found in some plants, particularly cereal grains, which binds minerals into an unabsorbable form.

Phytoquinone — Any compound with vitamin K activity in the K-1 group. Also called phylloquinone.

Pigment — A deposit of colored compound.

Pignolias — Pine nuts, the edible seeds of certain pine trees.

Pine nuts — Pignolias, the edible seeds of certain pine trees.

Pituitary — A small endocrine gland attached to the base of the brain, whose secretions control other endocrine glands.

Placenta — An organ in female mammals that lines the uterine wall and is attached to the fetus by an umbilical cord.

Plantain-eaters — An alternate common name for turacos.

Platelets — Blood cells smaller than the red blood cell and associated with the clotting of the blood.

Poison — Any substance that reacts in the body to cause positive harm to the cells and tissues.

Polarized light — Light that travels in a uniform straight path rather than in the random straight path followed by most light.

Politburo — The chief political and executive committee of a communist party.

Pollutant — Any substance that contaminates another substance.

Polycythemia — A disease characterized by a great excess of red blood cells, caused by a toxic excess of cobalt.

Polyneuritis — Inflammation of many nerves simultaneously.

Polysaccharide — A compound sugar composed of at least three, and usually more than six simple sugar or monosaccharide molecules.

Polyunsaturated fatty acid — A fatty acid with more than one open double bond linkage.

Potassium — A metallic element, atomic number 19, symbol K, a vital bulk element in nutrition.

Potassium chloride — One of the twelve tissue salts.

Potassium phosphate — One of the twelve tissue salts.

Potassium sulfate — One of the twelve tissue salts.

Potential Hydrogen — A measurement of the acidity or alkalinity of a solution, usually shortened to pH.

Precursor — A substance that can be chemically changed into a vitamin by a body process.

Pregnancy — The condition of a female mammal carrying developing fetuses.

Prenylmenaquinones — Compounds in the K-2 group with vitamin K activity.

Proline — A non-essential amino acid.

Proso — The Russian term for millet, most frequently seen in the description of large millets, such as those in parakeet mixes, e.g., white proso millet.

Prostate — The gland in male mammals located just before the neck of the bladder which produces an alkaline fluid which is discharged with the sperm.

Protein — A very complex combination of amino acids, which consists of carbon, hydrogen, oxygen, and nitrogen.

Protons — The positively charged particles in the nucleus of an atom which dictate the characteristics of the atom.

Proventriculus — The true glandular stomach of birds, located between the crop and the gizzard.

Provitamin — A substance that can be transformed into a vitamin by a process in the living body.

Pseudomonas — a genus or family of short, rod-shaped bacteria.

Psittacines — Birds of the parrot family.

Pterin — A compound that forms folates in the food supply together with para-aminobenzoic acid.

Purified diet — A planned food intake for experimental animals, containing known amounts of the necessary nutrients in pure form for control and testing purposes.

Pyridoxal — A form of pyridoxine, vitamin B-6, found primarily in animal tissues.

Pyridoxal phosphate — A coenzyme form of pyridoxine that functions in many biological reactions.

Pyridoxamine — A form of pyridoxine, vitamin B-6, found primarily in animal tissue.

Pyridoxic acid — The form in which excess pyridoxine is excreted in the urine.

Pyridoxine — A vitamin of the B complex, also called vitamin B-6.

Pyridoxol — The primary form of pyridoxine, occurring in plant material.

Quinones — A group of aromatic compounds found in many plants.

Radiation — The emission of rays or particles.

Radium — A rare, radioactive, metallic element, atomic number 88, symbol Ra, with no known nor suspected function in nutrition, though it is found consistently in body tissues.

Rancid — Unpleasant in odor and taste, as in the decomposition of fats and oils.

Rancidity — The decomposition of oils and fats which results in unpleasant odor and taste.

Rape seed — The seed of a Eurasian plant, botanical name
Brassica napus, usually called simply rape in aviculture.

Recessive — Concerning a latent genetic trait, which
cannot appear visually or physically unless both
parents possess the gene for that trait.

Red blood cell — An erythrocyte, the disc-shaped cell in
the blood lacking a nucleus, which holds hemoglobin
and gives the blood its color.

Regeneration — The regrowth of a dead or damaged portion of tissue in the body.

Reproduction — The process by which members of a
species create others of their own kind.

Residual ash — The dry mineral remainder after all organic
material is burned away or otherwise removed.

Resorption — The process of absorbing again.

Retina — The light-sensitive membrane lining the interior
of the eyeball and connected by the optic nerve to the
brain.

Retinal — An aldehyde form of vitamin A, also called
vitamin A aldehyde.

Retinoic acid — An acid form of vitamin A, also called
vitamin A acid.

Retinol — An alcohol form of vitamin A, also called vitamin A alcohol.

Rheumatoid arthritis — A chronic nutritional deficiency
disease characterized by inflammation of the joints,
with stiffness, weakness, deformity, and loss of
mobility.

Rhodanese — An enzyme which breaks down cyanide
in the cells of animals and bacteria.

Rhodium — A metallic element, atomic number 45, symbol Rh, with no known nor suspected need in nutrition. Rhodium will displace cobalt in its metabolic
functions.

Rhodopsin — An alternate name for visual purple.

Riboflavin — A vitamin in the B complex, also called vitamin B-2.

Ribonucleic acid — Any of the complex compounds found in all living cells, whose structure determines protein synthesis within the cell.

Ribose — A simple sugar, or monosaccharide, important as the base of riboflavin and the nucleic acids.

Ribosomal RNA — A form of ribonucleic acid that is the machinery for the synthesis of proteins within the cell, also written rRNA.

Rickets — A vitamin deficiency disease caused by lack of sufficient vitamin D in the diet. It can also result from poor calcium-phosphorus balance.

RNA — Ribonucleic acid.

Rod cells — The cells of the retina of the eye that respond to dim light.

Roentgen — A unit of radiation dosage, now rarely used.

Rosicrucian Fellowship — A philosophically oriented group headquartered in Oceanside, California, whose students hold that all living things have higher spiritual bodies invisible to normal human vision, and that rebirth is continued through many lifetimes until the individual achieves perfection, as Christ personified.

RRR-alpha-tocopherol — A new name for d-alpha-tocopherol, the natural form of vitamin E.

Rubidium — A metallic element, atomic number 37, symbol Rb, that will displace potassium in metabolic functions. It is suspected to be a necessary trace element in nutrition, but not yet proven to be.

Rutin — A bioflavonoid found in especially large amounts in buckwheat.

Safflower seed — The seeds of the safflower plant, Carthamus tinctorius.

"Salt sick" — A wasting disease of ruminants caused by cobalt deficiency.

Saturated fatty acid — A fatty acid with all available bonds filled.

Sciatic nerve — The main nerve in the region of the hip.

Scurvy — An acute nutritional deficiency disease caused by vitamin C deficiency.

Sea squirt — A member of the family of sea creatures called Ascidians, unique in using vanadium as an oxygen carrier in the blood.

Selenite — A nutritionally essential anion with a selenium base.

Selenium — A non-metallic element, atomic number 34, symbol Se, vital in nutrition in trace amounts.

Selenium oxides — Highly toxic compounds of selenium, a vital trace mineral.

Seminal fluid — The fluid which carries the sperm cells.

Serine — One of the non-essential amino acids.

7-dehydrocholesterol — The provitamin irradiated to form vitamin D-3, cholecalciferol.

Shen-nung — A legendary Chinese emperor who lived about 4,700 years ago. He is remembered for a treatise on herbal medicine.

Siderosis — A disease caused by excess iron in the body.

Silica — A silicon and oxygen compound.

Silicic oxide — One of the twelve tissue salts.

Silicon — A non-metallic element, atomic number 14, symbol Si, essential in nutrition in quantities larger than trace minerals.

Silver — A transitional, metallic element, atomic number 47, symbol Ag, found consistently in body tissues with no known nor suspected biological function. It is a copper antagonist in the diet.

Silver sulfide — A compound of silver and sulfur which causes the dark stains on silverware used for eggs.

Skeletal muscles — The muscles attached to the bones that allow movement.

Slipped tendon — A manganese deficiency symptom in birds in which the tendon slides out of place.

Smooth muscles — The involuntary muscles of the internal organs, such as those controlling intestinal rhythm.

Society Finch — An alternate name for the Bengalese Finch, whose origins as a domesticated bird are lost in antiquity. They are presumed to be domesticated forms of the Striated Munia, Lonchura striata.

Sodium — A metallic element, atomic number 11, symbol Na, vital as a bulk element in nutrition.

Sodium chloride — A compound that supplies a substantial amount of both sodium and chlorine in the diet. It is one of the twelve tissue salts.

Sodium fluoride — The compound in which fluorine occurs in sea water.

Sodium phosphate — One of the twelve tissue salts.

Sodium sulfate — One of the twelve tissue salts.

Softbill — Any bird whose diet consists of insects, fruits, and berries.

Soybean — The seed of a legume native to Asia which is very nutritious and high in protein.

Species — A particular kind, or variety of bird, or any other living thing.

Spermatozoa — Usually called sperm or sperm cells, they are the male cell which fertilizes the egg. Singular term is spermatozoon.

Spine — The backbone.

Stannic sulfate — A compound of tin, sulfur, and oxygen which can be used as a dietary tin supplement.

Starch — A polysaccharide, the only one that the avian metabolism can use efficiently. The most important carbohydrate in nutrition.

Starvation — Suffering and dying from extreme or prolonged lack of food.

Stearic acid — A non-essential saturated fatty acid with 18 carbon atoms in its chain.

Sterile — Infertile or incapable of reproducing sexually.

"Stiff lamb disease" — A fatal disease of newborn lambs caused by vitamin E deficiency.

Strain — A group of birds or other organisms of the same species that have a distinctive set of inherited characteristics.

Streptomyces bacteria — A family of one-celled mold organisms that produce the antibiotic streptomycin and cobalamin as a by-product.

Stress — Any distress or a mental and emotional influence which disrupts normal biological functioning.

Strontium — A metallic element, atomic number 38, symbol Sr, found consistently in the body, with no proven essential function as of this writing.

Strontium-90 — The radioactive isotope of strontium.

Sub-clinical scurvy — Severe vitamin C deficiency with symptoms just below the level which would be diagnosed and defined as scurvy.

Sucrase — The enzyme which as a catalyst splits the glucose and fructose molecules of sucrose apart. It is also called invertase.

Sucrose — A disaccharide composed of one glucose molecule and one fructose molecule.

Sugar — A general term for any of the monosaccharides or disaccharides.

Sulfa compounds — Any of a group of synthetic organic compounds which are capable of inhibiting bacterial activity and growth.

Sulfates — Anions with a sulfur base.

Sulfur — A non-metallic element, atomic number 16, symbol S, which is an essential bulk element in nutrition.

Sulfur-containing amino acid — A group of amino acids which contain sulfur in their composition. The three most important in nutrition are methionine, cystine, and cysteine. Taurine is another.

Sunflower seed — Any seeds from commercially grown plants of the genus Helianthus.

Sunshine vitamin — Vitamin D.

Supplement — An additional substance added to the diet to supply a nutrient or group of nutrients that may be deficient in the diet.

Synthesis — The manufacture within the body, when referring to nutrients.

Syphilis — A chronic venereal disease usually transmitted by sexual contact.

Tannic acid — An acid compound which the body cannot metabolize, derived from many plants and also called tannin.

Taurine — A non-essential amino acid which contains sulfur.

Testicle — A male reproductive gland, which produces spermatozoa and the androgen hormones, normally occurring in pairs.

Theralin — A commercial vitamin-mineral supplement marketed by Lambert Kay.

Thiamin — A water soluble vitamin in the B complex, also called vitamin B-1.

Thiamin hydrochloride — A more stable chemical form of thiamin.

Thiamin mononitrate — A more stable chemical form of thiamin.

Thiaminase — An enzyme found in certain raw fish that splits and destroys thiamin. It is inactivated by heat.

Thioctic acid — An alternate name for lipoic acid.

Threonine — One of the essential amino acids.

Thyroid gland — A gland located in the throat which requires iodine for the production of thyroxine to control body growth and metabolism.

Thyroxine — The thyroid hormone formed from iodide and tyrosine.

Tibiometatarsal joint — The foot joint in birds where the toes join.

Timnodonic acid — A non-essential, polyunsaturated fatty acid with 20 carbon atoms in its chain.

Tin — A metallic element, atomic number 50, symbol Sn, an essential trace element for rats and probably for all birds and animals.

Tissue — A group of cells functioning as a collective unit in the body.

Titanium — A transitional, metallic element, atomic number 22, symbol Ti, found consistently in body tissues, but with no known nor suspected biological function.

Tissue Salts — A group of twelve compounds necessary for the proper health and functioning of body tissues.

Tocopherol — The chemical name for vitamin E and its close chemical relatives.

Tortillas — A corn-based, thin, unleavened pancake, characteristic of Mexican food preparation and used in a variety of ways.

Toxemia — A condition in which toxins or poisons are not eliminated from the body, but provide fertile ground for the multiplication of disease microorganisms.

Toxic — Harmful or poisonous.

Toxicity — The condition of being poisonous.

Trace minerals — Those elements essential in nutrition in trace amounts, usually a few milligrams or less daily.

Transfer RNA — A type of ribonucleic acid that serves as an adaptor, often written tRNA.

Transitional metals — Those metals having an incomplete or unfilled outer electron shell, and are thus reactive in nature.

Transmutation — The change from one element to another through the addition or removal of protons from the nucleus of the element.

Triglyceride — A glycerol base with three fatty acids attached.

Trivalent chromium — The type of chromium that forms the basis of the Glucose Tolerance Factor.

Trypsin — An enzyme produced in the pancreas for food breakdown in the small intestine.

Tryptophan — One of the essential amino acids.

Tungsten — Also called wolfram, a transitional metallic element, atomic number 74, symbol W, with no known nor suspected biological function. It is a molybdenum antagonist.

Turacin — A unique color pigment, neither melanin nor lipochrome, with a copper salt base, found only in the turacos.

Turaco — A family of African birds related to the cuckoos, also called plantain-eaters.

Turacoverdin — An iron-containing pigment unique to the turacos.

Turacus corythaix — Scientific name of a particular species of turaco.

Tyrosinase — An enzyme needed for the conversion of the amino acid tyrosine into melanin.

Tyrosine — A non-essential amino acid used by the body to form melanin and thyroxine.

Ubiquinone — An alternate name for coenzyme Q.

Ultraviolet light — Light rays just beyond the violet of the visible spectrum. They are invisible to the normal eye.

Unsaturated fatty acid — Any fatty acid that has any of its double bond linkages unfilled.

Uranium — A metallic element, atomic number 92, symbol U, found consistently in body tissues with no known nor suspected biological function.

Uric acid — A nutritional waste product of metabolism, excreted through the urine.

Urine — A fluid containing dissolved waste products excreted as a liquid in mammals and primarily as a white
semi-solid material in birds.

Uroflavin — An old, now outdated term for riboflavin,
derived from its source of isolation, the urine.

U.S. Pharmacopoeia Unit — A measurement unit equal to
an International Unit, used to measure vitamin A. One
unit is 0.3 micrograms of retinol.

Utilization — When referring to nutrition, the use within
the body of a particular nutrient.

Valine — One of the essential amino acids.

Vanadium — A transitional metallic element, atomic number 23, symbol V, which is an essential trace element
in nutrition.

Varicose veins — Blood or lymph vessels that are abnormally
dilated, knotted, and winding.

Vascular — Concerning the vessels for the circulation of
plant and animal fluids such as blood, lymph, or sap.

Verdoflavin — An old name for riboflavin, resulting from
its extraction from grass.

Vertebra — One of the bones forming the spinal column.

Vionate — A commercially available vitamin-mineral
supplement formulated by the Squibb Company.

Viosterol — An alternative name for ergocalciferol, vitamin D-2.

Viral infection — Any manifestation of disease caused by
the invasion of viruses into the cells.

Virucide — Also spelled viruscide; any compound that will
kill viruses.

Visual purple — Rhodopsin, a compound which enables
the eye to see in dim light.

Visual yellow — A chemical compound formed when light
strikes rhodopsin.

Vitamin — Any of numerous complex chemical compounds

essential in small amounts for the control of metabolic processes.

Vitamin A — A group of fat soluble substances vital for life in humans, birds, and animals.

Vitamin A acid — Retinoic acid.

Vitamin A alcohol — Retinol.

Vitamin A aldehyde — Retinal.

Vitamin A palmitate — A combination of vitamin A and palmitic acid in which form vitamin A occurs in animal sources in the food supply.

Vitamin B-1 — An alternate designation for thiamin.

Vitamin B-2 — An alternate designation for riboflavin.

Vitamin B-3 — An alternate name for niacin.

Vitamin B-5 — An alternate, infrequently used designation for pantothenic acid.

Vitamin B-6 — An alternate name for pyridoxine, a group of water soluble substances that are essential for nutrition.

Vitamin B-12 — Cobalamin or cyanocobalamin, a water soluble substance containing cobalt, essential for life in birds, animals, and humans.

Vitamin B-13 — An alternate name for orotic acid.

Vitamin B-15 — An alternate designation for pangamic acid.

Vitamin B-17 — An unofficial, popular designation for amygdalin, also called Laetrile.

Vitamin C — Ascorbic acid, a vital, water soluble nutrient.

Vitamin D — the fat soluble substances cholecalciferol and ergocalciferol, which perform vital biological functions.

Vitamin D-2 — Ergocalciferol, found in vegetable sources.

Vitamin D-3 — Cholecalciferol, found only in animal sources and essential in the nutrition of birds.

Vitamin E — A fat soluble vitamin, chemically known as d-alpha-tocopherol.

Vitamin E acetate — The more stable form of vitamin E.

Vitamin F — An alternate term for the essential fatty acids, used especially in Europe.

Vitamin G — An old, now outdated name for riboflavin.

Vitamin H — A seldom used designation for biotin.

Vitamin K — A group of fat soluble substances with essential metabolic functions.

Vitamin L-1 — A presumed essential factor needed for lactation and derived from liver.

Vitamin L-2 — A presumed essential nutrient, derived from yeast and necessary for lactation in animals.

Vitamin M — An essential factor from the folacin group.

Vitamin P — The bioflavonoids.

Vitiligo — A skin disorder characterized by irregular spots of white, totally lacking in pigment, appearing on the skin.

Wasting disease — A disease of ruminants caused by cobalt deficiency.

Water soluble vitamins — The vital vitamin compounds not synthesized in the body, which are soluble in water and insoluble in fats.

Wattles — Fleshy folds of skin hanging from the neck or throat, often brightly colored.

Wax — Any ester formed by the combination of any alcohol other than glycerol with fatty acids.

White proso millet — A form of large, white millet, normally used in parakeet mixes and wild bird feeds.

Wilson's disease — An inherited disease characterized by chronic, long-term copper toxicity.

Xanthine oxidase — An enzyme containing molybdenum which is an essential catalyst for the oxidation of a number of substances in the body.

Yaws — A tropical skin disease characterized by multiple red pimples.

Yellow fat disease — A fatal disease of mink caused by vitamin E deficiency.

Zein — A protein found in corn.

Zinc — A metallic element, atomic number 30, symbol Zn, vital in trace amounts for the nutrition of birds, animals, and humans.

Zirconium — A transitional metallic element, atomic number 40, symbol Zr, found consistently in body tissues, with no known nor suspected biological function.

BIBLIOGRAPHY

Arnall, L. & Keymer, I.F. *Bird Diseases*. T.F.H. Publications, Inc. 1975

Chaney, Margaret S., Ross, Margaret L., and Witschi, Jelia C. *Nutrition*, 9th Edition. Houghton Mifflin Company. 1979

Davis, Adelle. *Let's Get Well*. Harcourt Brace Javonovich, Inc. 1965

Ellis, John M. *The Doctor Who Looked at Hands*. Vantage Press, Inc. 1966

Guthrie, Helen Andrews. *Introductory Nutrition*, 2nd Edition. C.V. Mosby Company. 1971

Harper, H.A., Rodwell, V.W., and Mayes, P.A. *Review of Physiological Chemistry*, 17th Edition. Lange Medical Publications. 1979

Kervran, Louis. *Biological Transmutations*. Swan House Publishing Company. 1972

Krippner, Stanley, and Rubin, Daniel. *The Kirlian Aura*. Anchor Books/Doubleday. 1974

Morris, William, Editor. *The American Heritage Dictionary of the English Language*. American Heritage Publishing Company, Inc. 1969

Morrison, F.B. *Feeds and Feeding*, 20th Edition. The Morrison Publishing Company. 1944

Nutrition Search, Inc. *Nutrition Almanac*. McGraw-Hill Book Company. 1975

Pfeiffer, Carl C. *Mental and Elemental Nutrients*. Keats Publishing Company. 1975

Pfeiffer, Carl C. *Zinc and Other Micro-Nutrients*. Keats Publishing Company. 1978

Picton, Lionel James. *Nutrition and the Soil*. The Devin-Adair Company. 1949

Random House, numerous editors. *The World Atlas of Birds*. Random House. 1974

Rodale, J.I. *The Complete Book of Minerals for Health*. Rodale Books, Inc. 1972

Rodale, J.I. *The Complete Book of Vitamins*. Rodale Books, Inc. 1974

Romanoff, Alexis L. & Romanoff, Anastasia J. *The Avian Egg*. John Wiley & Sons, Inc. 1949

Schroeder, Henry A. *The Trace Elements and Man*. The Devin-Adair Company. 1973

Scott, Milton L., Nesheim, Malden C., and Young, Robert J. *Nutrition of the Chicken*, 2nd Edition. M.L. Scott & Associates. 1976

Sturkie, P.D., editor. *Avian Physiology*, 3rd Edition. Springer-Verlag. 1976

Underwood, Eric J. *Trace Elements in Human and Animal Nutrition*, 4th Edition. Academic Press. 1977

United States Department of Agriculture. *Food, The Yearbook of Agriculture*. U.S. Government Printing Office. 1959

United States Department of Agriculture. *Handbook of of the Nutritional Contents of Foods*. Dover Publications, Inc. 1975

Voitkevich, A.A. *The Feathers and Plumage of Birds*. Sidgwick & Jackson. 1966

Williams, Roger J. *Biochemical Individuality*. University of Texas Press. 1956

INDEX

For items with multiple references, the page numbers entered in bold-faced type indicate the primary coverage in the text. Italicized page numbers indicate a glossary entry.

A

136, 138, 139, 143, 148,
149, 152, 153, 179, 181,
182, 186, 187, 192, 193,
195, 197, 199, 200-1, 202,
204, 211, 214, 218, 219,
220-1, 227, 228, 229, 230,
231, 233, 234, 235, 237,
240, 242, 245, 246, 250
Chitin, 72, *271*
Chloride, 166, **194**, 195, 250,
271
Chlorine, 33, 107, 166, 168,
190, **193-95**, *271*
Chlorophyll, 66, 195, 196,
198, 199, *271*
Chlorosis, 225, *271*
Chlortetracycline, *see* Aureomycin
Cholecalciferol, *see also* vitamin
D *and* vitamin D-3, 92, 94,
97, 98, *271*
Cholestrol, **61-2**, 63, 206, 207
226, 241, 242, *271*
Choline, 60, 81, **119-122**, 127,
131, 140, *272*
Chondrodystrophy, 227-228,
272
Choroid tissues, 2̶4̶4
Chromic acid, 129, *272*
Chromium, 62, 129-130, 135,
204-208, 241, 242, *272*
Chromosomes, 161, *272*
Cilia, 85, *272*
Cirrhosis, 104, 120, *272*
Cirruline, 41, *272*
Citrovorum factor, *see also* folinic acid, 126, *272*
Citrus fruits, *see also* lemons,
156
Cleft palate, 128
Cloves, 229
Clupanodonic acid, 56, *272*
Coagulation, 110, *272*
Coal, 203, 205, 216, 234,
236, 241, 249
Cobalamin, 20, 43, 80, 120,
121, **122-5**, 127, 130, 141,
153, 159, 162, 168, 175,
205, 209, 210, *272*
Cobalt, 122, 123, 168, 205,

208-10, *272*
Cobalt chloride, 210, *272*
Cocoa, 168
Coconut, 56
Cod liver oil, 90, 94, 97, 99,
Coenzymes, 70, 75, 120, 126,
141, 147, 152, 182, *272*
Coenzyme A, 138, *273*
Coenzyme Q, *see* ubliquinone
Collagen, 41, 76, 113-14, **115**,
189, 201, *273*
Colostrum, 102, 243, *273*
Comb, 88, 143, 152, 201,
273
Comfrey, 123
Complete protein, 38
Compound lipids, 60, *273*
Connective tissues, 63, 115
Constipation, 151, *273*
Conures, 18
Convulsive seizures, 67, 142,
143, 196, 199, *273*
Cooking, 28, 42, 76, **77-79**,
84, 101, 102, 115, 118,
125, 128, 136, 137, 139,
140, 144, 153, 158, 188,
199, 209, 258, 259
Copper, 57, 142, 156, 166,
211-15, 223, 232-3, 238,
244, 248, 251, *273*
Copper sulfide, 214, *273*
Coprophagy, 111, 117, *273*
Cordon blue finches, 28
Corn, *see also* sweet corn, 36,
39, 69, 91, 134, 181, 202,
241
Cornea, 88, 105, 148, 206,
207, *273*
Cows, *see also* cattle, 102, 180
Cramps, 98, 135, 143, 187,
192
Cranberries, 156, 168
Craving, 26, 262, *273*
"Crazy chick disease," *see* encephalomalacia
Cretinism, 221, *274*
Crop, *see also* diverticulum, 18,
274
Crude protein, 46, *274*
Cucumbers, 31

Cutthroat finches, 28
Cuttlebone, 47, 179, 183
Cyanide, 156, *274*
Cyanide group, 122, *274*
Cyanocobalamin, *see also* cobal-
   amin, 122, *274*
Cysteine, 41, 108, 129, 167,
   189, *274*
Cystine, 40, 41, 189, *274*

Doves, *see also* pigeons, 24, 28
   45
Dream recall, 141
Droppings, 32, 47
Ducks, 136, 138, 143
Duodenum, 19, 93, *275*
Dwarfism, 246

E

D

Dairy products, *see also* milk
   and cheese, 99, 233
d-Alpha tocopherol, 100-1, 102,
   274
Dates, 188
Decalcification, 202, *274*
Dehydration, 30, 34, 192, 193,
   274
Dementia, 134, *274*
Deoxyribonucleic acid, 160-2,
   274
Depigmentation, 214, *274*
Dermatitis, 134, 136, *275*
Deuterium, 282
Diabetes, 206, 226, *275*
Diarrhea, 20, 47, 89, 98, 134,
   136, 148, 187, 192, 213,
   248, *275*
Digestion, 18, 38, 50, 60, 68-
   70, 84, 102, 158, 168,
   173, 194, 245, 256
Diglycerides, 58, *275*
Disaccharides, 67-72, *275*
Diverticulum, *see also* crop, 18,
   275
dl-Alpha tocopherol, 100-1, *275*
DNA, *see also* deoxyribonucleic
   acid, 127, 141, 160-2, 182,
   197, 233, *275*
Dog food, 44
Dogs, 126, 133, 223, 244
Domestic animals, 209, 213, 227
   232, *see also specific varieties*
Domestic fowl, *see also specific
   varieties*, 9, 15

Ears, 228
Earthworms, 40
Edema, 143, 152, *275*
Egg eating, 46, 48
Eggbinding, 9, 64-5, *275*
Eggs — food, 25, 27, 29, 31, 36,
   43, 44, 45, 72, 84, 89, 90
   91, 99, 101, 112, 118,
   120, 122, 125, 126, 137,
   141, 146, 149, 169, 180,
   188, 192, 207, 209, 210,
   213, 214, 221, 222, 229,
   233, 238, 247, 248
Eggs — reproduction, 24, 26, 45,
   49, 56, 63, 64, 65, 84, 87
   88, 96, 97, 107, 114, 117,
   121, 125, 137, 138, 143,
   148, 179, 180, 187, 189,
   195, 197, 200, 202, 213,
   214, 216, 219, 220, 222,
   227, 228, 237, 250
Eggshells, 96, 179, 183, 186,
   187, 189, 197, 200, 202,
   245
Egypt, 246
Elastin, 212, *275*
Electrolytes, 166, 170, 184,
   275
Electrons, 166, 167
Electrophotograph, 259, *275*,
   see also Kirlian photography
Emaciation, 138, 148, 152,
   237, *276*
Embryos, 45, 49, 87, 88, 107
   114, 129, 148, 220, 227,
   228, 236, 246, 250, *276*
Encephalomalacia, 108, 131,
   276

England, 93
Enrichment, 258, *276*
Enzymes, 18, 19, 33, 47, 60, 69
    70, 71, 84, 85, 88, 96,
    109, 114, 115, 116, 124,
    126, 135, 141, 142, 147,
    152, 153, 156, **157-58**,
    170, 173, 174, 175, 177,
    183, 197, 212, 214, 216,
    223, 226, 231, 237, 244,
    245, *276*
Epinephrine, *see also* adrenalin,
    71, *276*
Equisetum, *see* horsetail
Epithelial cells, 85-6, *276*
Ergocalciferol, 92, 93, 98, 99,
    276
Ergosterol, 94, *276*
Esophagus, 18, *276*
Esoteric teaching, 81, 259, *276*
Essential amino acids,   **38-40**,
    41, 42, 47, 50, 78, *276*,
    see also individual names
Essential fatty acids, *see also
    individual names*, **62-65**, 76,
    80, 81, 140, 142
Ester, 60, *276*
Estrogen, 107, *276*
Europe, 62, 76, 208
Exudative diathesis, **108-9**, 131
    237, *276-7*
Eyelids, 89, 90, 117, 138,
    148
Eyes, *see also* eyelids, 85, 86,
    87, 88, 89, 105, 117, 148,
    206, 244, 246

F

Factor R, *see* folacin
Factor U, *see* folacin
Fast, 17, 53, 69, *277*
Fats, 19, 31, 32, 39, 52-65,
    66, 69, 70, 76, 77, 84, 85
    93, 102, 103, 104, 108,
    109, 111, 119, 120, 124,
    131, 135, 137, 142, 146,

150, 151, 152, 168, 173,
    175, 182, 184, 207, 209,
    213, 218, 226, 241, 246,
    277
Fat soluble vitamins, *see also
    names of individual vitamins*,
    62, 64, 76, 80, **82-112**,
    277
Fatty acids, *see also individual
    names*, essential fatty acids,
    84, 106, 116, 132, 135,
    138, 147, 152, 170, 182,
    206, 226, *277*
Feather plucking, 28, 46, 47
Feathers, 26, 36, 41, 46, 47, 48,
    49, 83, 94, 97, 128, 136,
    147, 152, 189, 213, 214,
    223, 242, 244, 246
Feet, 90, 94, 117, 138, 143,
    144, 246
Female reproductive organs, 218
Ferritin, 223, *277*
Ferrous sulfate, 223, 229, *277*
Fertility, 26, 44, 87, 109, *277*,
    see also sterility
Fingernails, 189, 203, 244,
    245, 248
Fingers, 98, 144
Fischer's Lovebirds, 24
Fish, 53, 58, 97, 118, 131,
    153, 194, 217, 244
Fish liver oils, *see also* cod liver
    oil, 56, 89, 90, 97
Flavonoids, 249, *277*
Flavoproteins, 146, 147, *277*
Flax, 64, 156, 181, *277*
Fledglings, 44, 45, 228
Florida, 213
Fluorescent bulbs, 98, *277*
Fluorides, 181, **216-17**, *278*
Fluorine, 166, 180, **215-17**,
    278
Folacin, 77, 78, 80, 120, 121
    124, **126-29**, 131, 151,
    153, 162, *278*
Folates, 126, *278*
Folic acid, *see also* folacin, 126,
    159, 210, *278*
Folinic acid, *see also* citrovorum
    factor, folacin, 127, *278*
Follicles, 94, *278*

N

O

X

Xanthine oxidase, 231, *305*
X-rays, 112, 174, 202

Y

Yaws, 204, *306*
Yeast, *see also* brewer's yeast,
    77, 118, 126, 131, 132, 133,
    137, 146, 252
Yellow fat disease, 107, *306*

Z

Zebra Finches, 28, 44
Zein, 36, *306*
Zinc, 44, 132, 141, 166, 168,
    169, 176, 214, 240, 241,
    243-248, 251, *306*
Zirconium, 253, *306*